THE UKIMWI ROAD

DERVLA MURPHY

THE UKIMWI ROAD

From Kenya to Zimbabwe

JOHN MURRAY

© Dervla Murphy 1993

First published in 1993
by John Murray (Publishers) Ltd.,
50 Albemarle Street, London W1X 4BD

The moral right of the author has been asserted

A catalogue record for this book is available from the British Library

ISBN 0-7195-5250-8

Typeset in 11½ on 13 pt Baskerville by
Colset Private Limited, Singapore
Printed and bound in Great Britain at
the University Press, Cambridge

For Jo and Oisin,
who rallied round

Contents

Acknowledgements

Sustenance on several levels was lavishly provided *en route* by Maire and Eamonn Brehony, Pauline Conway, Maura and Jim Culligan, William Howlett, Michael Kelly, Audrey and Michael O'Dowd, Mary and Seamus O'Grady, Betty and Michael O'Meara, Anne and Michael McInery, Joy and John Parkinson, Geraldine Prenderville, Brendan Rogers, Isabelle von Prondzynski and Sean White. To all, affectionate thanks for their considerable contributions to my survival and enlightenment.

Hallam Murray provided invaluable advice on the bicycle-buying level; then he taught me how to use derailleur gears after fifty years of Sturmey Archers.

Diana, Jock and John Murray performed their usual heroic feats on the editorial level; 'What they do/Still betters what is done.'

One of the more obvious areas of Africa's decay is the infrastructure. The road is fundamental to the nation and yet it is in large parts in utter disrepair, for mile after mile. It tells us a lot about the state of communications in Africa. It tells us a lot about the African condition. It was Julius Nyerere, founder President of Tanzania, who once said that while the great powers are trying to get to the moon, we are trying to get to the village. Well, the great powers have been to the moon and back, and are now even communicating with the stars. In Africa, however, we are still trying to reach the village. And the village is getting even more remote, receding with worsening communications even further into the distance.

Ali A. Mazrui

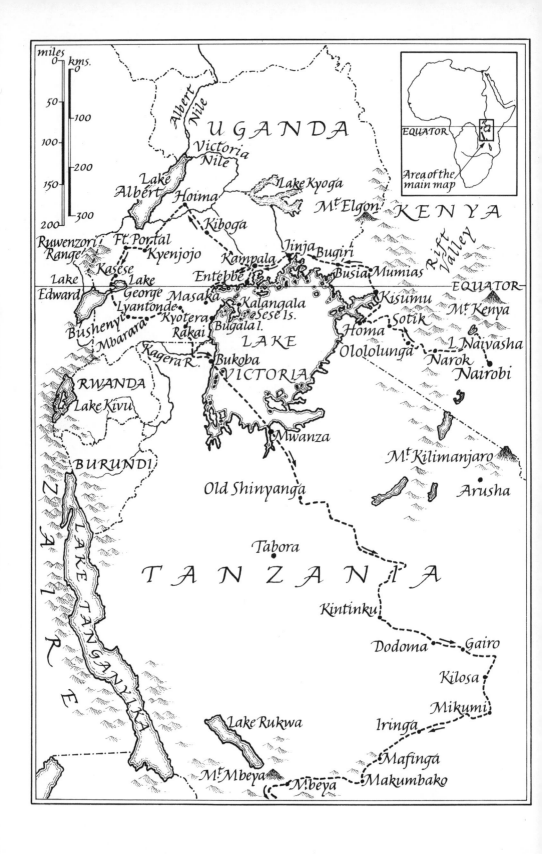

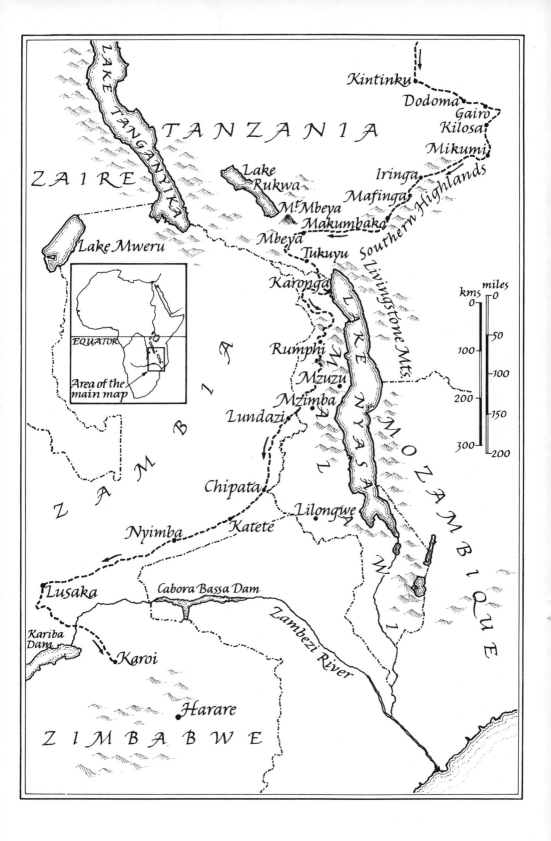

1

A Rough Welcome

Nairobi to Sotik

In the past it was taken for granted that when travellers said goodbye they became inaccessible for an indefinite period, only sending back the occasional message (a year or two out of date) in a cleft stick. But now we are expected to remain in touch with home, friends and problems; our escape is merely physical, the mental and emotional shackles staying firmly in place.

On and off, over the years, I have brooded on this constraint. Then suddenly I was vouchsafed a blinding glimpse of the obvious. 'Ease of communication' could be defeated by not telling anybody – not even one's nearest and dearest – where one was going. If nobody knows which continent a traveller is travelling on, enjoyment of the present cannot be threatened by calamities back home, like news of your dog being run over, your house being burned to the ground or your bank going into liquidation.

In January 1992 I craved this degree of isolation. During the previous few years a combination of circumstances (not least my involvement in Rumania's post-Ceausescu problems) had put me under some stress and my self-prescribed unwinding therapy was a cycle tour from Kenya to Zimbabwe via Uganda, Tanzania, Malawi and Zambia – a carefree ramble through some of the least hot areas of sub-Saharan Africa. I therefore presented myself, for my sixtieth birthday, with a Dawes Ascent mountain-bike, the cyclist's equivalent of a Rolls-Royce, named Lear. Then I bought a ticket to Nairobi and told all concerned that I was about to indulge in a four-month mystery tour.

At once all concerned rose up in arms. I was being, they alleged, perverse, selfish, irresponsible and neurotic. They needed to keep in touch, to know that I was safe. The illogic of this attitude

escaped them. If I were unsafe – diseased, injured, jailed, robbed, murdered – their knowing about it would not materially alter my situation but would distress them. So my insistence on not keeping in touch was a kindness; every sensible person assumes no news to be good news.

I was, I suppose, trying to create an oasis in time. However, it didn't work out quite like that; if you leave your own problems behind, other people's come along to fill the vacuum – a lesson that lay in the future as my airbus took off from Heathrow on 2 March. It was three-quarters empty: worrying for Kenya Airways but agreeable for us passengers. After a tolerable dinner and several free Tusker beers I slept well, lying luxuriously along three seats.

A pair of Heathrow scaremongers had warned me that most Nairobi airport officials are surly predators. But as we landed at 7.30 a.m. I had another concern: would Lear be grievously maimed by the baggage-handlers? Most cyclists are capable of attending to their machines' injuries; I am not. Anxiously I asked a tall, handsome uniformed official – his precise function unclear – where bicycles could be collected. He gazed down at me reflectively, then wondered, 'Why did you bring a *bicycle*? It is better for old people to travel in vehicles.' Already I was streaming sweat, in no position to dispute his next comment. 'It is too hot to cycle. Even for us it is too hot before the rains. Why did you come with a bicycle in the hot season?'

For cat-sitter reasons (my home is owned by three cats) this journey had been started a month earlier than originally planned. That a traveller's timing should be determined by feline whims is plainly absurd but it seemed unnecessary to expose this deranged area of my psyche to an airport official. Meanwhile, as we chattered unproductively, someone might be bikenapping Lear . . .

The young man nodded towards the conveyor-belt and said, 'All luggage comes there.' Spatially a bicycle could not 'come there' so I hurried to the Information kiosk where a small round amiable man observed, with a twinkle, that in Kenya lions eat cyclists. Then, intuiting that I was in no mood for banter, he indicated a nearby doorway.

In a grey concrete hanger I found decrepit tractors drawing trailers of luggage through greasy diesel clouds. At last one of them returned with Lear – only Lear – on board. When I eagerly leaped forward, the tractor-driver required no documentary proof of ownership; perhaps my joyous relief was proof enough. Beside the kiosk I set about unwrapping Lear from those many layers of plastic sheeting in which he had been dressed for his journey. Despite this precaution, two nasty gashes marked the saddle and the right-hand gear lever had been dented. Mercifully, neither injury affected his performance. A small but fascinated crowd gathered to watch me adjusting the handlebars before beginning a humiliating struggle to screw on the pedals.

Eventually, the tall handsome official was moved to intervene. 'You don't understand bicycles,' he said triumphantly, taking over the spanner. 'They are not suitable for women. Pedals must be *straight* and you are putting them on crooked. It is better if you use vehicles and sell me this bicycle. In Africa we can't buy such strong bicycles.' A jolly air-hostess, off our flight but showing no sign of fatigue, fell about laughing and diagnosed, 'She has a hangover! So many Tuskers, now she can't see straight!'

By the time I had loaded Lear – his pannier-bags go as hand-luggage – all my fellow-passengers had disappeared and so had the customs officers. At Immigration a charming young woman gave me a three-month visa, said it could be extended indefinitely and sounded sincere when she welcomed me to Kenya. No one was interested in my health documents. So what was all that about 'surly predators'?

Huge brash advertisement hoardings infest the road into Nairobi and I winced on passing an 'interpretative centre' offering The African Experience. My immediate destination was a Christian guest-house on Bishop's Road where a room plus three palatable buffet meals cost only £8.50. Having locked Lear to my bed, the day could be spent ambling around Nairobi; after an intercontinental flight one needs to take it easy.

Where I had turned off the Uhuru Highway towards Bishop's Road, a thousand or so men and women were singing in perfect harmony near the corner of Central Park, one of Nairobi's many wide green spaces. Evidently something was being celebrated and I soon returned to that junction, known as Freedom Corner. The crowd, which had been standing, was now sitting or kneeling and at once several people urgently requested me not to stand.

This was no celebration but a movingly civilised demo, supported

3

by all classes and age groups. On a dais under a canvas awning five elderly women – the mothers of sons 'wrongfully imprisoned' for the past six years – were into the fourth day of a hunger-strike protest. At intervals they spoke to the crowd, vehemently and pleadingly, arguing for their sons' release. Yet the atmosphere was entirely free of aggression; this gathering was resolved to provoke no violence from any source, hence the directive to sit or kneel, to seem physically passive though spiritually assertive. One could not imagine a more orderly crowd, listening attentively to the mothers and their supporters – members of the opposition party, or coalition of parties, known as FORD (Forum for the Restoration of Democracy) – then rhythmically clapping while singing plaintive hymns. Three Whites were openly filming the scene under the impassive gaze of thirty-two heavily armed policemen, standing some fifty yards behind the dais in the shade of a blue-gum coppice. Emboldened by this free-ranging media activity, I gradually moved, on my knees, from the edge of the crowd to the front of the dais.

That was unwise. Half an hour later two lorry-loads of the dreaded paramilitary GSU (General Service Unit) troopers arrived to reinforce the police and we were savagely dispersed. The troopers were armed with rifles and sub-machine-guns, the police with rifles and three-foot-long wooden clubs, crudely hewn out of thick branches; all wore tin helmets and carried flimsy-looking plastic riot-shields. Without warning the sitting crowd was charged and as I scrambled to my feet I could hear all around me the sickening thud of wooden staves on innocent backs. Twice I was struck hard across the shoulders as we all fled in panic, leaving the mothers to be tear-gassed and beaten (one into unconsciousness) until in desperation they stripped naked – completely naked. This culturally symbolic gesture got massive media coverage and shattered Kenya; no amount of speechifying or hymn-singing could have drawn so much attention to their sons' cause. To be seen stripping naked is a woman's ultimate protest against injustice and it incorporates a powerful curse against those inflicting the injustice.

That barbarous attack gave the green light to hundreds of young males – cheered on by an interesting number of young females – who now felt justified in retaliating not only against the security forces but also against the affluent layer of society those were defending. In the city centre many shops were looted and I saw several

4

vans, belonging to firms suspected of donating large amounts to the
Kenya Africa National Union (KANU), being stoned or petrol-
bombed. Yet to me, comparing the vibes with Northern Ireland's,
there was an element of pretence, of fun and games, about that afternoon's lawlessness. For hours open-backed, orange-painted police
lorries patrolled the streets, pursued by gangs throwing sticks and
bricks and bottles and verbal abuse. Occasionally a lorry stopped
and policemen swarmed over the sides to chase the youths, who fled
at Olympic speeds wearing broad grins. Meanwhile Nairobi's élite
were out on their skyscraper balconies, cups of coffee or glasses of
something stronger in hand, observing the fray as an entertainment.
I decided then that I do not, and never will, understand the role of
violence in modern Africa.

It takes more than a riot to separate me from my evening intake
of beer. By finding the back entrance to an up-market alcohol
store – the front entrance was securely barred against looters – I
acquired four bottles of Tusker. These had to be smuggled into my
guest-house where a conspicuous notice in the hallway forbade the
bringing of alcohol or tobacco on to the premises. East Africa's
Christianity still bears the stamp of those earnest evangelicals who
imported it a century ago.

Prudence prompted me to get off the streets before sunset; at the
best of times Nairobi is unsafe after dark, especially for foreigners,
and my way back to Bishop's Road led through one of the unsafest
areas, between Central Park and Uhuru Park. Having left the
excitement behind, I became aware of my throbbing shoulders. The
day's activities had coated me with sweat and dust but, alas, Nairobi
was then drought-stricken; only the guest-house kitchen had water,
drawn from some distant source by two donkeys. Unfortunately a
bathroom adjoined my bedroom and the stench from the loo
suggested that this was no recent shortage.

Most of Kenya's Christian Churches had by then come out openly
against President Moi and in favour of multi-party democracy, and
my fellow-guests seemed twitchy as we gathered in the dining-room.
Among those missionaries my inelegant cycling garb marked me as
an outsider and I was handled, conversationally, with caution. A
few dozen mildly manic Christians were sitting around balancing
plates on laps while solicitously offering one another more filtered
water and blandly discussing non-political topics. About half

were Whites – from Britain, Scandinavia, Germany, Switzerland –
whose female component vied for the attentions of a tubby, bouncy
Kenyan bishop. Black church workers from up-country – teachers,
nurses, lay-preachers – loudly discussed fund-raising. Four Nigerians, in Nairobi for a theological conference, were conspicuous
because several shades darker than the average Kenyan and many
shades more sophisticated. They also seemed outsiders and spon-
taneously we got together over our kedgeree and salad. These high-
powered theologians immediately sought my opinion of Teilhard de
Chardin, Hans Kung and other pioneering Christian thinkers; then,
realising that this was an unequal meeting of minds, they turned
down the heat with typical African courtesy. A history lesson
followed. In West Africa, they proudly told me, the Freetown and
Lagos grammar schools had always upheld European academic
standards and at Fourah Bay Institution, affiliated to Durham
University since 1875, Hebrew and Greek had formed part of the
ordination course since the 1840s. By 1890, West Africa's seventy-
six Anglican priests included several Durham or Cambridge graduates. In East Africa the missionaries never demanded the same
educational standards of Blacks as of Whites, or even tried to give
a sound theological training, and the first barely literate deacons
were ordained only in the mid-1890s.

After dinner a small energetic Kikuyu woman of indeterminate
age herded us all into the adjacent sitting-room for a Holy Time.
Beaming ferociously at her captives, she set about arousing fervour:
'Have we any soloists who can please Jesus by singing beautiful
hymns?'

We hadn't. My eyes wandered to the television set high above us,
near the ceiling. Julie Ward's father was being interviewed outside
Nairobi's imposing courthouse. On that flickering screen the poor
fellow seemed to have St Vitus's Dance. The Luo teacher beside me
muttered angrily, 'Why so much fuss about this one murder? Only
because she was White and killing her is bad for the tourist trade.
Every day Kenyan people are murdered in Kenya and there is no
fuss!'

Inexorably our shepherdess drove us towards a semblance of
fervour. 'Now, all together, let's clap for Jesus! And now we'll
stamp the feet for Jesus! Show him how your love for him carries
you away!'

I glanced around the room; my fellow-Whites seemed as much at ease with this charade as their Black colleagues. Then I caught the eyes of the Nigerian quartet and it was clear that they, too, were planning their escape.

At last our opportunity came: 'Now let's sing and dance for Jesus! Everyone hold hands and jump around for joy!' Within five minutes I had jumped to and beyond the door. The Nigerians, at the far end of a long room, had farther to dance but soon passed my bedroom, laughing quietly. The source of their amusement was not hard to guess.

I hadn't planned to linger in Nairobi and Day One did not tempt me to change my mind. At dawn, psychopathic drivers were already racing each other up and down Cathedral Road. Negotiating the junction to cross Kenyatta Avenue brought me out in a cold sweat. On the Uhuru Highway, which would lead me out of the capital, I funked cycling and walked. Then came a four-lane motorway in the making; on both sides of this Prestige Project unschooled children swarmed between homes ingeniously constructed in varying combinations of tin, plywood, cardboard, canvas and plastic sheeting. A local man who had appointed himself my escort ('There are criminals here!') complained that before the official opening of the motorway this area would be 'tidied': the shacks bulldozed, the inhabitants banished beyond sight of foreign visitors.

In Britain's anti-racist circles it is often said that Afro-Caribbean children should be shown photographs of African city centres where sleek limousines create traffic jams between skyscraping architectural extravagances. These, it is argued (usually by people who have never set foot in Africa) would enhance Black children's self-esteem, allegedly damaged by pictures of shanty towns, mud huts, medicine men in sinister attire, women carrying water from distant wells and other such 'stereotyping' images. Yet city centres like Nairobi's illustrate the most shameful aspect of modern Africa, not its achievements. Millions live in shanty towns, patients must depend on medicine men and women must carry water because African politicians are so addicted to motorways, limousines and architectural excesses. However, facing such facts is as distasteful to extreme anti-racists as to the West's donor governments, the World Bank, and the many UN and other agencies who find it expedient to evade or distort African realities.

7

Where construction work was still in progress two lanes of the Prestige Project were closed to motor traffic but open to cyclists, pedestrians and beasts of burden. Scores of fine-boned donkeys, their crosses conspicuous on short, sleek oaten coats, carried charcoal, brushwood, vegetables or plastic jerry-cans of water, three or four on each side. Some were teamed in twos or threes to draw crude wooden carts, each bearing several tar-barrels. Elsewhere, Kenyan donkeys look privileged; here many were overworked, underfed and dreadfully afflicted by sores. Urban life takes its toll among all species.

In the busy scruffy little town of Limuru I tried to buy a newspaper but already the day's editions had been sold out, a measure of the interest taken in the Mothers' Protest and its sequel. Turning west off the motorway towards the Mau Escarpment, my spirits rose as I pedalled upwards – slowly, being not yet accustomed to the weight of the panniers. Soon the tarred surface gave way to loose large stones, ridges of sharp rock and stretches of deep dust – suffocating and blinding when the occasional truck passed. Lear had to be pushed for two gruelling hours through apparently uninhabited grey-green scrub, the gravelly soil desiccated below thorn trees, the silence broken only by raucous or plaintive or alarmed bird-calls. At intervals a group of children or a couple of youths waited hopefully for some passing driver to buy their little cellophane bags of mangoes or small hard sweet pears; evidently this bush concealed dwellings. One smiling young man presented me with three pears and said, 'No money from Mama!' In Africa numerous benefits accrue to the granny generation.

On the edge of the escarpment tarmac reappeared, allowing me to freewheel for miles, weaving between the sort of mega-pot-holes that unnerve drivers but leave cyclists relaxed. The steep slopes above the road were darkly pine-covered; far below on my left stretched the Rift Valley's immense heat-hazed flatness. Even while descending at speed I was aware of the rising temperature.

A small township on the valley floor marked the junction where I was to turn west for Narok. Here a mud-brick, tin-roofed shack-bar tempted me to pause for a Tusker, in defiance of colonial folk-wisdom. Crude wooden trestle tables and benches wobbled on the earth floor and a vast earthenware jar of cold water, covered with drenched sacking, served as refrigerator. The owner, Ruth, was a vigorous, voluble Kikuyu woman, long since deserted by her husband and now feeling let down by her 14-year-old son.

'I saved and saved to send him to boarding-school but he won't study. I tell him he can leave school and go to Nairobi and look for his father to feed him. My daughter is 9 years old and a good student. I will spend the money on her. Kenya needs educated women. The men are lazy and weak, only pretending to be important. The women know how to work. So our girls should learn how to work with their brains, then they can take over the government and show men how to do things sensibly!'

As I was applauding this viewpoint, an anti-AIDS poster on the opposite wall caught my eye. It depicted an emaciated young man surrounded by his grieving family. 'That came from Uganda,' said Ruth. 'Even in the villages there people are dying. Here it's a city disease, brought by Americans – and now they try to blame *us*! To save money for education I had to work with many men, now I won't have truck-drivers or city men though they pay most. I have a brain, I can see how this disease goes. If you get it money won't cure it – OK?'

Emphatically I agreed, then wondered if I should remark that by now working with *any* men is dangerous. But I hesitated to throw my White weight about. Kenya is – or was then – reluctant to admit the extent of its AIDS problem. In 1988 a rash of sensational Western press reports, describing the epidemic sweeping through East Africa, caused a 30 per cent decline in tourism earnings – normally around £220 million a year and Kenya's main source of hard currency.

A strong cross-wind tempered the sun's ferocity as I followed a narrow, smooth tarmac road through Hell's Gate National Park. Few vehicles disturbed the peace and there were neither dwellings nor people, only scores of fat placid zebra and statuesque eland, and hundreds of graceful Thomson's gazelle wandering through the sparse bush. To me those last are among the most beautiful of creatures, their russet flanks darkly striped, their horns elegantly curved, all their movements exquisite. Even as a child, long before conservation became fashionable, it baffled me that Europeans could regard the unprovoked killing of such animals as a boast-worthy personal triumph.

Hell's Gate National Park, recently established at the expense of the local Masai's grazing rights, is named after that spot on Lake Naivasha where a German explorer, Gustav Fischer, was forced by the Masai to retreat in 1882. The earlier explorers of the Lake Victoria region had cautiously skirted Masailand because these pastoralists, who migrated from Southern Sudan a few centuries ago, long remained determined to prevent any European encroachment on their territory. However, by the early 1890s the clan quarrel between the Ilmasai and the Iloikop – combined with epidemics of cholera, smallpox, rinderpest and consequent famine – had so reduced Masai numbers and vitality that the British were able to negotiate a treaty with Olonana, their *laibon* or religious leader-cum-chief. The subsequent construction of the Mombasa-to-Uganda railway bisected Masailand and, when the settlers arrived, the Masai were banished to two reserves, north and south of the railway. As settler demands increased, the colonial authorities compelled the Masai to leave the northern reserve and move south. Ever since, they have grazed that reserve and parts of northern Tanzania, but having to share their territory with protected wildlife naturally causes some conflict between tribesmen and game wardens.

In regions with any considerable Masai population I was to hear frequent references to 'those stupid backward people'. Their conspicuous presence, wandering proudly across the landscape in traditional dress, irritates those eager to seem Westernised. There must also be some underlying envy. In general, the Masai spurned Christianity, one of the colonists' main control levers, and for generations remained untempted by mission education, 'status'-bestowing European dress and first names, the cash economy and its concomitant consumerism. Supremely confident of their superiority to everyone else, Black or White, only they have preserved their integrity as Africans. When they meet the *mzungu* (foreigner) their gaze is direct, calm, assured, untroubled by the confusions that beset too many of their more adaptable fellow-citizens. But inevitably Masailand is now changing. It has become a sad region where a tribe long celebrated for its dignity, courage, endurance, physical beauty and independence of spirit is gradually being overwhelmed by the demands of game parks, agribusiness and tourism.

At 4 p.m. I rejoiced to see a bank of dark cloud spreading up from the eastern horizon. By then I was flagging; that deceptive wind had

not really protected me from the perilous equatorial sun. Longingly
I watched those clouds; their blackness seemed promising. All afternoon my destination had been visible: a jumbled range of blue
mountains rising dramatically from the level plain. Near the edge
of the plain, hundreds of fenced-in acres were planted with arti-
ficially fertilised and irrigated grass and wheat; a Nairobi tycoon had
recently developed this ranch, I later learned.

As the road rose and the sun sank, the air cooled and I revived.
Here, on the scrubby hillsides, unkempt shambas (small farms) surrounded the square huts of Masai families who had been forced to
settle and cultivate – a shaming occupation for pastoralists, some of
whom hire Kikuyu women to work for them. The road wound from
ridge to ridge, each higher than the last, and the pedestrian traffic
consisted mainly of Masai. An aura of privilege and aristocratic
poise surrounds even the younger generation – tall, lean young men
with features that seem carefully sculpted. Each carried a long
herding stick and a short polished knobkerrie, the only weapon now
allowed to men who in former days would never have been seen
without a spear. Some, too, had ear mutilations that involved the
lower half being completely cut off, not merely elongated. So there
is no hope for the local donkeys, many of whom have cropped ears –
only one-third left – as this is believed to check braying.

Towards sunset the breeze became a strong wind, thunder
growled above the distant Aberdares, lightning danced among the
swelling clouds – and at last a deluge came, quickly dissolving my
patina of salt crystals. The map showed no village ahead and neither
the terrain nor the weather favoured camping. I realised then how
different was Kenya from tourist-free Cameroon where I had
trekked in 1987. There, at sunset, one can be sure of a warm if
puzzled welcome in any remote compound. Here, only some
extreme emergency could adequately explain a *mzungu*'s seeking
hospitality in the bush. Because tourists are amply catered for by
Kenya's smart hotels, the notion of any White curling up happily
in the corner of a hut would shock and upset; I knew that intuitively.
On my return to Kenya four months later, for a longer period, I
realised that this potential for embarrassment between the races is
not entirely based on the existence of an organised tourist industry.
A half-century of White settlement created a racial chasm unknown
in Cameroon.

It was almost dark when I panted on to the highest ridge-top, by then resigned to camping damply. But there – hurrah! – stood a guest-house, surrounded by a six-foot wooden fence. This was the biggest building in a newish trading centre not marked on any map. In the empty wick-lit bar I was welcomed wonderingly by Ed and Gin. Gin spoke no English; Ed's was quite fluent. He wheeled Lear across a wide flooded yard to our £2 room – the walls and floor concrete, the barred window unglazed, the tin roof supported by stout beams, the only furniture a hard but comfortable single bed with clean cotton sheets. This being a modern establishment, three toilet bowls had been installed in cubicles at the far end of the yard and there were two open-air wash-basins with chrome taps: an expensive mistake, Ed admitted, since running water remained a pipe-dream. The usable latrine was a hygienic forty yards away, in the bush.

Supper consisted of a one-egg omelette and a small tomato. The family had already eaten, Ed explained apologetically, and there were no left-overs. Abraham arrived as I ate, introducing himself as 'a Christian pastor'. He was tall, fortyish, quiet spoken, careworn and teetotal, but tolerant. 'From Nairobi is seventy miles,' he observed, as Ed opened yet another Tusker. 'You need much liquid, cycling in the hot season.'

My companions were pessimistic about Kenya's future. 'We have eighteen millionaires and eighteen million paupers,' quoted Ed. '*That's* our problem!'

Abraham added, 'But the West helped to make this problem and still subsidises our corrupt leaders – *why*?' Then he fulminated against the staffing of Nairobi's Kenyatta Hospital (the biggest in the country) by expatriates whose monthly salaries exceed what Kenyan doctors can earn in a year, even Kenyan doctors more highly qualified than the expatriates. Ed laughed and said, 'Some Whitemen like Africa very much – here they can get big pay for a little learning.'

Both men were riveted by my 'very big adventure', as Ed described it. They pored over the map by lamplight, considering my proposed route. Then Abraham straightened up and sighed. 'For most of this way,' he said, 'you'll be on the *ukimwi* road.'

Ed translated. 'In KiSwahili, we say *ukimwi* for AIDS.'

Abraham accepted another Coca-Cola and asked, 'Are you going to help people about this plague?'

'How can I? I'm only a traveller, not a medical person.'

'That I understand,' said Abraham. 'But I meant help with *information*. You are from the West, educated, old enough to be respected. You must know all about this plague and many of our people are ignorant. They need information and may listen to you. You must help them. I have thought about this in my own work, as parson. By changing the way only *one* person behaves, we can save many lives.' He moved the lamp closer and stared at me. 'Now you don't like what I'm saying. But you cannot follow the *ukimwi* road and be silent! There is no medicine for this plague, only *information* to stop it. You have that information and must share it. All our Western visitors should do this but for tourists it's not so easy, especially young tourists. They cannot talk about certain things without giving offence. But for you, an old woman staying in villages, there will be many opportunities. I believe God has sent me here tonight, to give you this guidance.'

When Abraham had left, carrying a dozen Coca-Colas for his son's birthday party, Ed asked me, 'Why do you look so worried?'

I prevaricated; it would be difficult to explain that the role of 'educated White woman informing ignorant Africans' did not appeal to me. Yet I saw, too clearly for my own comfort, that Abraham had reason on his side. One day out from Nairobi, my therapeutic journey seemed at risk.

I emerged into a chilly pale world. Above the eastern horizon lay long lines of pale primrose cloud; young pale green grass grew by the roadside; a pale blue sky arched over an immense undulating expanse of low, dense grey-green bush. Now I could see that this was not a ridge-top but another wide plateau, tilting westwards. For twenty-five miles the traffic-free road to Narok descended gradually through country inhabited only by massive tusked warthogs, dainty gazelle and a multitude of brilliant birds darting and swerving through the tangled vegetation.

Narok in its broad valley, overlooked from the north by forested slopes, seemed almost metropolitan: a large, straggling, crowded place, untidy and undistinguished. As in all East African towns, one is aware of an imported way of life having been suddenly grafted on to a culture unprepared to receive it. This alien flavour is strengthened by the visual assertiveness of decaying colonial offices, incongruous European-style churches, thriving Asian business premises. East Africa, when taken over, was not at the stage of building administrative centres or running commercial enterprises. Apart from the Arabs' coastal cities, it had no centuries-old strongholds of indigenous culture, like Kano and Timbuctoo; it is hardly surprising that its towns lack character.

In a cramped, ill-lit hoteli, four meat samozas and four cups of sweet weak milky tea broke my fast. (Hotelis offer food but no accommodation, which is rather confusing for the newcomer.) Neither the staff nor my fellow-customers – three men eating mounds of rice and strips of gristle – spoke English. Faced with a language barrier, Kenyans tend to be aloof, almost hostile, I fancied later, wandering around Narok in search of groundnuts. But perhaps I was mistaking unease for antagonism. Abraham had warned me that 'uneducated Kenyans' (many Africans are fond of this academic class distinction) expect elders to behave with dignity. And travelling by bicycle is not dignified for any European, least of all a female elder; one rarely sees an African woman cyclist.

Just beyond Narok I paused to observe a small Masai cattle-fair. On a dusty common, encircled by soaring blue gums, a few score cows and calves – long-horned, glossy though thin, as beautiful to look on as their owners – were being denigrated by Nairobi traders whose trucks waited nearby. The Masai listened in haughty silence. 'They won't bargain,' said the elderly Kikuyu by my side, who had also stopped to watch. 'When they don't get their price they are happy. They want not to sell, they only try because of the drought. They love their cattle more than their families. They are primitive people with no education.'

As he spoke, several Masai women of all ages converged on me, offering bead necklets and wristlets. They were quietly courteous, despite my declining to buy. A young man then appeared, wearing a red plaid cotton tunic, slit up the sides to reveal his copper flanks, and a complicated phoney-looking head-dress of twigs and leather thongs. In happier times he would have been a *moran*, jointly responsible, with the rest of his age group, for defending herds and homesteads. Five US dollars was his price for being photographed but he too accepted 'no deal' with a polite smile, then spotted a safari van in the distance and hurried towards it. Many such vans stop briefly in Narok, *en route* for the Masai Mara Game Park. Ed had

14

grumbled that Asian tour operators and the Masai gain most from Kenya's tourist industry. He couldn't see that the Masai deserve as big a slice as they can get of the tourism cake, their traditional resources having been so grievously depleted by the development of game parks, Kenya's main tourist attraction.

It was already cruelly hot, at 9.30, as I pushed Lear up a long precipitous hill towards the turn-off on to a traffic-free (I hoped) earth road. Near the junction, outside a posh new Tourist Lodge-cum-petrol station, two minibus-loads of Germans, returning from Masai Mara, were queuing to photograph jewellery-laden Masai women and ersatz warriors bearing pretend spears. Ingeniously, the broad wooden blades had been covered in glittering tinfoil.

My earth road was indeed traffic-free; after a few smooth miles the surface became acutely motor-deterring. Again I was on a high, wide plateau, cooled by a steady breeze. No dwellings were visible but small herds of cattle wandered through ragged scrub, avidly cropping the short new grass. An occasional cow ambled on to the road to drink from muddy lakelets, then stood surveying me with that intense bovine curiosity which seems so absurdly flattering – why should one be of such interest to any fellow-creature? Previously, young warriors guarded the herds; now, in this area, no predators remain and the children in charge – usually boys, sometimes girls – smiled at me shyly, or waved from a distance; none begged for money. The Masai are shocked to hear that in our 'advanced' countries it is no longer always safe for children to roam alone.

Soon after midday a hamlet appeared, another of those isolated settlements where dispossessed Masai have reluctantly put down roots. Tin-roofed shacks of rough-hewn planks or concrete blocks lined the road and between them flourished many gawky papaw trees, which need no care. But all the maize was too close-planted and disastrously weedy. As I sought some non-alcoholic drink an ancient Asian Muslim, wearing a long white gown and embroidered skull-cap, stared derisively at me from his cubby-hole clothes shop. The other store was a Masai grocery, stocking only soap, Vick, salt, razor blades, weevil-infested biscuits, blighted Irish potatoes and warm Coca-Cola. A degenerate-looking young man charged me double for a Coke (fair enough in the back of beyond) and then tried to short-change me. The *mzungu*'s arrival had drawn the entire population on to the road but it did not form a welcoming crowd

15

and my usually successful efforts to surmount the language barrier received no co-operation. As a group of ragged youths gathered around Lear, discussing his unfamiliar features without reference to me, I mused on the vulnerability of cyclists: the loot itself provides the getaway transport.

Not far beyond the hamlet I lay in the bush for an hour, reading my Nancy Mitford Omnibus – carefully selected as ideal escapist literature – and marvelling at the quantity of sweat flowing off my body; when I stood up, the dusty patch where I had lain was turned to mud. Then suddenly clouds rode to the rescue. On an earth road these provide instant relief; on tarmac the heat is retained and radiates up, relentlessly, for hours after the sun has been obscured. Happily I pedalled on, the track plunging in and out of mini-ravines and the bush now an impenetrable tangle, through which protruded aeon-smoothed monoliths of bare rock.

Two hours later my cloud-shield delivered a tropical storm of blinding violence. I was then pushing Lear up a steep slope through deep yellow dust and within moments he had been immobilized by sticky mud tightly packed under his misnamed mudguards. Mercifully the hilltop village of Olololunga was near; through horizontal sheets of gale-driven rain I could dimly see a long, low concrete building. The stricken Lear had to be half-dragged, half-carried to the shelter of this health-centre from which, as I arrived, an unconscious little boy was being borne to a pick-up truck by distraught parents. (The district health-worker was not available that week; he had gone to a wedding in Narok.) For twenty minutes I cowered on the veranda, sodden and shivering, watching the truck's desperate struggle to reach the hilltop. Time and time again the driver tried every manoeuvre he knew but each ended in a skid, the wheels slewing to left or right. Finally he gave up and the patient was moved to a nearby house.

Abruptly the wind dropped and the rain lightened. Olololunga lies at right angles to the road and, leaving the health-centre, I hauled Lear up its sloping street – a wide cart-track, now converted to a rushing torrent. Clearly this trading centre had seen better days; the steps leading up to the dukas (very small shops) were perilously broken, the tin roofs askew and patched, the cigarette and patent medicine advertisements almost illegible. When I asked about lodgings blank stares were the only response. Where the village merged into grassland I hesitated, then saw a young Masai in Western dress carrying a crate of empty beer bottles from the last house. At once my spirits rose. 'Tusker?' I shouted hopefully.

The young man stared, then abandoned his crate and leaped down to assist me. His name was Tambo and his English rudimentary though fluent enough for the occasion. Here was no lodging-house (nor, come to think of it, could I see any reason why there should be one) but yes, this bar stocked Tuskers. Nothing indicated that his house was a bar so I made a mental note for future reference: 'Even if no bar in sight, *ask* for beer.'

Tambo carried Lear, minus panniers, to the back entrance via a steep grassy incline. Then he showed me an empty storeroom smelling of musty maize and mouse-droppings; here I could sleep, free of charge, if I had my own bedding. And if I had my own lock the door could be secured. To please him I locked it, though the window had neither glass nor grille.

In the bar I collapsed on to a long horse-hair couch suffering from broken springs; it screamed in agony whenever anybody shifted position. At one end sat an ancient Masai woman, wearing a moderate amount of jewellery and a filthy tattered gown and clutching a bottle of Tusker. At the other end sat a burly dark-suited man, wearing a gold signet ring and a straw boater and drinking Guinness (expensive in Kenya) from a glass. The woman smiled at me, revealing a residue of jagged and blackened fangs, and we wordlessly shook hands. The man greeted me effusively in English and asked, 'What is your mission?' When I had explained myself he repeated, 'But what is your *mission*, what are you working for? Who is funding you? Or are you sponsored, cycling for charity?'

Ed had asked the same questions; scores of others were to repeat them all along my route. To Africans the concept of unsubsidised solo travelling seems a weird aberration. Sometimes I tried to explain that Westerners can save money on Third World journeys. This four-month 'African Experience' was to cost me less than £420, plus £470 for my air-fare; and the days have long gone when one could survive in Ireland for four months on less than £900.

The Masai mama took no further interest in me; that Tusker was not her first and she tended to doze. Matthew, however, waxed autobiographical. After 'the best' education at a Nakuru mission school his politician uncle in Nairobi helped to set him up in the

17

import business. Then a few years ago he sensed the coming slump ('I have a sharp brain, I see ahead') and Uncle arranged for him to go into an agribusiness partnership with two 'brothers', actually Uncle's sons. 'Tomorrow you'll see our ranch, it was neglected Masai land, now it is producing well with a foreign grant for aerial spraying.'

'A grant from whom?' I asked.

Matthew ignored that and hurried on to family details. He had married at 21 and his bride produced their first-born before she was 17. 'Soon we had four of each,' said Matthew complacently, 'which is sound economics. But eight is enough so I took my wife to Nairobi for the operation – she was only 30 and could have ten more!'

By then I needed another Tusker but Tambo had disappeared. I found him in the yard, beside a barrel of rainwater, painstakingly cleaning Lear. Having somehow unblocked the wheels and scoured the mudguards, Tambo was using a small paintbrush to clear every vestige of mud from gears, chain and brakes. I was speechless with gratitude. My Masai knight smiled up at me and advised, 'Rain comes on dust, you leave road and stand!'

Matthew's taciturn wife Ella ran Olololunga's hoteli, to which I was eventually invited, as a guest, for an excellent meal of beef stew, braised potatoes, greens and chapattis. In the lamp-lit bar, two earnest young teachers were awaiting my return. Both claimed to belong to minor tribes, thus distancing themselves from the regional Kikuyu/Masai land-based tensions. When they probed for my reactions to Matthew I was noncommittal. Only one spoke fluent English though both taught the language. Tobias said, 'New problems are coming here, the Masai don't like agricultural development. They don't want compensation, they want the land for their cattle. When the government makes them take money, what can they do with it? They have no education, no way to *use* money. In this district we have too many young Masai ready to be dangerous – no land, no cattle, no work, only compensation money. And with that they can buy weapons from Ethiopia or Somalia.'

My views on the FORD campaign for a multi-party democracy were eagerly sought. Sleepily I explained that I didn't understand Kenyan politics and therefore had no views on the subject.

Tobias scowled. 'But don't you understand that for us it's *bad*? It's making us kill each other! Our President sometimes does wrong and donor countries get angry and try to rule us with their ideas like in colonial times. Why not leave us to make our own mistakes? In the Cold War nobody cared about democracy in Kenya if anti-Communists were in power. Since Independence the West has supported tyrants in Africa – Amin, Mbuto, Barre, Banda – were *they* democrats? Do you think we're so primitive and stupid we can't see the way you play around with us?'

'It's my bedtime,' I said, 'you must excuse me.' I stood up then and they shook hands and smiled – but not with their eyes, which remained angry.

At 5.45 the morning star shone solitary and brilliant in a violet sky and from rain-revived vegetation drifted an aromatic complexity of scents. Lear, after a soothing supper of oil, was functioning faultlessly on the level earth road – bone-dry, apart from numerous crater lakes. To the west lay a faraway frieze of low, rounded, dusky-blue hills, marking the end of this almost unpopulated plateau. In the dawn coolness, gazelle herds crossed the road just ahead of me, moving unhurriedly in single file. But too quickly the sun climbed and the bush lost its soft shadowiness, becoming again all harsh thorny angularity – until suddenly it was replaced by irrigated wire-fenced fields.

Here the surface improved, for the benefit of the ranch's shiny new tractors and trucks, and a monoplane cruised low above the young wheat, trailing long yellow-green plumes of pesticide vapour. My watering eyes and itchy nose and throat stirred Rumanian memories. When a Landrover arrived at a cluster of buildings – also shiny and new – I dawdled to watch two agribusinessmen in pin-striped suits consulting thick folders while mud-stained foremen deferentially stood by.

At a crossroads on the edge of the plateau I was surprised to see a signpost – deformed and barely legible, one of only two observed in Kenya. It advised me to turn right for Bomet but said nothing about distance. Gradually the track descended, coiling around deforested slopes, their umber nakedness gashed by red erosion gullies. Beyond stretched hilly bush, much greener than usual, where two little boys were milking among the acacia. I hastened hopefully towards them with my half-litre mug and delightedly they sold me a litre of warm foamy milk for the equivalent of 50 pence, the standard price; bush cattle yield so little that milk costs twice as much as beer.

Forty miles from Olololunga we joined another Prestige Project and for the next three hours – the hottest of the day – Lear skimmed swiftly over velvet-smooth tarmac. This pukka road carried little motor traffic as it swept grandly, in expensively engineered curves, through a suddenly different landscape. Shambas crowded the fertile hillsides and narrow valleys and each ridge-top overlooked many other ridges, offering a study in green – dark green wattle groves, tender green tea-gardens, dull green plantains, emerald green young maize, faded green blue gums, pale green sugar-cane. When Herbert Binks, one of the earliest settlers, surveyed this region in 1901 he found the Kikuyu cultivators enjoying two or three harvests a year. In *African Rainbow* he records the purchase, by one settler, of 640 acres of the richest land for two rupees an acre, payable over fifteen years.

From beehive huts children came tumbling by the score to jump up and down on the verge, waving with both hands while chanting, '*Mzungu! Mzungu! Mzungu!*' The adults were no less friendly; several cyclists pedalled beside me for a few miles, asking the usual questions, deploring the region's politically unsettled state and warning me to be careful – 'Bad men could rob and kill you!' They were disbelieving when told that in Europe, too, we have bad men who rob and kill.

An uninhabited stretch, its precipitous slopes planted with coniferous junipers, separates this region from Sotik district. At a seedy T-junction trading centre, which I at first mistook for Sotik town, a disproportionate number of young Kipsigi males were hanging about, looking restive; on my dismounting to seek lodgings they yelled jeeringly, then gestured threateningly. I retreated towards two elderly nurses leaving a small mission hospital opposite the dukas and beer-halls. Quickly they looked me up and down, before curtly directing me to the Sotik Hotel, a few miles further on. Relieved, I sped downhill through a wood of blue gums and pungently resinous pines and arrived in Sotik proper with an hour of daylight to spare.

2

Graduates or Warriors?

Sotik to Maseno

———————

The small town of Sotik, half a mile off the main Kericho–Kisii road, overlooks hilly fertile farmland semi-encircled by gentle mountains. On the outskirts stands the Sotik Hotel, surrounded by piles of builders' rubble and malodorous restaurant garbage. Its five jerry-built storeys seem excessive; rumour had it that a local politician's son-in-law was the contractor. Wide black streaks on the concrete façade led my eye to defective guttering and the enormous square patio became an ankle-deep pond when it rained. However, the staff were amiable, though none spoke comprehensible English, and the wooden table and chair in my £3 room guaranteed a writer's comfort. Unfortunately, privacy was limited by a broken window pane through which inquisitive hands could (and often did) pull aside the flimsy curtain. In my *en suite* bathroom the shower worked but the lavatory had long since become a health hazard.

I was about to shower when a policeman knocked on my door and brusquely ordered me to remain in Sotik 'until further notice'. As I began to argue he added, 'For your safety, madame'. He declined to expatiate but later on, reading a borrowed copy of the *Daily Nation*, I saw his point. Between Sotik and the Ugandan border nasty things were happening. 'Tribal warfare', explained the *Nation*. My two Luo drinking-companions in the bleak third-floor hotel bar – up a concrete spiral stairway reeking of urine – had another explanation. 'It's Moi stirring trouble,' one muttered in my ear. 'He's trying to prove multi-party democracy won't work in Kenya.' Then two Kikuyus entered and the Luos fell silent.

Sotik is a Kipsigi centre and the Kalenjin-speaking, Nilo-Hamitic Kipsigis (President Moi's small tribe) are on the Kikuyus' side against the Luos. These last are not to be confused with the Western

21

Bantu Luhyas, though I personally wouldn't blame anyone for confusing tribes which to European ears sound identical. Much as it pains me to have to agree with the reprehensible Moi, it has to be said that none of Kenya's forty tribes is known for its devotion to Western-style multi-party democracy. Nor is it realistic to expect them to appreciate a political system so remote from their own traditions.

For £1.20 the hotel restaurant provided ideal cyclist-fodder: a tender giant steak (it covered the dinner-plate) with three helpings of crisp chips and carefully cooked cabbage. I complimented the cheerful young chef when he left his cockroach-busy kitchen to observe my gustatory reactions. He beamed and explained, 'Here we learned to cook the English way. My grandfather and father cooked always for the same family. They could serve you many complicated meals, now we have only simple foods.'

At the next table sat a bank clerk newly arrived in Sotik. He was doleful. 'My home is in Kisumu, a real town. This place is only a trading centre. What will my wife say when she sees it? Where are my children to get good education? The older ones must stay with their grandparents.' (At 34 he had six children and a seventh on the way.) 'My wife must stay in Kisumu to have this baby, here she might die. And how can we bear such cold nights? We have always lived in Kisumu.'

Another grievance concerned his youngest brother; on applying for a bank job he had been told he must have an AIDS test. 'These people say they cannot waste money training youngsters who may soon die. This insults my brother. He is a good Catholic boy, he lives like a Christian. Now he is looking for other work, he is too much afraid of the test. But he can find nothing else so secure and well-paid with nice promotion.'

I remained silent; it seemed not the occasion for drawing logical conclusions.

Sotik's night-life happens in its hotel and the inhuman decibels of amplified reggae and punk rock blared until 4.15 a.m. After that I needed my fortifying breakfast (for 70 pence) of two giant chef-made beef sausages, two slabs of bacon, two fried eggs, a pyramid of bread thickly buttered and a large pot of strong hot tea. Foodwise, I could have been delayed in no better place.

It took me all of fifteen minutes to explore the town. Poorly stocked ex-Asian shops, solidly built but neglected, lined the dusty, pot-holed main (and only) street. In significant contrast were two pretentious new banks (Barclays and KCB) and two garish new petrol stations (Esso and Caltex). Coca-Cola was yet to come; elsewhere, many township shop-fronts had recently been painted cream with the Coca-Cola script writ large and high in crimson lettering visible from afar. This jollification of otherwise dismal trading centres is rewarded by a prodigious consumption of the liquid advertised, which costs exactly ten times as much as a more wholesome and equally refreshing cup of tea.

To the chagrin of President Moi – uncomfortably aware of donor scrutiny – Kenya now enjoys a more or less free press, though its freedom was hard-won and is always under threat. The literate public values this aspect of democracy and every morning I saw newspapers being attentively read on the streets, in tea-shops, around the marketplaces. Moreover, even in Sotik, reputedly a pro-Moi stronghold, those papers which try to be objective seemed the most popular. Kenyans are shrewd folk who know a propaganda sheet when they see it and prefer to acquire the facts – if possible – and do their own interpreting: which augurs well for the long-term political future of their country.

To state that most Africans are noisy is an allowable generalisation; whatever their mood – usually cheerful – they like to give tongue. Yet Sotik that day was strangely quiet. Although I sensed no hostility to the *mzungu* everyone was being uncommunicative, not only with me but with each other. Apart that is from Albert, who ran a cramped but busy general store and seemed something of an enigma. He was tall, well-built, grey-haired, exceptionally black and forcefully eloquent. He should, I felt, have been lecturing at some university rather than selling pints of kerosene, half-pounds of rice and quarter bars of soap behind a Sotik counter. I hinted as much, but he only slightly enlightened me.

'You're right, I'm not a local man. So I don't have to get involved in all this present nonsense. And I'm not afraid to talk. It's good for foreigners to know what's going on, though not many give a damn about Kenya unless they want a holiday here – looking at *animals*! Who cares about Kenya's endangered humans? Yet now we're sliding to the edge of the abyss. You must avoid Sondu, a small town but dangerous now. At midday yesterday, when the

23

market was crowded with Luo, the Kipsigi attacked, using pangas, spears, poisoned arrows. Eight Luo were killed, scores badly wounded. Forty of their huts were burned. Those Kipsigi were trucked in from elsewhere, they weren't residents. In fact many were unemployed graduates, disguised in warrior garb. My son was there – he's studying these developments – and he recognised nine of his classmates among the "warriors". Trouble was expected in Sondu but the police kept off the scene, no doubt obeying orders. Take my advice and move fast to Uganda. Hundreds of Luo work on Sotik's tea estates – maybe the next targets?'

In 1882, Joseph Thomson wrote to his Royal Geographical Society patrons requesting copies of *Punch, The Illustrated London News, The Athenaeum* and *The Graphic*: 'A bundle of such, coming across my path in the Masai country, would indeed be a boon and a blessing.' Following the same line of thought, I spent the hot noon hours on my bed engaged in *The Pursuit of Love*. Then a sadness shadowed my day; calling on Sotik's Mill Hill missionaries, I heard that a young colleague of theirs and good friend of mine – first met in Cameroon – had recently died of malarial complications.

Back at the hotel, a compactly muscular young man was awaiting me in the bar. He wore a neat but shabby grey suit, its open jacket revealing a Harvard University T-shirt.

'They told me you come from Ireland,' he said. 'My name is Moses and my teachers were Irish – Father Declan, Father Pat, Father Malachy. They were good teachers and now I love Ireland.' He sat opposite me and added, 'You will give me a beer.'

That demand grated; within moments I would have offered a beer. Repressing my annoyance, I ordered two Tuskers while Moses lamented his fate – in the same health-worker job since his marriage nine years ago, with no hope of advancement because he couldn't afford bribes and knew no Big Men.

When I suggested taking our beers outside to enjoy the sunset, Moses declined to move. The balcony overlooked level common-land, dotted with tin-roofed shacks and thatched huts, each in its little vegetable plot. As I was being awed by the conflagration above the western hills, Joseph joined me – a loquacious government vet first met the previous evening. Together we watched a prosperous-looking gentleman in a city suit herding two cows with calves

24

towards a large colonial bungalow surrounded by a grassy acre, once no doubt a gracious garden.

'That's a Big Man at Barclays in Kisumu,' observed Joseph. 'Every weekend he comes home to his cattle. Cattle are still important here, owning even a few makes us calm. His father got that house from an English farmer. Some families were lucky at Independence, the English going home gave them presents of buildings and land. They just had to promise to treat the dogs and cats and horses very well, and to *talk to them*!' (This last concept vastly amused Joseph.) 'The English are very religious about pet animals – is it the same in Ireland? My grandfather says they're afraid animals will curse them if they're not treated like humans – is that true? Anyway we did look after them, we felt so grateful for the land. Their children are still around, mixed in with our own animals.'

I glanced sideways at Joseph, whose neat oval face was bronze in the afterglow. At first I had suspected irony but he was being utterly sincere. Evidently no one had ever told him that in many cases the retreating settlers had originally acquired their land through robbery with violence. In 1906 a British army captain, Richard Meinertzhagen, was busy 'pacifying' this Sotik region and wrote in his journal:

26 Feb. A ring of posts is being established round the reserve and Nandi found outside it are to be shot at sight . . . Though the Government have achieved their purpose in punishing the Nandi and confining them to a reserve, I am not so sure that it has finally disposed of the Nandi question.
6 March. We have been most successful against those Nandi who broke out of the reserve . . . When it was just light enough to shoot we surprised a party in a hollow not more than forty yards from us. I at once ordered rapid fire and the whole party of thirteen were shot down . . . By this time Wilson had reached the vicinity and the enemy was completely surrounded. They lost thirty-two killed. I took my position on Chebarus Hill, whence I could overlook the operations . . . [which] . . . I hope will convince the Nandi of the futility of breaking out of their reserve . . . We effected a complete surprise, finding many of the enemy still in their huts. We killed nineteen Nandi and captured thirty-four. We also bagged 542 sheep and goats. We had

25

two men wounded. When natives are surprised like this they have little heart for opposition, especially when they find themselves surrounded. Having taught these Nandi their lesson we came on to Nandi Fort in the evening.

When the 24-year-old Captain Meinertzhagen arrived in East Africa from Burma in 1902 the Protectorate Commissioner was Sir Charles Eliot, he who first designated the Kenyan Highlands as ideal 'White man's country' where European interests should always be given priority. In 1904, Sir Donald Stewart succeeded Eliot and was reminded by the Foreign Office that Britain's presence in Africa could be justified only by 'a most careful insistence on the protection of native rights'. Unluckily for the 'natives', Meinertzhagen seems never to have heard of these emphatic written instructions. In those days London was a long way from Mombasa and many were the cracks through which inconvenient directives could fall.

No settler could have farmed without local labour, so a variety of unsavoury methods were used to force Africans to work for wages – a bizarre new concept which outraged their dignity and quickly wrecked their social structures. In 1913, Karen Blixen recorded:

> I had 6,000 acres of land . . . About one thousand were squatters' land, what they called their *shambas*. The squatters are Natives, who with their families hold a few acres on a white man's farm, and in return have to work for him a certain number of days in the year. My squatters, I think, saw the relationship in a different light, for many of them were born on the farm, and their father before them, and they very likely regarded me as a sort of superior squatter on their estates.

Only a generation separated the 'pacification' of Kenya's Highlands and Karen Blixen's departure from her failed farm. Yet by 1931, as she poignantly illustrates, most Africans had accepted European domination and been drained of initiative:

> The Natives of the farm looked to me for help and support and did not, in a single case, attempt to arrange their future for themselves. They tried their very best to make me stay on . . .

26

A flock of sheep may be feeling the same towards the herd-boy, they will have infinitely better knowledge of the country and weather than he, and still will be walking after him into the abyss. The Kikuyu sat around my house and waited for my orders . . . You would have thought that their constant presence, when I knew I could not help them, and when their fate weighed heavily on my mind, would have been hard to bear. But it was not so. We felt, I believe, up to the very last, a strange comfort and relief in each other's company. The understanding between us lay deeper than all reason.

As the first stars twinkled I said to Joseph, 'I'm glad people here remember the settlers kindly. But I'm sad Europeans made so many Africans feel inferior.'

Joseph smiled wryly. 'But we *are* inferior! Before, we had no civilisation, nothing but wars and superstitions. Why do you pretend? I'm not stupid, I don't want to be told sweet lies to make me happy!'

'You've just proved my point,' I laughed, turning back into the bar.

Sotik's electricity supply had failed yet again and two smoky oil-lamps were being lit. Moses had ordered himself another beer; indicating the bottle he said cheerfully, 'On your account!' Even in the dim light I noticed annoyance flickering across Joseph's face. Pointedly he declined my offer of a beer, shook hands with both of us and was gone.

'You must meet my children,' said Moses then. 'I have nine, the eldest aged eight.'

Promptly I fell into the trap. 'So you have two wives?'

Moses gurgled with laughter and clapped his hands in the air above his head. 'No! No! I am a good Christian, I have only one beautiful wife! You forgot about twins and she gave me *two* pairs! So for seven births we have nine children – good value!' He sucked the last drop from his bottle and stood up. 'Come, we will eat together, my home is near.'

Moses's home was an hour's walk away, in the bush, and only a few stars peered through the drifting clouds. The terrain was hilly; the rough narrow path was lined with thorn bushes; half-rotten tree trunks spanned a wide shallow stream. Without my pencil torch I would probably have twisted an ankle and possibly broken a leg. Moses led the way, needing no light. On particularly confusing stretches he turned gallantly to take my hand. We passed two compounds of round Luo huts where fires glowed under pots of posho (maize porridge), its appetising aroma mingling with the scent of blue-gum smoke.

Moses talked of his ambition to become an AIDS counsellor. 'This is a big problem, brought to us by tourists and the British Army having exercises here. In the clinic I see how many are dying with doctors calling it something else – like pneumonia, malaria, TB, cancer, brain tumours. We need *so* many people to teach the *wanachi* about this dirty disease! But to counsel I need special training, in the West. You can please arrange for me to go to Ireland – OK?'

I forebore to argue with Moses about the mysterious origins of the AIDS virus; its present and future control are incomparably more important than its past. When I told him that there is nothing new to be learned about AIDS in the West he protested plaintively, 'But I know you have special training for counsellors! An American *nun* said so in our church!' He fell silent when I suggested that techniques developed for helping Whites might not help Blacks, given our radically different cultural backgrounds. I later discovered that he knew more about the medical aspects of the epidemic than most Western lay people and was free of those calamitous notions so common in Africa, such as anal intercourse being 'safer' than vaginal.

Kerosene is expensive in Kenya and the living-room, when we arrived, was illuminated by a flickering wick in a tiny tin of tallow. Moses lit a lamp before introducing me to his Kikuyu mother-in-law, a gracious old lady (she turned out to be two years my junior) who rose to greet me from her stool in a corner. A tightly tied headscarf showed her strong handsome features to best advantage and she had the exaggeratedly looped ears that some fashionable Kikuyu women of her generation indulged in by way of competing, jewellery-wise, with the Masai. You can display an enviable load of earrings if your lobe-hole is four or five inches in circumference.

Then Jenny entered, looking astonished – as well she might, I being the family's first ever White guest. Despite all that child-bearing she remained remarkably beautiful, a slender, serene 28-year-old, considerably taller than her Luo husband. Neither she nor her mother spoke English but Moses proved a diligently non-sexist interpreter, keen for his womenfolk to have their say.

Then the children came crowding in, their eyes aglow with excitement. In sequence they shook hands while saying 'My name is Ann' – or Paul or Rebecca or Timothy or James or whatever. Even the toddler, Simon, managed to squeak 'Si' before noticing something comic about me and rolling on the floor in a fit of giggles. They were an enchanting quiverful, however ecologically excessive, and their faded and threadbare clothes, I noted uneasily, were considerably cleaner than my own. Eagerly the older ones questioned me about my tribal territory and looked anxiously sympathetic when I admitted to owning no cattle. For them, too, Moses was a patient translator; seen as father, husband and son-in-law, he seemed a much more congenial and relaxed person than the Luo government employee met in a Kipsigi town.

A giant thermos provided oddly stimulating herbal tea. Granny had collected the herbs in the forest, then dried and blended them; anyone could *pick* herbs, she stressed, but only an expert could *blend* them. After my third cup a selection of pious pictures, torn from mission magazines and pinned to the walls, began slowly to gyrate . . .

Granny felt an exile in Sotik. Only two years previously the family had moved from their village by Lake Victoria because the unschooled tea-pickers from the same area knew little Swahili and needed a Luo-speaking health-worker. Then Moses, assisted by Luo neighbours, had built the two-roomed hut in which we sat and the adjacent kitchen shack; Granny and the children shared a nearby beehive hut. Now Moses was gathering stones for 'a big house'. Eight of his acres supported five cattle; the other four were cultivated by Granny, Jenny and the older children. All of which indicated a second source of income, *pace* that tale of woe in the bar.

The children queued to shake hands again and say 'Good-night, Dervla' – they had been practising that odd name – while Granny fetched the statutory basin and water-jug. As we adults dug into three communal dishes – stodgy maize dumpling, watery greens, hunks of tough beef – I noted guiltily that the meat was being reserved for Moses and me; we had bought it *en route*, from a wayside stall lined with sleeping bluebottles. I little thought that three months hence, in drought-stricken Zambia, I would look back on such meals longingly, as banquets.

Moses reproached me for having no camera. 'I need pictures of my beautiful children!' That grievance was easily remedied; we arranged to meet for a photographic session at the market at noon next day. After an expedition to the distant latrine – roofless and odourless, encircled by creeper-bound stakes – I slept soundly on the living-room couch, between freshly laundered sheets.

At this arid season Sotik market offered only low mounds of bananas, onions, greens, tomatoes, potatoes, chillies. No one could hope to make any significant profit from the day's dealings, yet the women squatting beside their produce looked cheerful. 'They are happy', remarked Moses, 'because on Sundays they needn't work on their shambas. They can spend all day here, talking with friends.' The briskest business was being done by second-hand clothes dealers whose prices, for well-worn American garments, were quite high. The same money spent on locally made garments would have procured something more durable and becoming but lacking the cachet of imported cast-offs. Again I noticed an uncharacteristic quietness. Normally market crowds are audible a mile away; here the bargaining and attendant badinage were subdued.

On that Sunday afternoon Sotik's shops were shut and its street almost deserted. In a squalid hoteli I ordered four cups of tea, the teapot being there unknown. All the other customers – mostly men, a few with wives and children – were intently watching a hyper-violent film on a fuzzy blank-and-white television set. Then real violence impinged.

Truckloads of the General Service Unit, bristling with guns, raced recklessly up the pot-holed street. Hastily the hoteli door was closed and barred and the women hauled their toddlers away to the safety of a back room. As the men rushed to the wide window an agitated waiter sharply ordered them back to their seats. Moments later we saw scores of Luo men, of all ages, being pursued up the street by a heavily armed foot patrol carrying tear-gas canisters. I looked questioningly at my companions but everyone avoided my eye; within that group mutual mistrust was palpable.

When the door was unlocked twenty minutes later I strolled up the street, past gatherings of tensely silent men and women standing outside shop entrances staring in the direction of the man-hunt. Soon I was overtaken by another platoon in full battledress, half-running, their sweating faces ugly with hate. Waving rifles and staves, they shouted threateningly at everybody and one deliberately kicked me as he passed. Then they were out of sight, over the dip in the road where it descended to the Catholic mission. At the end of the main street two complacent-looking well-dressed urban types, wearing KANU badges in their lapels, stood conferring by the kerb. Both shrugged and turned away when I ventured to ask, 'What's happening?' A moment later several shots came from the direction of the mission. There was an odd non-reaction; no one retreated into doorways, no one exchanged words. I stood still, acutely aware of being *de trop*, a resented witness. Then a young clergyman, hurrying around the corner, noticed me and stopped. 'Leave this place,' he said. 'Come with me.'

On the way back to the hoteli my protector anxiously enquired, 'Are you saved?'

To soothe him I said 'Yes', then asked, 'What's going on?'

'It doesn't matter,' he said. 'God will protect us because we are saved.' But his body language contradicted his words. When another yelling truckload jolted past, as he was lifting his tea-cup, half the contents spilled on to his lap and there was terror in his eyes. 'I now go back to my family,' he said. 'You go back to your group. Tourists are very safe in Kenya, we like them very much, but you should not leave your group. I give you God's blessing and also to your group.'

I thanked him for his caring and spared him the knowledge that I was ungrouped.

All afternoon I read and wrote in my room, while heavy rain flooded the hotel patio. The *Sunday Times* ('The Voice of the People'), the *Sunday Nation* ('The Newspaper that Serves the Nation') and the *Standard on Sunday* all devoted many pages to the attack on the hunger-striking mothers and the significance in African tradition of women stripping naked. In a *Standard* article on 'Female Stripping' Mumbi Risa wrote:

> Among some African communities, when a woman strips it is a sign of extreme anger – a choking anger. A sign that she is ready for anything including death. It is viewed with fear especially if the stripper is older than one, a mother or

31

grandmother. Among the Kikuyu, when a son abuses his mother or grandmother the greatest threat she can issue to him is, 'Do you want me to strip in front of you? Do you dare me do that?' In the Luo community when a woman bares herself it is regarded as a terrible curse. It is the most fear-instilling thing a woman can do. In the Masai community, even if a man would be beating his wife and she bares herself, he stops and runs away. Every effort is made to cleanse him of the curse because they believe that if this is not done death will surely befall him. The choicest of goats is slaughtered to cleanse him of the curse.

After the attack, the mothers were given refuge in the crypt of the Anglican All Saints' Cathedral, a courageous gesture on the part of the Church authorities. According to the *Sunday Nation*:

A Government minister, Mr Nabwera, said he supported the Government's eviction of the hunger-strike mothers of political prisoners from Uhuru Park. He also supported the storming of the All Saints' Cathedral compound by anti-riot police to disperse supporters of the hunger-strike mothers hiding there. Mr Nabwera said, 'Let the police throw tear-gas at the churches which some Kikuyu have been using to spread evil. Stripping naked is the final madness which cannot be allowed even in the Luhya community. Do the Kikuyu think they are the only ones with women capable of giving birth to presidents?

The *Sunday Nation* also carried a full-page advertisement, inserted by a Mombasa women's group, registering the strongest possible condemnation of 'the abhorrent and ghastly behaviour of our menfolk'.

All the papers described a riot that had taken place on Nairobi's Dandora estate on the previous Saturday afternoon when a KANU rally provoked anti-KANU mobs to go on the rampage. The *Sunday Nation* reporter, Willys Otieno, was himself badly beaten up, as a photograph proved. He wrote:

The GSU squad embarked on a patrol of the estate in which they hit everybody in sight. Police arrested a lorryful of suspects including a European who spoke with a markedly French accent. The barefooted European, dressed in blue jeans, white shirt and green jacket, pleaded for mercy as the police rained baton blows on his head. 'I have done nothing! Why do you want to kill me? Don't kill me please!' he pleaded as the beating went on. At least six policemen were seriously injured during the fracas.

The *Sunday Times* printed a press statement signed by Professor Philip Mbithi, Permanent Secretary in the Office of the President, Secretary to the Cabinet and Head of the Public Service:

> The Government is disappointed by the story carried yesterday in the *Standard* and expects the press to present news objectively and factually. At Uhuru Park the police had instructions only to ensure that chaos did not break out in the city and to oversee the pursuance of law and order. At no time were the striking mothers dispersed. The women were protected from the demonstrations and riots and were peacefully taken from the park to their homes. The Government wishes to reassure members of the public that during the demonstrations and riots which emanated from the political highjacking of the women's hunger-strike, the police exercised exemplary restraint and discipline.

Five days after that exercise of restraint my upper back was still sore and multi-coloured. Yet I had been lucky. A *Standard on Sunday* photograph showed one of the hunger-strike leaders, Professor Wangari Maathai, leaving hospital wearing a neck-brace; necks are more vulnerable than shoulders. Professor Maathai went straight from her hospital bed to the crypt to rejoin her comrades.

The political prisoners were at last released a few days before my return to Nairobi in July. I rejoiced then with them and their mothers – still living in the crypt, though they had long since given up their hunger-strike. (Apart from the Irish, few protestors anywhere take hunger-strikes to their logical and lethal conclusion.) Having talked at length with several of these remarkable men, I could see why President Moi had been so keen to keep them off the political scene, by fair means or foul, for as long as possible.

That evening the hotel bar was almost empty. When Joseph appeared, and heard that I planned to continue next day, he asked uneasily, 'You have permission?'

'No, but since there's trouble here I may as well push on.'

Joseph glanced around and, judging our two fellow-drinkers to be out of earshot, confided, 'Today was a mistake! This morning two Kipsigi were speared and killed outside the hospital, in revenge for Sondu. Yesterday the Kipsigi attacked there again, killing with one arrow a 12-year-old girl and the 2-year-old brother on her back. They have a new kind of arrow, made from big flattened nails dipped in vegetable poison. But here, this morning, we had no crowd trouble, after the killings. Then someone sent a wrong message, about big gangs of Luo attacking Kipsigi all over Sotik. The GSU came quickly, all stirred up to punish the Luo – any Luo. That message was sent to spread the trouble, maybe to frighten Luo workers away from our tea plantations. But why? The local Kipsigi don't want that sort of hard work with low pay. It's all a plot to make anarchy.'

A week later, in Kampala, I bought a Kenyan newspaper and read that hundreds of Luo workers had fled in panic from Sotik's tea plantations.

I left Sotik by starlight, my breath cloudy in the cold air. The map showed an unmotorable track, bypassing Sondu, and quite apart from tribal warfare such a route appealed. In Kenya the main threat to life comes not from the spears or poisoned arrows of inflamed warriors but from the average driver's attitude to cyclists and pedestrians. Both are expendable, as is proved by the road-death statistics printed daily in the national newspapers. When matatus (mini-van taxis) or buses or trucks are intent on overtaking each other (which is all the time), the presence of wayside travellers is ignored. However narrow the road, overtaking is the name of the game, as though each driver were racing for a valuable prize. The matatu-drivers do indeed have an economic motive for their madness; the more miles they can cover in a day the more they earn. And then the bus- and truck-drivers' macho distaste for being outsped causes the whole stream of traffic to become homicidal. The drivers' own death-rate, to say nothing of their passengers', is not much less horrendous; that willingness to dice with death which spreads the AIDS virus also prevails on the road.

34

Most of that day's eighty-eight miles were downhill, the first fifty
or so through intensively cultivated rolling country – the many
ascents short, the many descents long, the thronging natives
friendly, the beauty memorable. Unsuccessfully I tried to imagine
this region as it was when Meinertzhagen first arrived, eager to join
in the 'Sotik Expedition' – organised because 'the people of Sotik
raided the Naivasha Masai and carried off a lot of their cattle. On
being asked to return them they refused and sent insulting messages
to the Government.' Finding his martial arts superfluous on that
occasion, Meinertzhagen sought consolation, as was his wont,
in killing large numbers of animals, triumphantly listed – 'oribi,
bohor reedbuck, Jackson's haartebeeste, waterbuck, topi, warthog'.
How different the landscape must have looked when its lavish fertility was supporting an abundance of wildlife and comparatively
few humans!

It is easier to imagine colonial Kenya a decade or two later, so
vividly has that era been described in books that have become minor
classics. There is a mystical quality about many Europeans' descriptions of 'their' Africa; almost they hypnotise one into forgetting the
realities in the background – the destruction of delicately balanced
relationships between land and people, herds and people, wildlife
and people. These love-affairs with Africa's more salubrious areas
were essentially perverse; the settlers became besotted by the physical environment while refusing to treat the inhabitants as fellow-
adults. Notoriously their workers, of all ages, were referred to as
'boys'; and probably few Whites are immune, even now, to this
dangerous virus. I had diagnosed it in myself while staying with
Moses's family. After supper he borrowed my pencil torch, I
assumed for some practical purpose. On realising that he merely
wanted to play with it I insisted on having it back – for me it was
a scarce resource – and as he poutingly surrendered it I caught
myself thinking, 'He's just like a *child*!'

In Kenya most 'natives' seem to have been quite well treated
when employed as loyal servants. Then they became part of the idyll
and were affectionately described in much the same tone as devoted
dogs or beloved horses. Their ceremonial dances, sometimes performed as part of the celebrations for a European twenty-first
birthday party or wedding, were relished as another delicious ingre-
dient of the African Experience, and later in my journey I was

disconcerted to find this attitude persisting. An assiduously kind sisal plantation host went to great trouble to organise a display of tribal dancing, by his 'boys', for my entertainment. Without giving offence I could not express what I felt about tribal dances being thus degraded for the benefit of the Bwana's guest. I have rarely spent a more uncomfortable hour, outwardly feigning interest, inwardly resenting my false position as a spectator of this sad parody.

Among certain missionaries – usually of American bible-belt extraction – contempt for 'evil African superstitions' also persists. Yet I, as an agnostic, can see no qualitative difference between believing in witchcraft and the power of the ancestors and believing in the Virgin Birth and the Resurrection, never mind transubstantiation and papal infallibility. However, America tends to produce the best as well as the worst. Vincent J. Donovan, an American Roman Catholic priest who lived for years among the Masai, admitted in *Christianity Rediscovered*:

As I witnessed the work of the witch doctor I felt sad and slightly sick, if not ashamed. Every single thing I saw him do, I recognized, not from my acquaintance with other pagan religions, but from my experience as a priest in our own Christian religion . . . The ordinary people, especially women, completely at the mercy and whim and arbitrariness and exclusiveness of the holy one; the offerings for the sacrifice and the daily sacrifice itself; the manipulation of sacred signs and relics; the air of unfathomable mystery about it all. There is scarcely a pagan trick that we Christians have overlooked.

By now a few generations have absorbed, most notably from Karen Blixen and Elspeth Huxley, the settlers' view of the African – however likeable – as immeasurably and irredeemably inferior to his European master (or mistress). Both women wrote as supremely cultivated and sensitive representatives of their own culture, people incapable of crude racism – and thus, incidentally, reinforced the image of the 'primitive' African all the more subtly and strongly. To experience colonial thinking in the raw one has to read something like Erika Johnston's deservedly forgotten *The Other Side of Kilimanjaro*, published in 1971. There one encounters, unadorned

36

by mellifluous prose and unfiltered by poetic sensibilities, the White settlers' conveniently narrow definition of 'property'.

Piet Hugo was the only farmer who continuously suffered at the hands of the Masai. He has carried on a ceaseless struggle with them for they trespass with their cattle on his farm, bringing with them the danger of disease to his own herd . . . and as fast as he mends his fences so the Masai break through them again. Perhaps it is because Piet's farm stretches further down into what used to be Masailand, and they do not seem to comprehend that the land they had freely grazed over for centuries now has an owner.

So, if you cultivate land you 'own' it. If you freely graze your cattle over the same land, as your ancestors have done for countless generations, you do not 'own' it; it is public property, to be appropriated by any enterprising, energetic White who covets it.

The White Highlands' beauty, fertility and – at most seasons – agreeable climate of course made them alluring to Europeans. Yet it takes no great insight to discern another element at work in the colonial psyche. In very different (and frequently conflicting) ways, many of these administrators, missionaries and farmers were on lifelong ego-trips, inordinately proud of bringing law and order, Christianity and agricultural improvements to the 'savages'. Should we take the *Zeitgeist* into account? It is always comforting, when reviewing ancestral sins, to be able tolerantly to murmur, 'Father, forgive them, for they knew not what they did!' No doubt we would like our own descendants to do the same for us, as they review the vicious injustices and ruthless ecological vandalism of the twentieth century. But how valid is this apologia? Our generation knows exactly what it is doing, but to do it is politically and/or commercially profitable so we bash on regardless, often not even bothering to devise those self-justifications so important to the early exploiters of Africa.

In her Preface to the 1983 Eland edition of Meinertzhagen's *Kenya Diary*, Elspeth Huxley wrote:

One has only to dip into these diaries to apprehend how profound has been the revolution in our attitudes within the lifetime of many still alive . . . Today the tally of slaughtered animals, then present in such astonishing abundance, seems nauseating . . . [In Africa] literacy was unknown, superstition rife, and almost all the aids to a more civilized way of life were lacking. A great gulf then separated the pale and dark skinned races. Now it has been bridged by education.

A revolution in our attitude to animals has had to take place, so few remain. But has there really been a revolution in our attitude towards the 'dark-skinned races'? And can it be argued that 'the great gulf . . . has been bridged by education'? The quantity and quality of education on offer to Africans, either during or since colonial times, could build only an imitation bridge, unsafe to walk on.

A recent 'international bestseller', Kuki Gallmann's *I Dreamed of Africa*, reveals how little has changed. In 1972, when the author migrated from Italy to farm 90,000 acres in independent Kenya, she reacted to her surroundings, as many reviewers admiringly noted, in a way 'vividly reminiscent of Olive Schreiner, Karen Blixen, Elspeth Huxley and Beryl Markham'. One of her European friends was 'warm as the earth, artistic and inventive . . . She loved Africa, *the land and its animals*, with a passion' (my emphasis). The success of this book indicates that Kuki Gallmann's image of Africa is the one with which, even in the 1990s, White readers are most comfortable. This endangers the Africans who, as I write these words, are being indirectly killed, in considerable numbers, by relentless First World profiteering.

Freewheeling down the day's last incline, to the shore of Lake Victoria, I told myself, 'Looking backwards is futile'. Yet to make any sense of East Central Africa's shambolic present, one must be aware of the past. The disorienting pioneer missionaries, the ambivalent Protectorate Commissioners, the brutal German plantation farmers and thuggish 'pacifying' soldiers were active during the lifetimes of people still living. In historical terms, the Africans' trauma is very recent. So why are we surprised when they sometimes behave like people collectively in shock?

My first glimpse of Africa's biggest lake – almost as big as Ireland – disappointed me. Joseph Thomson, too, felt a sense of anti-climax when, on 10 December 1883, he reached the summit of a low hill after a fifteen-month walk from the coast, and saw only the Bay of Kavirondo – itself bigger than most European lakes yet seeming tame and cosy, shut in by several wooded islands.

Here my track joined a new road at a T-junction where a gaudy petrol station dwarfed the few nearby dukas. There was no hoteli, hence no tea. At 2.30, at lake-level, the heat was lung-searing. Sitting on a plastic crate outside a duka, I reminded myself that alcohol would be unwise. But four Coca-Colas proved unwiser still, activating an unpleasant digestive disorder (I think it's known as heart-burn) which had never before afflicted me.

On this straight, level, treeless road the sun seemed to be attacking me personally. Occasionally Lake Victoria's muddy shore appeared beyond lines of giant euphorbia candelabra, or plantain groves, or a papyrus swamp, or an expanse of yellowed grassland on which many cattle grazed – so many that none had adequate sustenance. Over-grazing is among Africa's major problems yet herds are unlikely to be reduced while owning a few cows has a calming effect on senior bank officials.

Poor Thomson was suffering from malaria while foot-slogging through Kavirondo. Some warriors tried to block his way to the lake, fearing he might bewitch it, but their halfhearted opposition didn't diminish his joy at having 'opened up' the route through Masai land. He had thus exposed Buganda to what was euphemistically known as 'European initiative'. Hitherto the region had been shielded by the Masais' exaggerated reputation for ferocity – exaggerated by the Swahili ivory- and slave-traders who wished to keep Europeans off their patch. Thomson noticed that in fact the coastal traders in his party were much more afraid of the Kikuyus' poisoned arrows than of the Masai spears; the Masai were known to be disciplined warriors whereas Kikuyu attacks were arbitrary and treacherous. Having enjoyed 'the supreme satisfaction of drinking the waters of Victoria Nyanza', the 25-year-old Thomson could legitimately boast, 'Without the loss of a single man by violence or the necessity of shooting a single native I have penetrated through the most dangerous tribes in Africa.' He had called the coastal traders' bluff. 'The most dangerous tribes', if treated as Thomson (but few other Europeans) treated them, were not so dangerous after all. The young Scotsman's rare empathy with the Masai enabled him to describe their esoteric initiation rites and novel (to him) sexual predilections – in the customary Latin appendix. Presumably

39

this was a device to prevent the Victorians' womenfolk from acquiring knowledge of such matters; it cannot have been imagined that a classical education rendered people immune to 'corruption'.

At 3.30 I collapsed for an hour under a giant mango tree overlooking the lake. Water was being fetched by processions of small children, head-carrying containers almost as big as themselves. Daily I marvelled at the Africans' physical strength; both sexes and all age groups achieve feats that most Europeans couldn't even attempt. But what are the side-effects? It cannot be good for any children whose bones are still soft to carry such weights. As the loaded children passed, one could see their stamina being tested to the utmost – and they were not enjoying the test. Yet while scampering down to the grassy shore, bearing empty containers, they exuded *joie de vivre*.

Beside me, on another segment of that tree's massive root system, a pensive young woman awaited a bus. She wore purple lipstick and nail-varnish, a fussy frilly raspberry-pink blouse and a tight lime-green skirt; golden sandals matched her large plastic handbag. Having done well at school she wanted to 'go into business' but – 'How can I start without capital? My father is rich but spends everything on my brothers. He tells me to marry now, he doesn't like a daughter making her own money, living independently. I want to be rich because *I* work, not because my husband is a Big Man. In Kenya educated women know about that Women's Liberation, but how can we find it?' She looked over the lake. 'There is only one way to get capital and now they say that's dangerous. But people who have no choice take chances.'

The bus appeared and my companion jumped up. 'So I go to Kisumu to work!' As she waved from her privileged front seat, beside the driver, I felt cravenly relieved. Had our conversation been prolonged Abraham's strictures would have compelled me to 'share information'.

At 4.30 the sun felt bearable yet an hour later I stopped again, debilitated by the tarmac's stored heat. A bar stood at a junction, twelve miles from Sondu, and I was about to enter it when two open-backed lorries came at speed from the Kisumu direction, halted at the junction and disgorged scores of warriors (or graduates?). These were clad in animal skins and armed with bows and arrows (not the sort used by hunters) and formidable six-foot-long broad-bladed

40

spears. For an instant I felt afraid. Then the men loped away – off the road, into maize fields, moving silently and purposefully.

Turning back to the bar I saw a small, slim young Luo in the doorway, staring at the vanishing warriors. 'Who are these people?' I asked.

The young man blinked and moistened his lips and hesitated. Then he said, 'I didn't see them.'

This windowless, earth-floored shebeen was comparatively cool. Behind the bar stood a tall grim-looking elderly man who spoke no English. In a corner two giggling young women were drinking ersatz orange juice, the sort that stains your teeth for a week. I ordered two Tuskers; the young Luo seemed to need a drink. His name was Isaah and he claimed to have a BA in 'History, Comparative Religion and Eng. Lit.' He couldn't have passed an O Level examination in any of these subjects yet he wanted – *longed* – to do a postgraduate course in Britain. Listening to him I felt a sort of despair, tinged with that guilt which, like the dust, gets into all one's African reactions. Isaah was not stupid but had been messed up by an educational system that was irrelevant, inadequate, confusing and ultimately deeply frustrating. When I had explained, as gently as possible, that a postgraduate course in Britain could not possibly be organised, by anyone, he looked at me with a mixture of grief and resentment.

'Why do tourists never want to help us? We like to help you, when you visit. But you just have fun in Kenya and then forget us. I go sometimes to the Masai Mara to try to meet very rich tourists – not like you, on a bicycle. But no one wants to help. *Why?*'

I must have looked as unhappy as I felt because suddenly Isaah leant forward to press my hand and said, 'Don't worry! I think you are too poor to help but you are a nice lady!' He advised me to spend the night in Katika's John Jameson lodging-house, ten miles further on, where he would join me later with his girlfriend ('a very clever scientist') and two of his brothers who had recently lost their government jobs for making mildly anti-Moi remarks. 'They were lucky,' grinned Isaah. 'Before, people went to prison, or worse, for that . . .' I never saw him again, which didn't surprise me. That's life, in Africa – as often as not.

Katika proved to be a shabby little township at a crossroads; the John Jameson seemed the biggest as well as the most respectable of its several lodging-houses. An agreeable quartet welcomed me on the long, narrow veranda, netted against mosquitoes. I sat beside a young Baptist minister who drank only 'sodas' and believed the IRA to be funded and trained by the Vatican. Opposite were an elderly teacher, a retired army officer (I wondered which army: he looked like an Amhara) and a down-at-heel businessman called Murphy Odiyo. To celebrate this coincidence Murphy stood me a beer (an unusual gesture in such a setting), then begged me to become his agent in Ireland, selling zebra-hides as car-seat covers. It was a treat, they all agreed, to have foreign company for the evening. The teacher observed, 'Ordinary Kenyans meet few *mzungus*. We only *see* them, millions of tourists staring at us as if we were part of the wildlife.'

'And thousands of expats,' added Murphy, 'living in their rich reservations and rushing around in their luxury vehicles to meet our Big Men.'

When a young Kisumu doctor joined us I sought information – to the evident discomfiture of my companions – about the workings of Kenya's National AIDS Control Programme. I could have asked no better man. Dr Shikuku had spent the day collecting blood in the bush from young donors whom he described as 'relatively low risk'. Blood donations in Nairobi, he said, had dropped from 26,000 units in 1981 to 8,000 units in 1991 'because people fear they can get the virus from giving blood'. (A not unreasonable fear, I reckoned, but tactfully didn't say so.) The most recent HIV + figures were 7.5 per cent of blood donors and 12 per cent of pregnant women attending ante-natal clinics. 'And worst of all,' said Dr Shikuku, 'the high-risk group mostly *don't want to know and won't be tested.*' Wearily he shook his head. 'So our carriers will go on increasing fast. We used to think the high-risk age group was 25 to 40, now we know it's 15 to 60. The National AIDS Control Programme was given enormous funding – KSh. 800 million. Most of that's spent on big salaries, air fares to international AIDS conferences, hotel bills and "expenses", Pajeros serviced and run for personal use only. Millions of Kenyans now imagine the virus is going away, we've so little publicity about the rate of spread. Our government is the most irresponsible in Africa, things are much better organised in Uganda, Tanzania, Zambia.'

Certainly nobody in the large grubby restaurant off the veranda 'wanted to know'. My two fellow-diners were truck-drivers being

42

eyed hopefully by five adolescent girls in tawdry attire, clustered around the courtyard doorway. 'Two into five won't go,' I reflected. But perhaps two would go into these five if their charges were low enough.

I devoured a mound of glutinous lukewarm rice and two greasy skinny chicken-wings. Then, crossing the courtyard to my room, I observed the truck-drivers each linking an expensively dressed bar-girl; one sensed long-term arrangements. Resignedly the teenagers drifted off to the veranda where my respectable friends had been replaced by a gathering of rumbustious young men drinking a col-ourless, sinister-smelling liquid; something similar gave me severe gout in Madagascar.

For 80 pence one can't expect too much and it took time to manoeuvre Lear into my windowless cell, ventilated by spaces between the filthy walls and the tin ceiling. On the narrow sagging bed I wrote my journal by the light of my own candles; writing in public almost always drew a distracting crowd. At intervals during the night I was half-awakened by the impassioned quarrelling of two men in the next room or by drunken arguing, singing and laughter from the restaurant. All-night parties were a feature of such lodging-houses; doubtless the locals slept throughout the heat of the day.

The heat of the next day had wrecked me by ten o'clock, when I was struggling out of big, bustling, sweltering Kisumu, Kenya's main port on Lake Victoria. From Kisumu to Maseno the threaten-ing traffic was constant, the many townships were dreary, my brains felt fried and I hardly registered the landscape.

Seeing me drinking yet another litre of water under a wayside tree, several passersby paused to converse.

A Church of God freak reproved me for wearing trousers and asserted that alcohol is the sole cause of the AIDS epidemic – 'If all remain sober, there is no filthy business.'

A hydraulics engineer begged me to find him a job in Ireland – 'I am very much afraid of this AIDS killer but in Europe the women are still clean so I would be safe.'

A 30-year-old post office clerk had seven children ('two others died of malaria') and wanted no more. 'But now we have *ukimwi* it is hard. If I go to other women I can get sick, if I stay with my wife she can get sick from too many children. *Ukimwi* makes

43

educated people who understand it have more children – they are afraid to leave their wives. Bar-girls know how to stop babies so it was better for the over-population when we went to them. Now I am confused, people tell about so many different ways to stop babies. Which is best? You must have good information.'

'Tube-tying,' I said succinctly. The young man beamed and thanked me and went on his way. Then it occurred to me that I should have lectured him on his wife's right to make these contraceptive decisions. My brains, as I have said, were fried that day.

At 3.30 I was slowly pushing Lear up a long steep hill to the town of Maseno, an educational stronghold founded by the Church Missionary Society (CMS). Maseno straddles the Equator, but even on the Equator how could the sun be so brutal at 5,000 feet? I wished I were cycling in Ireland, well wrapped up against the March east wind.

Then Damian came towards me, a willowy young man wearing blue jeans, a Berkeley University T-shirt and a slightly odd expression. He passed me with a civil greeting and a look of great curiosity, then a moment later was back by my side. 'You look too tired,' he said. 'Go no further! Spend the night with John, our world-famous artist, a painter and sculptor. He likes to entertain foreigners.'

It seemed Damian was also an artist who had been apprenticed to John and was planning to settle in Uganda where, he fancied, tourist hotels would employ him to paint giant murals; thus he too would soon become world-famous. 'Fame and popularity are the most important things in life,' he assured me. 'John is no longer a Christian because he is famous. I still believe in Christ because I am not yet a success and secure.' As we turned towards John's shamba I hoped the artist had little in common with his apprentice.

A steep rough track led to a wide ledge under a dramatic rock escarpment. The garden was more obvious than the house. Candelabra cacti towered over three other sorts; tall smooth grey papaya trees looked like telegraph poles decorated with tufts of vegetation; jacaranda, bougainvillaea and hibiscus spouted high fountains of colour between less familiar shrubs and trees; purple-flowered ground-creepers coiled between beds of scarlet salvias. At first all seemed wild and unplanned; in fact the whole had been carefully designed to act as a background to John's work. Several pairs of wooden figures, fifteen feet tall and carved from single

44

tree-trunks, formed archways over the paths. Particularly moving were two women with arms outstretched, hands meeting and clasped, one with a suffering face turned aside, avoiding the stern gaze of the other; and an old, dignified, devoted couple, each with one hand on a hip, the other hands joined. Under a flame-tree, carved from some wood resembling bog-oak, a naked musician sat on a low stool, legs wide apart, stringed instrument being played with exaggeratedly huge yet sensitive hands, eyes closed and mouth slightly open in ecstatic response to the beauty he was creating. Among the cacti were a totem pole hinting at the various stages of pregnancy; an exultant mother suckling her baby; an elder in Western dress enjoying a joke. Everywhere were weirdly beautiful abstract sculptures in both wood and stone – dreamy, sinuous, secretive pieces.

John's wife Teresa – a secondary school headmistress – was small, neatly built, self-possessed. She welcomed me with a generous smile, explaining that John had driven to Maseno to deliver milk to an invalid relative. Then she apologised because I would have to wait for hot water; water was very scarce now, there was none running in the taps. It took time to persuade her that I did not need hot water, or indeed any washing-water, in view of the drought. Those of us who come from cold climates do not share the Africans' obsession with personal cleanliness.

The large bungalow, starting from a colonial nucleus, had been extended at different times in different directions. In the spacious guest-room a row of books – mainly early British writing on Africa – stood between the twin beds. Children and servants swarmed; the latter, I came to realise, were poor relations. In John's studio a display of international press-cuttings proved his fame but Teresa remarked that he wore it lightly. 'It pleases him, but it doesn't really matter – only his work matters.' Often people urged him to move to Nairobi, to get on to the cosmopolitan scene, to look for commissions from expats who would pay lavishly for such unusual 'souvenirs'. 'But if he did that', observed Teresa affectionately, 'he wouldn't be John.'

I was glad to have seen John's work before he returned – a middle-aged man with a goatee beard who engagingly blended shyness as an individual and authority as a creator. It is always more satisfactory to respond solely to an artist's work, detached from its human envelope. Had I met John first I might have wondered, afterwards, if my appreciation of his sculptures had been partly influenced by my appreciation of himself.

We were soon joined by John's doctor brother and a writer friend who worked in both Swahili and English. That stimulating evening more than compensated for a hellish day. My heat-exhaustion forgotten, we talked until 1.30 a.m. – about Northern Ireland, the effects of Structural Adjustment on the African poor, the Rushdie Affair, the profit motive and commercial hype in relation to artistic endeavour, AIDS, the American constitution, the status of women in Africa, the impact of Christianity on East Africa, the catastrophic state of education throughout most of the continent. My four companions – witty, well-informed, articulate – were people content to live simply, secure in their African identity and proud of it, yet intellectually open to the whole wide world. Between them they didn't have even one chip about anything: a rare enough form of liberty in Black Africa. They taught me much that illuminated the rest of my journey.

3

Across the First Border

Maseno to Entebbe

I crossed the Equator at 6.10 a.m. and six hours later – helped by a strong tailwind – arrived at the Ugandan border. Those were fifty-five exhilarating miles, again through densely populated, rich farmland with many coffee plantations, a reassuring wealth of trees – sometimes mercifully shading the road for long stretches – and superb views over deep forested valleys or gentle green hills festooned with webs of winding red paths.

The listless border town of Busia was long, dull, dusty and very, very hot; by then I had lost 1,500 feet. Beyond stood a pleasingly rural border-post, shaded by ancient fig and mango trees. Only trucks – mostly petrol tankers – were entering or leaving Uganda and now all their drivers lay asleep in the roadside bush. Yet my pushing Lear into the cramped immigration office enraged a corpulent sweating officer who sat behind a rickety little table picking his teeth. Rejecting my passport he shouted 'Take that bicycle out! You get no stamp before you take that out!'

'Sorry,' I said, 'it can't be left unguarded. There are too many young men hanging about.' When I again proffered the passport he detached a morsel from between his molars and spat it in my direction. 'If you had a car would you want to drive it in here?'

I felt two kinds of irritation coalescing: that produced by the equatorial sun at noon and that produced by bloody-minded petty officials. Controlling myself, I pointed out that if I had a car my luggage would be locked in the boot.

'You think Ugandans are all thieves? In what other country would you behave like this?'

'In every other country. There are thieves everywhere.'

47

'In *what* countries? Where else can you put a bicycle in everyone's way? Now no one else can enter this office!'

This was a slight exaggeration but I confined myself to remarking, 'No one else wants to enter it. And if you'd stamped the passport at once, instead of arguing, my bicycle and myself would've been well out of the way by now.'

Mysteriously, this logic amused him. He slapped his thigh, roared with laughter, laid aside his toothpick (it seemed to be a large fish-bone) and stamped my passport without even glancing at it. 'You *are* a funny old woman!' he chuckled then, leaning forward to shake hands.

Young Forex sharks cruise around most African border-posts, operating under the noses of customs officers – with whom they doubtless have an arrangement – and urging in a stage-whisper, 'Change money here! From me the *best* rate!' Quickly a dozen jostling youths surrounded me, waving six-inch-thick rubber-banded wads of indecipherably filthy Ugandan shillings; the rate was then 2,100 to the pound sterling. I would have liked to oblige one of those pleading youngsters but to count so many illegible notes by the roadside seemed impractical. They accepted their dismissal good-humouredly, wishing me a happy time in Uganda.

The smooth tarmac road, built with 'Reconstruction Aid', ran level through sun-scourged scrub, sparsely populated. Eventually a fig tree offered shade and as I lay reading five little boys gradually came closer and closer, through rustling dead maize, speculating in whispers about this bizarre phenomenon. They couldn't conquer their timidity and were malnourished and ragged; I never saw their equivalent in rural Kenya. There the benefits of three peaceful decades, sheltering under the capitalist wing, are as evident as the settlers' indelible markings, physical and psychological. On this first afternoon in Uganda my impressions – confirmed during the weeks ahead – were of far worse poverty and far less servility towards the *mzungu*.

Yet the poverty was not as extreme as I had feared, given the unpeacefulness of Uganda's post-Independence decades. So much of the country is so fertile that since the Terror ended in 1986, when the National Resistance Army (NRA) brought down the second Obote regime, it has been able – under President Yoweri Museveni – to regain a degree of stability and prosperity.

Pre-Independence, Uganda was a tragedy waiting to happen. During the 1950s the Ganda – the people of Buganda, who speak Luganda – made up less than 18 per cent of the Protectorate's total population yet would accept a united Uganda only if they were guaranteed its political leadership. As this could not reasonably be arranged, Buganda decided in 1960 to reclaim its pre-colonial sovereignty and declared itself a 'separate autonomous state'. Britain said 'Nonsense!' – a Uganda without Buganda would have been an economic cripple – and then quickly cooked up a constitutional dog's dinner which satisfied no one.

After a few uneasy years of Independence the first Prime Minister, Milton Obote, whose supporters were the Acholi and Langi, used the national army commanded by Idi Amin to suppress the Ganda. (Their Kabaka was exiled to Britain.) In 1971 Amin overthrew Obote, who was given asylum in Tanzania, and filled all the lucrative political posts with his own supporters, the Kakwa and Nubi. He also issued decrees of legal immunity which enabled heavily armed soldiers to terrorise the population, looting government and private property, burning crops and homes, robbing motorists at gunpoint, shooting or stealing cattle, slaughtering villagers. Extermination squads, mainly Nilotic and Sudanic, toured the army camps murdering officers and men suspected of loyalty to Obote. In 1972 the International Commission of Jurists reported: 'There has been a total breakdown in the rule of law throughout the country.' According to the *Africa Contemporary Record, 1982–83*, some 350,000 Ugandans were killed under Amin's regime – many after tortures one can hardly bear to read about – and thousands of others went into exile. 'Virtually the whole of the modernizing élite was either killed or fled abroad.'

In 1982 Amnesty International found that human rights in Uganda 'were still being violated with impunity, mainly by the army'. Then Obote was again in control (the Tanzanian army had got rid of Amin in 1979) so the Acholi and Langi were killing the Kakwa and Nubi, and of course lots more besides. One Ugandan scholar, Ali A. Mazrui, Professor of Political Science at the University of Michigan, sees the Terror as an unusually lethal brew of tyranny and anarchy: too much government and too little. For a generation Uganda endured not only political and economic collapse but also, as Professor Mazrui puts it, 'a basic moral collapse

49

among those who wielded weapons'. He traces the roots of the tragedy back to the colonial period, when Britain disarmed the warriors of the well-organised Buganda and Bunyoro kingdoms, turning them instead into civilian officials co-operating in the administration of the Protectorate along the 'indirect rule' lines prescribed by Lord Lugard. Simultaneously, the British were recruiting for the King's African Rifles from among the primitive Nilotic tribes in the north. These tribes had nothing in common with the developed southern kingdoms, whose efficiently run administration astonished Speke when he first arrived at the Kampala court of the Kabaka of Buganda. As Professor Mazrui explains:

> While the Baganda and the Banyoro were being demilitarized and losing their warrior tradition, the Acholi, Langi and Kakwa among other northern Ugandans underwent militarization of a new and modern kind. They were being absorbed into the colonial security forces, with guns rather than spears. This change was destined to have enormous consequences for the future of Uganda. By the time the British were leaving, the armed forces of the newly independent country were disproportionately Nilotic in composition. Although all the Nilotic tribes in Uganda together add up to only a small minority of the population, the stage was already set for a Nilotic supremacy in at least the first few decades of post-colonial Uganda . . . It was a case of precolonial stateless societies inheriting the post-colonial state. The Langi (Obote's tribe), the Kakwa (Amin's tribe) and the Acholi (Okello's tribe) were all fundamentally stateless in their precolonial incarnations. It was their militarization during British colonial rule that prepared them – quite unwittingly – to inherit the post-colonial state. The European experience played havoc with the different traditions of Africa, casting old groups into new roles, and 'mis-casting' decentralized people into centralizing functions. This whole cultural disruption had a lot to do with the decay of the post-colonial state in countries like Uganda.

The five little boys were still crouching in the maize, watching my every move, when gathering clouds encouraged me to continue at three o'clock. Soon I was in broken country where green jungle

50

covered steep slopes and baboons wandered over the road, as usual looking disgruntled and having noisy family squabbles. On the main Mbale–Kampala road the stifling smoke of pre-rains bush-burning made my eyes water. Here I observed a curious ritual. Four small boys, squatting by the roadside around two distorted doll-sized figures of mud men, were drumming rhythmically (wood on wood) and looking solemn and intent, as though engaged in a ceremony rather than a game.

I was now in Busoga, historically one of the Buganda kingdom's tributary states and known to early explorers as 'the backdoor of Buganda'. It was then notoriously hostile territory. Bishop James Hannington of the Church Missionary Society was murdered here in 1885, having walked from the coast in a mere eleven weeks, following Thomson's route. Foolishly he ignored the emphatic advice given him by, among others, a friendly Chief in Kavirondo – 'Avoid Busoga at all costs!' By temperament he was at least as much an explorer as a bishop and Busoga, being hitherto untrodden by White feet, fatally tempted him. He and his small team of porters were murdered – hacked to death with spears – by order of the alarmingly unstable 20-year-old Mwanga, the Kabaka of Buganda. Any European who tried to use the forbidden 'backdoor' could only be a spy.

Apart from petrol tankers, the local traffic was mainly two-wheeled. Most cyclists carried improbable loads: a passenger or two, huge jerry-cans of water or home-brewed alcohol, long sacks of charcoal, formidably heavy bunches of matoke (green bananas) reaching almost to the ground on both sides, pyramids of firewood, unidentifiable cloth-wrapped bundles, hens in wicker coops and, on one carrier, a sleek chestnut kid curled up in a shallow wooden box and apparently enjoying his excursion. As the land became more fertile, untidily thatched square or round mud huts huddled in unfenced compounds amidst unkempt shambas. In the few drab, destitute townships rusty tin roofs were balanced, often precariously, on disintegrating grey shacks. Busoga's almost bare shelves made Kenya's rural dukas seem like Harrods. Only the women brightened this landscape, all wearing spotless ankle-length dresses with exaggeratedly puffed-up shoulders and wide sashes tied in a big bow above their conspicuous buttocks, or, occasionally, tied diagonally across their equally conspicuous bosoms. As they walked gracefully

51

by the roadside this shimmering flow of contrasting colours – rose-pink, deep yellow, pale green, crimson, royal blue – made a glorious mobile pattern in the dappled shade of mango, fig and blue-gum trees. By comparison, Kenyan women seem dowdy and shapeless in their shoddy mass-produced Western garments. I later learned that this Ugandan fashion was instigated by missionaries in the 1890s and designed by a Goan tailor.

At dusk I arrived in Bugiri, a candlelit village – and candles were scarce. The one tiny lodging-house stocked no beer but an obliging young woman offered to fetch my evening fix from elsewhere. No washing water appeared and I requested none, visualising the distance that young woman might have to walk to fetch it – probably, given the drought, all the way to Lake Victoria, through some five miles of bush and swamp.

News of the *mzungu*'s arrival spread fast and soon a self-proclaimed smuggler hurried in, avid for Kenyan shillings. I only had sterling; resigning myself to being cheated I changed a five-pound note, enough to get me to a Jinja bank – where I felt suitably guilty, on realising that the smuggler had given me a little more than the official rate. In a corner of the yard food was being cooked over a tin of charcoal; supper consisted of a small dish of soggy rice and a giant bone to which adhered a few fragments of fat and gristle. As I ate, an elderly man entered, sat in the corner by the door, beyond the candlelight, and used the smuggler as his interpreter.

Was it true that Europeans and Americans were also dying of AIDS and had no cure? When I confirmed that this was indeed true the smuggler translated, 'He doesn't believe you, he believes Western doctors have cures for their own people.' (This misapprehension is widespread in Africa.) 'He asks if you can get him some of that medicine. Last year his first-born died, now another son is dying in Kampala. The dying boy won't come home, he saw how much his brother's slow death made his mother sad. A sister cares for him.'

That was a harrowing encounter, the first of many such; villagers frequently mistook the grey-haired *mzungu* for a touring AIDS expert.

Again I had difficulty fitting Lear into my room, one of a row of eight mud-brick cells. Inexplicably, no mosquitoes attended me despite ill-fitting shutters on the unglazed window.

I breakfasted at eight, two hours beyond Bugiri, in a hoteli facing many half-built red-brick dwellings, abandoned by families fleeing from warfare. A friendly young man provided weak but real coffee and scraps of cold omelette sandwiched in a stale, kerosene-flavoured bun. Above a showcase displaying two more stale buns hung an anti-AIDS poster, handwritten in the local language and illustrated with clumsy drawings. I enquired about its provenance. 'My father made it,' said the young man. 'He is a minister of God and tries to warn and teach people. Here most of us can't read posters from Kampala in English so we must translate.'

The wide smooth road switchbacked on through miles of sugar-cane, maize, arid bush and papyrus swamp, in which glistened an evil black sludge instead of the normal quota of water. Each climb seemed longer and steeper than the last. At 11.15 I diagnosed imminent heat-stroke and retreated into the thin bush – too thin to give full protection. Significantly, I couldn't read. For four hours I lay in a strange stupor, no more than semi-conscious yet not sleeping and feeling oddly *content*.

Continuing at 3.30, I could keep going for less than an hour. Heavily sweating fellow-cyclists, of whom there were many, assured me that I was not being unduly feeble; they too were wilting. 'And we were born here!' said one. 'And you live always in the snow in Ireland! So our terrible heat can kill you – we hear stories how Europeans drop dead in the sun, like they were shot!'

I smiled and nodded, too dehydrated to rectify this faulty image of Ireland. Alarmingly I had ceased to sweat, despite having drunk six litres of water since dawn. In the next township I stopped for another hour and drank six more litres to the giggling wonderment of the girl who drew it from a tar-barrel at the back of her half-built hoteli. (I had given up purifying my intake and after four months of drinking whatever came my way, with no ill-effects, I wonder if the contamination of Africa's water supplies, about which we hear so much, is not perhaps exaggerated?) As my body absorbed the liquid I could feel myself coming out of that curious semi-comatose state. The final thirty miles to Jinja, over some punishing hills, were accomplished non-stop.

Jolting along Jinja's main street through a pink haze (traffic dust tinted by a flaring sunset), I reproved Uganda's second city for not maintaining its streets to match the excellent motor-road. In the rambling Lake View Hotel my £2 room had a bath – alas! *sans* water. This welcoming Muslim establishment was teetotal, a snag dealt with by giving one of the staff 2,000 shillings and telling him that if he brought me two beers (costing 1,000 shillings) I wouldn't expect any change. In the humid restaurant I supped off more soggy rice and an extraordinarily nasty fish stew. Then I fell into bed and had an unique experience.

Switching off the light, I was resigned to the inevitable; one learns to live – even to sleep – with mosquitoes. Moments later the fleas became apparent; several fleas, simultaneously settling down to their evening meal. I resigned myself to those, too. Given their way, fleas soon become replete and desist; to interrupt them merely wastes energy and prolongs the agony. And anyway the mosquitoes were going to give me an itchy night. Then something else made itself felt, something unfamiliar and dreadfully numerous. Switching on the light, I found the bed swarming with mites – creatures much too small to be lice, so minuscule that one could see them only because they were moving. I looked at my naked body; they were swarming on it, too. Then another movement caught my eye: truly this room was an insect game-park. Down the wall from the wooden ceiling scores of red-brown bedbugs, the size and shape of a little fingernail, had been marching – until the light went on. Bedbugs are allergic to light and now they were in disarray, scuttling to and fro instead of proceeding in an orderly fashion to their destination. Experienced travellers maintain that bedbugs and fleas cannot co-exist; this fallacy I am now in a position to disprove. Having rid myself of the mites (that took time) I slept in the bath with the light on. Only the mosquitoes followed me.

In Jinja the source of the Nile must be saluted and I had booked into that insect game-park for two nights. However, my Nile pilgrimage was delayed by numerous lengthy social encounters beginning with an eager-looking young man, met in the bank, who said he had seen me arriving the previous evening. His office-boy job in a sugar factory bored him so please could he interview me? He wanted to become a journalist and if he could write something really exciting about a brave old European mama cycling alone through Africa maybe that would be the turning-point in his life. Few of us can resist the possibility, however remote, of being the turning-point in someone else's life. We therefore settled down in a corner of the bank where my answers to his questions were carefully inscribed on the back of several Foreign Exchange Permit forms provided by a genial bank clerk. The young man's questions were excellent; many professional journalists could learn from him. But his grammar was so original that I doubt if I served my turning-point function.

After that I sought a second breakfast; at dawn the hotel menu had been restricted to weak tea and a flaccid left-over chapatti. Not far from the bank a clean and pleasant little café provided a three-egg omelette, fresh bread, strong coffee and good company.

James, the café owner, was a tall, blacker-than-usual young man with a pot belly. His year-old daughter roved the floor as we talked and his beautiful wife, expecting her second at any moment, was carrying beer crates from a truck parked outside.

A retired teacher asked my occupation, then frowned. Travel writers ignorant of local languages, he opined politely but firmly, often give misleading impressions. 'Only about 20 per cent of Ugandans can hold a conversation in English. And no African can express *African* thoughts and feelings in any European language – not even people as fluent as I am. That's one reason why so many donors go astray, wasting billions of dollars – or turning our politicians into billionaires. Most expats plan on a false basis.'

James was standing by the door, watching his wife woman-handling another load of crates. He turned and beckoned me to join him. 'Look!' he said, pointing across the street. 'See those people? They're waiting for the AIDS clinic to open. Go and talk to them, they'll give you something *real* to write about. Even if you can't talk to them, you can understand their problem – OK?'

I shook my head. '*Not* OK! I'm not a journalist looking for a story, I'd prefer not to intrude.'

Impatiently the teacher said, 'So you'll only write about "the Pearl of Africa"? A pretty picture for your readers? But isn't it dishonest to censor out AIDS? It'll spoil the pretty picture, but it's affecting most Ugandans, directly or indirectly.'

A young man who had been listening, saying nothing, now laughed derisively. 'She's afraid she'll get infected if she goes near those people – she only wants to know about funny native customs.' He looked at me angrily and added, 'In the past four months, three of my friends have died.'

55

'She's not afraid,' said the teacher sharply. 'She's an educated woman. Or if she is afraid it's of seeing suffering, not of the virus.'

Thus challenged, I crossed the street as the clinic door opened. A queue of forty or so – three-quarters of them men – edged into a large room with three small rooms opening off it. No notice was taken of my arrival; evidently Jinja had had its fill of 'interested' foreigners. The staff – a young male doctor and two older nurses – all wore starched white coats. One small room was for testing; another for giving the news of test results; the third for dispensing to those with full-blown AIDS whatever alleviating medicines were available.

Eventually Dr Mulumba acknowledged my presence. 'You represent which organisation?'

I explained myself rather incoherently, wishing I were anywhere else.

The doctor smiled. 'Just relax and talk to people, if they want to talk. Say what you feel. Then they can say what they feel. It's good for them to talk to outsiders. Don't be frightened if some get very angry – with themselves or their families or partners or you as a European. After we close I want to talk to you myself, about Irish bishops.'

I can think of more relaxing situations. True, many were eager to communicate with a *mzungu*, sometimes more by looks than words. And it was easy enough to cope with the anger, the men's blaming of women, even the occasional outbursts of semi-hysteria. But the quiet bewildered despair was devastating, as was the terrified tension among many queuing for the test, who noted that only two came out of the 'results' room looking relieved. Others, however, confidently claimed to be 'clean'; the test was a mere formality to reassure a parent or partner. More and more arrived. One young man told me, 'At first people were too ashamed to come here. Now in the cities everyone knows someone . . . It's got like malaria, not a disgrace.'

Afterwards the doctor and I sat drinking tea out of a megathermos; the nurses had hurried away to prepare their husbands' lunches. One commented, '*We'd* like to talk to you, too. But African *women* can never sit around!'

Dr Mulumba was understandably baffled by the Irish approach to AIDS. 'In *Time* I read about Irish bishops not letting the government give people condoms – they'd prefer people to give each other AIDS! Is this true?'

At the end of my long dissection of that lamentable controversy Dr Mulumba observed, 'So you are a Protestant, not a Catholic.' Like most Africans with whom this subject came up, he refused to believe that I have no religion. Refilling our cups he said reflectively, 'AIDS is unlike all other diseases. When healthy people hear they're positive they don't react like sick people told they're dying. It's like being sentenced to death for a crime you didn't commit. That's why some men – and women – say "I'm not going alone!" and deliberately infect others.'

I stared at him, too appalled to comment. He seemed to find my reaction surprising. 'Isn't it the same in the West?'

'Maybe it is – I don't know, I've never heard of this before. To me it's very shocking, unless the person was already mentally ill.'

'I can understand it,' the doctor said calmly. 'They feel an *injustice* and having revenge makes life seem more balanced. What shocks me is some men now going for school girls only – men never tested. They're so afraid of infection they look for virgins. In this clinic we've three girls, aged 12 to 13, infected by their teacher. He threatened to throw them out of school if they didn't. And virgins always get infected because of the bleeding. Now that man's dying and nobody's sorry. Of course his wife's positive too. She's gone back to her family in Masaka with the four children.'

I looked at my watch and invented an appointment. Dr Mulumba may have had lots more to say but I didn't want to hear it.

The noon heat deflected me from the source of the Nile to a source of beer. In a small Western-style bar genuine-looking bottles of whisky, gin, vodka and brandy lined the shelves but were so expensive that only tourists (of whom there are few in Jinja) could afford them. In a rear room a clergyman was giving scripture lessons to a dozen little girls. At the bar counter larger girls were working on three young Asian businessmen from Leicester. These, I soon discovered, hoped to retrieve family properties in Busoga, their parents having been expelled in 1972. The Museveni regime, they said, was encouraging Asians to return and help put Uganda's economy together again, an irony they savoured. For generations Asians have been arousing jealous resentment throughout East Africa; only when a country finds itself bereft of their entrepreneurial energy are they appreciated. However, many confiscated properties were used to buy support for Uganda's military tyrants and their recovery, after twenty years of anarchy, is beset by every sort of difficulty: administrative and moral, economic and social, political and philosophical. Those three young men were pessimistic. They foretold that the Asians who answered Museveni's call would belong not to the rich exiled families but to the poorer segments of the Asian communities in Kenya and Tanzania, people hoping it would be easier to succeed in the new Uganda, free of competition.

This up-market bar cared for its image; an old crippled beggar who sidled in, his bloodshot eyes fixed pleadingly on the *mzungu*, was promptly ejected. The sleek bureaucrat sitting beside me, studying a thick FAO 'Comprehensive Plan', looked approving and remarked, 'We've no social security here, as in your countries.' He leaned towards me then and murmured, 'For one pound sterling 3,000 shillings? Tomorrow I'm colgating to Kisumu.' (In Uganda 'to colgate' means to cross the border, either licitly or illicitly, to buy coveted items of Western origin now manufactured in Kenya.) When I shook my head he looked resigned and asked, 'Where in Uganda are you visiting?' On my mentioning Karamoja his reaction was so extreme that everyone else in the bar turned to stare at us.

'No, no! A permit is impossible, the people are naked murdering savages! Men and boys all have two or three of the latest weapons – from Zaire, Sudan, Somalia, Ethiopia – so many that for three US dollars they can buy the best! Then they shoot everything that moves, the aid agencies have ordered armour-plated vehicles for driving through on humanitarian missions! Also they are pagans and sometimes need bits of outsiders. Lately a young Baganda priest was taken off his motor-bike into the bush and beheaded. I can't tell a lady what else they did. They're not thieves, they left his bike on the road, taking his head and other bits for their dirty religious ceremonies. No, no! Karamoja is not for tourists!'

All this sounded like the wildest exaggeration but was confirmed (and expanded upon) in Kampala, not by twitchy urban bureaucrats but by tough unfussy Irish nuns who had lived in the region for thirty years and spoke the language. One day (and it had better be soon) some authority will have to halt the flow of post-Cold War weaponry to every remote corner of the globe.

58

Sauntering back to the hotel, along wide arcaded streets, I paused by a pharmacy window to read a large, closely printed English-language poster. It explained every form of contraceptive, clearly stating all the pros and cons. Then the pharmacist came to the door – a tall, slim, elderly man – and said gloomily, 'Only foreigners stop to look at that.' He invited me in for a cup of tea and I asked if Uganda's pro-condom campaign was having an effect. To which he replied, 'In Africa the cultural barrier to condom use will almost certainly prove permanently insuperable.'

Squinting sideways, I could see the title of the book he was reading: *Adam Bede*. I was about to question him on Africa's cultural barrier, as distinct from the universal barrier of male selfishness, when we were joined by Dr Kivu, an old friend of his whose grandfather and father had also been doctors in Jinja' – But my grandfather was a medicine man, you'd say a witch-doctor!'

Dr Kivu had a message for the *mzungu*. 'In this one district, between 1900 and 1905, more than a quarter of a million died of sleeping-sickness. Africa has these plagues, they come and go. But now AIDS is fashionable in the West, so you people make it into a big drama. For us it's just one more calamity – we have them all the time. Wars, droughts, famines, locusts, human and cattle epidemics, crop disease . . . We must always be fatalistic, playing it cool as you'd say. But the West tries to make us panic about AIDS. You send teams of every sort of specialist, set up schemes for 'AIDS orphans', make TV films, write books and reports and theses, organise academic conferences and seminars and workshops, interview people on their death-beds, photo relatives looking at wasting bodies, conduct surveys, establish research institutes . . . Is this really helping *us*? Or is it another gravy-train for Westerners? Think about that!' The doctor put down his tea-cup, shook hands and departed.

I looked at the pharmacist. 'Do you agree with your friend?' He was so long silent that I expected an evasive reply. Then he said, 'I agree about the West behaving parasitically. But I do not agree that this epidemic can be equated with previous plagues. That notion is scientifically unsound. Nevertheless, it may be that without a cure being discovered, or any effective mass-immunisation, Africans will develop a natural immunity. It is too soon to make definite statements or predictions, as yet we know little about this virus. Possibly a percentage of HIV + will enjoy a normal life-span, while remaining a hazard to others. Decades must pass before that can be established.'

By now my main interest was focused on the pharmacist's use of English. He smiled when I asked where he had studied the language. 'I didn't study it, I was born in Cambridge.' Hopefully I waited for an explanation of this unusual event – unusual given his age and present occupation. But no further information was vouchsafed, as he himself might have put it.

My mid-afternoon walk to the Nile took me through the run-down city centre to a suburban area of once-handsome colonial and ex-Asian bungalows in spacious gardens shaded by blossoming trees; now very extended families have taken these over, with predictable results. In a more salubrious quarter, similar dwellings, well-maintained, overlook a golf course and sports ground. Then suddenly the scene before me was recognisable, though 130 years had passed since John Hanning Speke described it, on becoming the first European to see the White Nile at its source.

> Most beautiful was the scene, nothing could surpass it! It was the very perfection of the kind of effect aimed at in a highly-kept park; with a magnificent stream from 600 to 700 yards wide, dotted with islets and rocks, the former occupied by fisher-men's huts, the latter by terns and crocodiles basking in the sun, flowing between fine high grassy banks, with rich trees and plantains in the background . . . Though beautiful, the scene was not exactly what I expected, for the broad surface of the lake was shut out from view by a spur of hill . . . The expedition had now performed its functions, old Father Nile without any doubt rises in the Victoria Nyanza.

The source of the Nile has been only slightly developed as a tourist attraction; for most of the past thirty years Uganda was in no position to attract tourists. From the level crest of a high ridge a carefully tended public park marks the spot. Acres of mown grass – in March a thirsty brown – slope steeply down to the swift clear river. There are neat cacti hedges and weedless flowerbeds making ponds of deep pink or blue or scarlet under a wealth of shapely trees. Halfway down I paused to read the inscription on an uninspired, rather functional stone monument, four feet high:

THIS SPOT
MARKS THE PLACE FROM WHERE
THE NILE STARTS ITS LONG JOURNEY
TO THE MEDITERRANEAN SEA THROUGH
CENTRAL AND NORTHERN UGANDA
SUDAN AND EGYPT

For a moment I reacted Eurocentrically, feeling sad that poor Speke wasn't mentioned. But of course old Father Nile didn't begin his long journey only when a *mzungu* 'discovered' him doing so. And yet no African knew, in 1862, that here was the source of the White Nile. Indeed, none of the lakeside tribes met by Speke on his way north even knew the extent of Victoria Nyanza. So perhaps, after all he had suffered physically to reach this spot – and was yet to suffer emotionally, because of the controversy with Burton – he does deserve a mention on that monument.

There was no one in sight, a most unusual circumstance near any African town. Relishing this solitude I descended to river level and found a safe swimming spot – the water deep enough to slow the current. (Hereabouts crocodiles are now scarce; and this wasn't the sort of environment that much appeals to the bilharzia snail.) Black and white kingfishers dived repeatedly as I swam, herons waded nearby and overhead a fish eagle hovered, high up. The sky had half clouded over and when I emerged a strong east wind soon dried me. I sat opposite a rocky islet, some thirty yards offshore, which supported an ancient tree, its roots coiling like serpents among black boulders, its cascading outer branches almost touching the waters, its dense foliage home to a colony of large, raucous ungainly birds.

On the far side rose that high jungly ridge where Speke stood when first he saw the river and had his long-held hunch confirmed. Patches of matoke grew where the gradient allowed and at intervals slender fingers of rock stretched into the water, forming miniature bays in which a few fishermen were now visible, mending their nets or counting the day's catch. Exactly a quarter of a century earlier, on 20 February 1967, I had gazed at the source of the Blue Nile, where it flows out of Lake Tana in the Ethiopian highlands. Then Ethiopia was still an empire, Uganda's long agony had just begun and I remember wondering, that day, if I would ever see the source of the other Nile.

Introspection set in and I was comparing my 35-year-old self with my 60-year-old self when Peter arrived, in open pursuit of the *mzungu*. 'From my home near the golf course I saw you passing and thought maybe you could help me. You met my friend in the bank this morning, he said you are a writer.' Peter had just finished a novel, 'an important story which will interest people in the UK'.

As it is the duty of old writers to be attentive to young writers I made an encouraging noise. 'Why is it important?'

Peter beamed and sat beside me. 'It is about AIDS. That makes it important. The whole world likes to read about AIDS in Uganda – OK?' He looked at me hopefully. 'You are interested? You can help?'

'I'm interested, yes, but it's not easy to help. Tell me more.'

The novel was autobiographical. Peter's elder brother had died of AIDS. His 19-year-old sister was dying of AIDS. Two of his cousins were HIV +. He had been tested twice and was 'clean'. In September he planned to marry and had told his friends of his resolve to remain celibate until then, his fianceé being strictly controlled by her parents. 'But no one will believe me! My friends laugh at me! They tell me it is impossible not to have sex for six months and if I did I couldn't have good sex with my wife because I'd be damaged. You understand now why my novel is important? It explains *why* we have this terrible killer disease. And it is true and real, not from my imagination but from my experience. So how will you help me?'

It seemed a long shot, but I gave Peter my publisher's address and a scribbled note to enclose with the typescript.

'Typescript?' he repeated. 'My book must be *typed*?'

'I'm afraid so, nowadays. Otherwise it won't be read.'

'But that is too much money! Where can I get so much?'

We calculated; it wasn't very much in sterling. Peter however refused to be subsidised. 'No, no! I beg only for advice, never for money. I will work more to earn those shillings. My job is in a lawyer's office so I can work overtime. Too many Africans beg from the West. It's better to be independent.'

Just after sunset came a wondrous moment when the Nile shimmered a clear translucent blue and tall palms stood black against a silver-blue sky, their drooping fronds restless in the wind. Then the water changed to a sombre metallic grey-blue – and Peter insisted on

62

escorting me back to my hotel. 'It is too dangerous in our towns after dark, we have too many very poor, very young soldiers with guns.'

Ravening clouds of minute lake-flies tormented me on the road out of Jinja. I had to keep my eyes three-quarters closed, which was no bad thing as I crossed the Nile by a hideous hydro-electric dam that has obliterated the Owen Falls and supplies most of Uganda with electricity. ('But this is better', I reminded myself, 'than a nuclear power station on the lake shore.') The Owen Falls dam was completed in 1954; it took six years to build and cost £22,000,000. Industry developed in Jinja post-dam and, as many Ugandans are quick to point out, the wealthy classes benefited most; few others can afford electricity. Now this dam to a certain extent controls the Nile's flow, as does the Aswan dam. In the late nineteenth century control of the Nile was a major political issue and fear of some foreign nation seizing the source caused Lord Salisbury to change his mind about the desirability of Britain 'protecting' Uganda. This shows a certain vagueness about geography and engineering on the part of the noble lord; at that date the notion of the Nile's source being controlled to dominate the passage to India was absurd. Yet the geopolitics of the era were so eccentric (or do I mean neurotic?) that Uganda's strategic importance was imagined to be immense. In theory, whoever ruled Uganda controlled the Nile flow, and therefore dominated Egypt also – and whoever dominated Egypt controlled the Suez Canal, the passage to India. When the Kaiser sought British support against France and Russia in 1889, Lord Salisbury demanded that Germany first renounce all claims to Uganda. A deal was done in 1890, when Britain swapped Heligoland (three square miles of Europe) in exchange for Germany's not disputing British expansion into Zanzibar, Equatoria and Uganda (100,000 square miles of Africa). Given the fate of Tanzania, during its brief period under German rule, it has to be said that Uganda was lucky in 1890.

Beyond the dam stretched a magnificent Forest Reserve, green, shady and cool, the towering trees teeming with noisy multicoloured birds and four species of gambolling monkeys. Then came open, symmetrically hilly country, a pleasant enough though too predictable landscape. Slopes clothed in sugar-cane and matoke have their limitations, aesthetically. Thus far, the 'Pearl of Africa' was proving a trifle disappointing; modern Uganda's most 'developed' region belies the early travellers' descriptions. Remarkably, the seventy miles to Entebbe were without one level stretch and the heavy traffic, as homicidal as Kenya's, prevented my enjoying the steep downhills.

Until recently, much-feared military road-blocks were common on all Uganda's main routes. By 1992 these had become mere token reminders that the country was still ruled by its army, in so far as President Museveni depended on military support. Every twenty miles or so I passed three or four unarmed adolescent soldiers, wearing shabby uncoordinated uniforms and lounging under trees dallying with local lassies. Sometimes a small sign stood in the middle of the road saying: ROAD BLOCK or STOP! These simply added one more hazard to Ugandan motoring as drivers swerved sickeningly to avoid them. I, however, always stopped, hoping to get into conversation with the soldiers. Unfortunately none spoke English but they greeted me with friendly grins and waves, a few even exerting themselves to come forward and shake hands and gaze enviously at Lear. They were of an age to belong to what is facetiously known as 'Museveni's kindergarten'; countless 'Terror orphans' were adopted by the National Resistance Army and came to revere Museveni as 'Father'. They soon learned how to fire guns bigger than themselves and now some Ugandans worry about their being brutalised by exposure to the fighting in Karamoja – if not already brutalised by witnessing the atrocities of the 'lumpen militariat' (Ali Mazrui's phrase).

Kampala is conspicuous from afar, its several flat-topped hills cluttered with old ramshackle commercial buildings, new high-rise status symbols, the mosques of various sects and a Hindu temple. But for the moment I was bypassing Kampala; at Entebbe good friends awaited me – the Parkinsons, first met in Cameroon and now stationed in Uganda.

Even around its capital cities Africa is curiously allergic to sign-posts and by the time I had found my way through the industrialised suburbs and shantytowns it was 5.20. When I stopped for a quick Coca-Cola two elderly men worried about my safety; it is dangerous, they warned, to travel after dark. 'That is a very fine bicycle, you will certainly be robbed and maybe killed!' Beside me on the counter lay a new pro-condoms poster, just delivered by a health-worker. The duka-owner was scornful. 'I won't put it up, we get condoms not good enough for Western countries, dumped by Americans and Germans.'

Lear moved slowly over the last twenty hilly miles, through a perilous torrent of rush-hour traffic. Again the heat had taken its toll; clearly I was a write-off as a cyclist until the cooling rains came and it would make sense to remain with the Parkinsons while awaiting that relief. When darkness fell I donned my luminous vest though the traffic had almost ceased. On Entebbe's maze of unlit streets there was nobody around of whom to ask directions; during the Terror Ugandans developed the habit of retreating indoors at dusk. Then at last I was rescued by a kind askari who deserted his post outside the posh Victoria Hotel and leaped on his bicycle to lead me through impenetrable blackness to the secluded EC compound – so secluded that without guidance I might not have found it before dawn.

4

A Pause Insular and Urban

———————

For a few days I lapsed into two-tiered expat luxury: not only good food, strong drink, cold showers, attentive servants and a bird-rich garden but also (and much more important) reunion with dear friends who again pampered me endlessly, as they had done in Cameroon. Blessed are the travellers who can lay all their problems at the feet of such as Joy and John Parkinson and have them instantly solved.

Entebbe rests on its rather shrivelled laurels. In Protectorate times it was Uganda's administrative centre; now various government departments and aid organisations occupy the old colonial offices, while the President occupies the governor's residence on a grassy slope overlooking the lake. This august dwelling is so closely guarded that one hesitates even to glance at it lest some trigger-happy sentry might suspect the worst. Expats live in orderly oases of spacious bungalows and blossom-bright gardens, well-watered and green even in the dry season. One such oasis is the security-conscious EC compound, almost as difficult to get into as an Israeli nuclear weapons silo. Nearby, across the dual-carriageway leading to the airport, a trading centre lines a deep, wide hollow beneath a wooded ridge. Here I was extra-warmly welcomed on introducing myself as Joy's friend and I visited that market daily to keep in touch with the real Uganda, which fast recedes if one is being sybaritic in a White ghetto.

I rejoiced when John invited me to accompany him on a tour of coffee farms in the Masaka district, some seventy miles south of Kampala. He was then leading an EC project to introduce new and better strains of coffee to Uganda and, unlike many project leaders, he preferred practical work in the bush to writing theoretical reports in his office. From the little fishing-port of Bukakata, near Masaka, I could sail to Bugala Island – the biggest of the numerous Sese Islands – rejoining Lear in Entebbe when the rains came.

I shared the back of the Landrover with a smarmy agricultural officer intent on being EC-sponsored for some 'advanced' course in Britain. His efforts to impress and charm the EC Big Man were not, I intuited, being wildly successful. After thirty-five years in Africa John is a bona fide expert, no easy touch for sponsorship-seekers.

Halfway to Masaka we exchanged hilliness for miles of papyrus swamps containing the occasional tank corpse, relics of the Tanzanian army's anti-Amin invasion in 1979. Here a laden cyclist skidded in the loose stones of the verge and fell outwards; John reckoned we missed him by about four inches, through sheer luck. The driver, Albert, could not possibly have averted tragedy. (Albert was a most endearing character, gentle and handsome though shockingly thin; he needed sick leave increasingly often but was determined to keep his job for as long as possible.)

Throughout Africa drivers are recommended not to stop at the scene of an accident in populated areas, especially if Whites are involved. Instead, a statement should be made at the nearest police post. This may sound callous yet even people as soft-hearted as John see it as an essential precaution. Too many drivers – and sometimes their passengers, also – have been killed within moments of a fatal accident by enraged mobs. In just such circumstances, John himself had lost a friend in Nigeria.

The large – by local standards – town of Masaka remains grimly battle-scarred, though rebuilding had recently begun in a desultory way. John and I stayed in a pleasant little hotel (up-market for me, roughing it for John) far enough out of town to have come through the war unscathed. Our rooms had telephones and television sets and bedside lamps, none of which worked because Uganda's electricity supply had then been cut off for forty-eight hours. According to rumour, something crucial had fallen apart at Jinja's power-station, half the screws having been filched during construction. In the lamplit restaurant our fellow-diners were a harassed-looking Italian aid worker who spoke no English (we wondered how he communicated with the Ugandans) and a gaunt, tight-lipped Englishwoman who avoided everybody's gaze and studied tables of statistics throughout her meal. Next morning she drove away, alone, in an immaculate 'AIDS Prevention Programme' Range Rover. How many £2.50 AIDS tests could be provided, for those who wish to have them but can't afford them, if that 'Prevention Programme' lacked a Range Rover? And why don't more people – White people, not disregarded Blacks – ask such questions?

The local EC team (a woman and five men) had been requested, a week in advance, to assemble at 8.15 but it didn't surprise John that we set off at 10.30. I admired his capacity for being patiently courteous while gently chivvying. The new breed of expert tends to be much more short-tempered – and so would I be, if working with Africans. It is easy for the casually wandering *mzungu* to adapt.

John obviously inspired real affection among his colleagues, while making it plain that he knew exactly what they were up to. When it was claimed that repairs to extension-workers' motor cycles had cost an astronomical sum he blandly observed that the EC accountant would of course expect detailed statements of exactly how much each repair had cost and to whom the money had been paid. At this point the relevant official's body-language became interesting; I noticed his ankles being twisted around one another under the desk while he rapidly twirled a pen between his palms.

High in the hills, west of Masaka, our track overlooked vast expanses of broken country, fertile and patchily wooded. Deep little valleys suddenly appeared to left or right, low blue mountains lay along the horizons, rough red tracks climbed steep green slopes, a strong wind drove white clouds across the wide sky and I pined for Lear.

The prosperous shambas were scattered and we passed only one hamlet, a few dukas at a crossroads. The failure of the November and December rains had wrecked the maize crop but matoke and coffee can better withstand drought conditions and John was pleased with his project's progress. Only one pilot planting had ended in tears; an extension-worker had neglected to demonstrate how artificial fertiliser should be applied so it was sprayed on to the bushes, killing all fifty. Another illiterate farmer had been persuaded by a travelling salesman to buy a pesticide he could ill-afford against a worm unknown in East Africa; that spray did the baby bushes only temporary harm but gave the farmer a chronic cough. A third 'pioneer' warmed my heart by declaring that he would never poison his beloved land with chemicals. He believed in natural mulch and shade trees (unusual here) and his coffee was thriving. The Entebbe agricultural officer, well tutored by chemical salesmen, objected that natural fertilising wastes a lot of time, whereupon the Green farmer retorted that chemicals waste a lot of money.

It bothered John that while there was a bwana around his colleagues remained reluctant to take decisions. Repeatedly he reminded them that he was their adviser, not their leader, and that this project was for the benefit of *Africans* who must themselves take responsibility for its success or failure. However, as we went from farm to farm, encountering various small but important problems, it seemed that for this team to assume responsibility, with a White man on the scene, was almost a psychological impossibility.

Especially impressive were the achievements of one small, wiry, vigorous 60-year-old, described by John as among the most intelligent and innovative farmers he had ever worked with. Edward's coffee had flourished throughout the drought, he himself having devised an ingenious mulching system to cope with the crisis. Two hundred of his acres were grazing bush, the other sixty-nine (precisely!) were under coffee, apart from the matoke plantation behind a new breeze-block bungalow. He beckoned us to follow him into the matoke, where we admired his magnificent thirty-foot-high plants. As John pointed out to the team that this was how matoke should always be planted, with one or two juniors accompanying each senior, my eye was caught by a row of five graves on the edge of the plantation, near the house. Four were new, one so new that the mound of tawny earth had not yet settled. Three were marked by long terraced slabs of concrete, painted white; the headstones were blank. The fifth was much bigger and grander, a tomb of porous red brick where Edward's first wife awaited him; she had died of heart-failure in 1990. Angela, the one woman in the team, happened to be standing beside me. She whispered that the four smaller graves held Edward's two sons and their wives; all had died of AIDS within the past eighteen months, leaving him childless. (Two other sons were lost fighting with the NRA.) Medical workers have noticed that for some unexplained reason HIV + family members tend to sicken and die in clusters, even if infected at different times.

I looked at Edward, standing scarcely thirty yards from those graves animatedly discussing some new scheme with John. By then I had been in his company for an hour, without ever suspecting that he had recently endured such a tragic succession of bereavements. I remembered Dr Kivu, in Jinja, arguing that catastrophic epidemics are part of African life and accepted, even by those most afflicted, with a stoicism beyond the imagination of modern Europeans. 'We get on with the *present*,' he had said, almost defiantly. Edward was certainly doing that.

Back in the compound I noticed Albert sitting on the veranda step holding the hand of a frail 3-year-old, gazing into his eyes and talking softly to him. This was Edward's grandson, also dying. I found the gentle communication between those two victims – one aware, one unaware – almost unbearably sad.

We were welcomed into the house by Edward's fat cheerful second wife – in her mid-twenties, wearing a tight purple check dress designed to emphasise her obesity, hereabouts a mark of beauty. She hugged and kissed me before inviting us all to sit on green plastic couches, with slippery puce cushions. Above us hung a 1990 calendar, depicting the Duke of Edinburgh, and a Church of Uganda poster depicting the House of Bishops, their passport-size photographs tastefully arranged in the form of a cross. Alice spread a snow-white cloth on a long coffee-table and served Pepsi Cola, fried manioc and delicious banana fritters made with cassava flour. Meanwhile John was negotiating the purchase of a load of matoke.

Uganda's staple food was then very expensive in Kampala and Entebbe: 3,000 shillings a stalk as compared to 1,200 shillings in the bush. Therefore John had planned to pack the Landrover for the benefit of his wretchedly paid junior staff. But alas! on leaving Edward's house we found the vehicle already being loaded, under the supervision of Mr Smarmy, for the benefit of the well-paid Chief of the Department. There was nothing John could do, once his original polite though vigorous protest had been brushed aside. That marked the difference between being a colonial officer and an EC project director.

At the last shamba a 22-year-old English-speaking wife proudly introduced me to her three robust children and pointed towards the as yet invisible fourth. My suggestion that four might be enough amused her; at least four more would be needed to ensure an adequate labour force.

Before leaving for Entebbe John drove me (reluctantly) to a Murphy-type hotel, a quarter the price of his choice but equally comfortable though without a restaurant. As I went supper-hunting the rains came, only one day late – they are supposed to start annually on 17 March.

In a large, shabby, candlelit restaurant (the electricity was still off) I chose matoke and fishes' heads, in preference to rice and fishes' heads. Understandably, there were few customers and Professor Apollo Mugasha soon invited me to share a bottle of Nile beer (Uganda's best, but vastly inferior to Tusker). That was a noble gesture on the Professor's part, his bottle being the last in the bar.

It's not every day one meets a Ugandan Professor of Political Science, so tentatively I probed. Thus far, in Apollo's estimation, Museveni had kept his reputation for comparative incorruptibility and remained genuinely popular, if only as the best of a bad lot. Yet there was apprehension, among the politically sensitive, about the insecurity of his position, caught between smouldering tribal animosities and potentially treacherous ministers and army officers. For all his strenuous efforts to impose discipline on the army, troops were so badly paid that reports of looting and hold-ups appeared almost daily in the – happily uncensored – newspapers. In some areas (notably Karamoja) soldiers often engaged in cattle-rustling with the aid of helicopters and bombs, indiscriminately killing the pastoralists. The police force was regarded as less unreliable and unstable though by no means entirely trustworthy. The presence on city streets of so many policewomen, albeit heavily armed, reassured most people.

Old age is in some respects liberating and at that point I felt free to invite the Professor back to my room, where three Nile beers awaited us. Initially he recoiled from the sight of a *mzungu* – and a *lady* at that! – imbibing from the bottle; but soon he recovered and turned his mind to more important matters, such as the destruction of his home town by the Tanzanian army. 'Yes, we welcomed them here as our allies against Amin's army. But see what they did! Without discrimination they attacked not just military targets but hotels, banks, cinemas, government offices, little dukas and big stores, the homes of rich and poor alike. Yet in Africa, to this day, we manufacture only spears, pangas, bows and arrows. If no one had sold us armaments, how many fewer millions would've been killed in the past thirty years? Our towns and cities couldn't have been so devastated by attackers using the traditional arson. But the

71

"advanced" countries' armaments industries needed African purchases to balance their books. Do you realise that in the late '70s, when Amin was at his worst, the sale of arms to Africa, including Uganda, was twenty-five times higher – in dollars – than a decade before? And the British went on furtively supporting Amin's secret service and army, selling them sophisticated equipment, till his overthrow in '79. Then they backed Godfrey Binaisa's brief regime, which was nearly as bad. And worst of all, Obote's gang got British aid and military training long after his troops were *known* to be butchering tens of thousands of men, women and children. You expect such behaviour from Russians or Chinese, not from the country we were brought up to admire and imitate. Then the same support was given to Saddam Hussein till the eve of the Gulf War, only more so, since he was a better customer! Is there any difference between that sort of corruption and our sort?'

I poured petrol on the fire by reminding the Professor of the Western Cold Warriors' frequent and monstrous boast, 'Our nuclear capability has given us forty years of peace'. But then I assured him that to many Europeans the ethnocentricity of that 'us' is repellent.

He smiled grimly. 'You should also find it frightening. One day it may be punished.'

At 7.30 a.m. came another two-hour tropical downpour and the subsequent humidity, as I walked a few miles to the matatu stop, made me apprehensive. Was this what the locals meant when they talked about the rains 'cooling' things? Did they not know the difference between dampness and coolness?

The pick-up matatu for Bukakata was waiting under a mango tree outside a row of dukas at a crossroads. Approaching it, I got a nasty shock. I had imagined the Sese Islands to be *mzungu*-free yet in the back, squeezed between stalks of matoke, sat somebody red-haired and freckled. Only then did it occur to me that on the way from Nairobi I had met not one fellow-traveller.

As we talked – Ian came from Glasgow – the customary overload accumulated: sacks of bread and charcoal, more matoke, babies and hens and tins of kerosene, boxes of patent medicines and bales of cloth, much more matoke, innumerable items of personal luggage – and finally a bicycle, tied ingeniously to the outside back.

By the time we moved off at noon I had somehow lost my seat on an old tyre and been forced so to contort myself, while bearing the weight of three toddlers, that soon I had severe leg cramps. Now the rain clouds were gone but a frisky breeze helped as we jolted between plantain groves, or tea-gardens separated by patches of dense jungle from coffee plantations, or lush pastures on which dramatically horned cattle shone with good health; here the drought had been less extreme.

Bukakata is a village of crude wooden huts and non-committal people. Outside two of the shacks weather-beaten boards proclaim 'Maternity Clinic' and 'Dental and Chemist Care'; I would prefer to have a dental crisis elsewhere. The local industries are fishing and smuggling, though the latter has declined since Museveni took over. During the Terror these food-rich lake villages attracted many youngsters from the chaotic and starving districts to the west. The boys smuggled, the girls were 'employed' by, among others, Tanzanian soldiers. One hypothesis blames this migration for the spread of AIDS throughout those rural areas to which many youngsters returned when peace came. The Tanzanian hypothesis is of course different, suggesting that their unfortunate troops were infected, or bewitched, in Uganda.

In Masaka John had gone to considerable trouble to ascertain the ferry's departure time at the shipping company head office, but alas! there was no ferry. It had caught fire the week before, *en route* to Entebbe. How the head office could have remained unaware of this baffled me. It did not baffle John, however, when I told him on my return. 'So many bureaucrats had to pass that message from one office to another it never arrived where it was most needed – in Masaka.'

Near the little stone jetty a truck-driver, his vehicle half-filled with sacks of ice, was buying fish from the islanders. Tons of Nile perch, in packaged frozen fillets, are flown from Entebbe and sold as a delicacy in Paris, London, Brussels, Rome. The fishermen were being paid 300 shillings a kilo and the average fish that day weighed twenty kilo; post-Terror, the Sese Islanders are by far the most prosperous peasant Ugandans and they have the added advantage of their harvest being unaffected by drought.

The ferry's absence delighted the island boatmen, especially when Ian and I were joined by three Australian backpackers whose conversation reached such a pitch of banality that it finally toppled over into entertainment. There was much competition for our custom; we ended up in a crowded boat, twenty feet long, each having paid 700 shillings for the half-hour journey. Ian and I recognised many of the items on board, not to mention those toddlers, who happily sat on me again. Our destination was the nearest jetty, fifteen miles from the 'capital', Kalangala. The Australians already knew, from their *Lonely Planet* guide, that one could stay in a guest-house near the jetty before getting the early morning truck-bus to Kalangala. All these guide books seem to assume that the young travellers they cater for have lost the use of their lower limbs – which perhaps is logical, seeing the ludicrous amount of luggage backpackers carry. Some young women are incapable of lifting their own rucksacks at loading-up time, so it's small wonder they shirk carrying them a yard further than need be. And now there are not only backpacks but forepacks, bulky knapsacks hanging under the chin and alleged by their manufacturers to be an essential security precaution.

I moved off fast from the jetty, on a soft red track leading to a wall of fern-draped trees. Then bureaucracy struck. Peremptorily I was summoned to a small thatched hut by a very tall, barefooted young man in ragged jeans and T-shirt. 'Hey! You come! You register with police!' Evidently the hut was the police station and he the police officer. On a tiny table lay a grey kitten, who purred appreciatively when stroked, and a grubby exercise book in which *mzungus* were required to enter passport details. Feeling flippant, I described myself as a 25-year-old Russian astronaut. The policeman carefully scrutinised my entry and showed no trace of incredulity. As I left the hut my fellow-*mzungus* were slowly dragging their laden selves up from the jetty. I sped away into the forest and was greeted by a tumult of hornbills.

The guest-house, in a forest clearing, was a recent development inspired by the backpacking fraternity's discovery of Bugala Island. A tin-roofed shack comprising three bedrooms faced a large half-built brick edifice, overgrown with weeds. (By then I had been told why Uganda is strewn with these half-built homes, shops and godowns; one can lay claim to ownerless land – abandoned when the inhabitants of a district fled or were murdered during the Terror – by *beginning* to build on it.) The young couple in charge occupied an oblong two-roomed hut and behind it, in the round thatched kitchen hut, a primus stove gave status to the establishment. Beyond a muddy corral, holding four cows and three calves, the latrine was screened by unsteady stakes. The couple in charge spoke no English and seemed to regard tourists as an inconvenience to be patiently borne.

I strolled through high matoke and dense coffee bushes to a nearby hamlet where the few visible locals were friendly. The humidity was extreme; sweat flowed off me as I sat on a bench outside a duka drinking warm beer. Mr Etima appeared then, formally dressed and complacent-looking. He introduced himself as 'the local politician and administrator'; pre-Museveni he had been a teacher. 'It makes us very happy', he said, 'to see so many tourists coming back to our beautiful country. Now we have been in peace for six years and all have confidence in our present leader – all Ugandans, all *mzungus*! He is honest, kind, brave and clever. He manages very well the bad feelings between tribes and religions. At last we are lucky! For too long we lived badly, like savages. Even now mass graves are being discovered, full of families – even the babies.' He looked at his expensive watch. 'Excuse me, madame, I must hurry to Masaka, to an important meeting to get foreign money for our fine agricultural college in Kalangala. Thank you for coming to our beautiful country!'

Mr Etima is memorable as one of the few Ugandans who volunteered any comment on domestic politics. The average citizen simply seemed grateful for peace, while remaining sceptical about the motives of all politicians (including Museveni) and having no sense that as individuals they mattered on the political scene. A generation of bloody tribal turmoil does nothing for a new nation's self-respect. Nor did anyone want to talk about their own experiences during the Terror – in vivid contrast to the Rumanians, who needed the catharsis of re-living and analysing their worst moments. Perhaps the Ugandans' worst moments, involving much more physical violence, couldn't be shared with someone from another culture.

As I fetched a third beer (Nile is much weaker than Tusker), a tubby, worn-looking woman sat heavily on the bench, untied her small baby from her back and dumped him in the dust. When he stood up and sturdily walked away I asked his age. Agnes smiled at my astonishment. 'He was nine months yesterday – and walking the past ten days. We have babies more developed than yours, about six weeks ahead. And they go on developing faster. I got nursing training from Irish nuns in Masaka, that's how I know these things. I think you're Irish? You sound like the nuns.' She shouted to the duka-keeper, who at once hurried out with a large bowl of the best pineapple I have ever eaten. 'Tell me about the slim disease in Ireland – you know what I mean? We called it the slim disease before scientists gave it a smart name. I hear in the West it's different, only for drug addicts and men who behave like mad animals. We don't have those problems, except drugs in the coast cities brought in by Europeans and Asians. Your problems sound worse than ours, but is all I hear *true*?'

I ignored this typical African definition of homosexuality and said, 'Your slim problem is worse. It's not spreading so fast in Europe, we've fewer sexual relationships than you do.'

Agnes drained the bowl, then said broodingly, 'I've seven children – five too many, I used to think. Now I don't. This island is very bad because our men go to Masaka to enjoy themselves. Before that Tanzanian war there was no slim disease. Half my work now is giving condoms and information and talking to wives – all wasting my time! An American university man told me to tell women not to sleep with husbands who won't use condoms. I think he knew nothing about African women. They can't give orders to their husbands. And if they won't have more babies they'll be thrown away. That's what wives are *for* . . .'

Next morning torrential rain delayed both the arrival of the backpackers' truck-bus and my own departure. My journal records:

Off at 9.45 – a walk to remember! Pure joy all the way. None of Bugala's six motor vehicles disturbed the peace; four are on sick leave, I heard this evening. Without trying too hard I could imagine myself to be in pre-colonial Africa. The silence and overwhelming beauty put me in that magical mood where existence is reduced to the concentrated enjoyment of the present moment. I could do with more days like this. AIDS is beginning to get me down.

At first the narrow sandy track ran level through partially cultivated land: much healthy coffee, well-tended. Here a dozen laughing small children (sturdy, agile, charming) accompanied me for a mile or so, leap-frogging in and out of deep puddles. Then across many highish hills, covered in semi-rain forest, the dense foliage and tangled creepers and ferns allowing only glimpses of brilliant birds: turacos, greenbuls, weavers, wood hoopoes, grey parrots with scarlet tails – and others unidentified. A cool breeze tempered the humidity yet by noon dehydration threatened. Foolishly I left my water-container in Entebbe – no alternative then but to drink from a pure-looking pool of water in mid-track, being fed by a trickle coursing down from the forest.

Where lower hills were separated by sweeps of lush green grassland I wondered why no cattle? This can't be tsetse-fly territory, for I met none; but perhaps they are seasonal? Here, because Bugala is so irregularly shaped, the lake was sometimes visible on both sides, glittering sapphire beyond those curving downs. At the base of one hill huddled a few primitive huts with shaggy roofs. Nearby, in two forest glades, boat-builders were using methods developed millennia ago but none the worse for that. For a time I sat with a fisherman in his hut doorway, watching him weave an enormous net. The embryo, as it were, was wound around one big toe – deformed by years of such usage – and the whole process demanded swift, rhythmic dexterity. None of his seven children (eldest aged 10) is going to school: fees too high. His beautiful young wife seemed unworn by motherhood, perhaps because of the islanders' high-protein diet. He ordered a daughter to retrieve five small green oranges from under the charpoy-type bed in the two-roomed hut. Then wife washed them carefully in filthy water, cut off the tops as though beheading eggs and presented them on a plastic plate so worn it drooped like paper. Getting at the juice and flesh was hard work; why is this the favoured way of eating oranges in Africa? I tried to pay but that gave offence, a measure of how recently tourism has arrived.

A mile from Kalangala I stopped at the first duka for three Pepsis (the entire stock, that was) and the duka woman pressed a leaflet into my hand urging me to be Born Again. Reading it, I realised how that crusade could help, in relation to AIDS. People keen to change behaviour might get much support from the feeling that God was now helping them to live a different sort of life.

Hereabouts the country is extravagantly fertile, intensively cultivated. Half the 15,000 islanders live within a five-mile radius of their capital, a big village spread over high ground above a magnificent bay sheltered by steep forested slopes. The only guest-house, the Safari Lodge, was opened last year by Michael, a congenial retired teacher. I hope I sufficiently disguised my horror on finding *twenty-five* backpackers sharing the twenty rooms – jerry-built in three rows behind the old family bungalow. Michael is proud of his awareness of *mzungu* needs; each £1.50 room has a jug of boiled water, an oil candle and matches, a basin and chunk of soap. One fetches washing-water from a barrel in the yard. At a discrete distance the latrines (Ladys and Gentz) reek amidst giant matoke. Most African families keep their latrines (when they have them) clean and fresh; Michael apologised because the challenge of running a communal latrine is over-taxing his resources.

When Ian and the Australians arrived at 4.30 we sank several beers – kept in a barrel of water in lieu of a fridge – before supper was served at sunset by Michael's son-in-law. A long, wide veranda, high above the 'main street', is the dining-room – curtained at either end by swathes of crimson and gold flowering creeper. Mosquitoes savaged us as we ate (for 55p each) from heaped communal dishes of sweet potatoes, Irish potatoes, rice, beans, muscular chicken legs, delicately flavoured tapia fresh from the lake. Then a mega-fruit salad of bananas, papaya, oranges, pineapple. All these backpackers seem to be coming from or going to the same places and using the same guidebook – the *Lonely Planet*, ironically.

As the sun rose, a rough footpath led me straight down a grassy mountainside to the shore. Half a dozen boats were moored in the reeds beside a long jetty, built of stones and earth, and in a nearby hamlet of grass huts fish-bones littered the sandy ground. Beyond, a faint path wandered through waist-high golden grass, stretching for a mile or so to the edge of the semi-encircling forest. In a secluded corner, before the trees met the water, it was possible to swim unobserved. The clear lukewarm lake was disappointingly shallow near the shore and I dared not swim too far from my money-belt. Yet those were the best hours of each Bugala day – floating beneath the pastel morning sky, listening to the bird-calls in the forest, watching the fish-eagles gliding, gliding, gliding, then suddenly diving, splashing, swooping back to their young with a shiny catch.

The weather dictated my daily routine. Despite nocturnal downpours the midday heat remained enervating. Those hours were best spent strolling in the coastal forest, where only chips of blue were visible through the tropical canopy high above, or just sitting very still in the green-tinted shade, eventually being ignored by the many birds and few surviving monkeys.

One afternoon my path back to the Lodge passed the token Health Centre where Sister Mutembeya greeted me with a question – 'You have brought us medicines?' She was Bugala's Medical Assistant, a trained nurse and midwife who acted as locum when the doctor was AWOL – that is, most of the time. She invited me to admire the new 'maternity unit' – 'a gift from the kind people of Britain'. The bungalow comprised a twelve-bed ward and a small delivery room dominated by a giant refrigerator for use when/if electricity became available. The unit was empty and felt unused; Sister Mutembeya admitted that most women preferred to lie in at home, assisted by a traditional birth-attendant. She added sombrely, 'Maybe soon we'll turn it into a hospice for slim patients.'

In the cool of the evenings I explored further, crossing the island (narrow at this point) to the far shore. Here, from atop precipitous forested cliffs, one can gaze across Victoria Nyanza towards some of its seventy-seven other islands – none as big as Bugala, many uninhabited. According to Michael, one of the latter was being surveyed as a possible exclusive holiday resort for *very* rich tourists. It angered me to think of speedboats and water-skiers desecrating the blessed tranquillity of Victoria Nyanza. At least backpackers aren't ecological wreckers. Rich tourists must pollute before they can enjoy.

On my last evening I followed a wide path between shambas where children were weeding the maize, or driving cattle home, while their fathers relaxed – as they had been doing all day – and their mothers squatted over small fires, cooking matoke. Then a boy of about 12 came running after me – not begging, or cheerfully calling 'How are *you*? How are *you*?' but taut-faced. Seizing my arm he whispered urgently, 'Come! My mother to see you!'

We passed between tall glossy plantains, lanky papayas, spreading mango trees, an Irish potato patch. In an oblong hut his two older brothers, in their early twenties, were lying side by side on straw mats, both close to death. One was in a coma, the other conscious but speechless. Their bodies were skeletal, their feet hideously swollen. The anguished mother, seeing an elderly *mzungu*, had assumed me to be an 'expert' from some powerful Western organisation and in her despair was convinced that I could help. She spoke no English and the boy's was minimal. 'Medicine!' he pleaded. 'You give *medicine!*'

I could only state bleakly that no one has medicine for the slim disease. To see the momentary hope extinguished in that mother's eyes was unforgettably harrowing. I knelt beside the young men and held their hands, then looked up at their mother, trying to convey that I would have helped if I could. She seemed to understand. As I left the fetid hut she embraced me, then darted sideways into a corner and returned to present me with a hand of bananas.

I was walking on towards the Lodge, in an unhappy daze, when enthusiastic cheering drew me to a practice football match. The level brown-grassed pitch was of the required length but furnished only with goal-posts and bounded on three sides by a luxuriance of forest trees. On the fourth side lay the lake, darkly blue – then suddenly bright, streaked by an incandescent sunset.

Sitting with a group of friendly, articulate agricultural college students, from all over Uganda, I observed something extremely rare in Africa: public petting (rather heavy) between several couples; even odder, they were not at all inhibited by my arrival. It is generally assumed that all *mzungus* must be soccer fans, rather as they must have white skins, and my ignorance of the game puzzled everyone. Ignorance notwithstanding, I appreciated the spectacle of those twenty-two barefooted young men in action, all lithe muscularity and swift grace, their dark skins silken with sweat. Most islanders have magnificent physiques, attributed by Agnes to a high-protein diet from infancy. 'Too many African children', she had said, 'get *no* protein after weaning.' It was, however, impossible to forget Dr Mulumba's words – 'At present most HIV + victims are perfectly healthy.'

Two teenage couples accompanied me back to the Lodge through the brief violet dusk, richly scented and moistly cool as the night's rains approached. Feeling deinhibited by the youngsters' earlier uninhibitedness, I asked, 'Do you know how important condoms are now?' The girls giggled, the boys scoffed. One said, 'This is a big scare from the West, condoms against Africans. We know about this very well, about White people not liking to have too many Black people in the world!' No wonder Agnes had been despairing of her task.

Over supper on the veranda, testing was discussed.

An Australian nurse admitted, 'I daren't! In '86 I lived with a Kikuyu doctor in Nairobi for six months.'

This choosing not to know shocked an Englishman who had lavishly sown his wild oats while working in New York in 1985. Back home he had seen it as his duty to be tested before entering into a long-term relationship with a girlfriend.

A Canadian defended the Australian. As a postgraduate student in San Francisco he had lived unwisely, though heterosexually, but he too preferred not to know. 'Now I always use condoms so what's the point of knowing?' Then he had an afterthought: 'Until I want children, that'll mean thinking again . . .'

A Welshman, not in the business of discussing his own sex life, had yet to recover from his recent observations in Mombasa. 'There were these four Londoners, all middle-aged – just travelling for *sex*. Travelling to *Africa* for sex! Staying in that posh Castle Hotel, picking up different "high-class" virus banks every night. Me and my mate got after them, and asked, "Hey! What about AIDS?". They laughed at us like we were weak in the head. They said, "That's a youngsters' disease, only you kids have a problem!" So why are *Africans* criticised for being ignorant?'

Next morning, before dawn, seven of us made our way down to the jetty; a boat was to leave early for Kasenyi, nine miles from Entebbe. The fifty-foot battered-looking vessel, powered by an outboard motor, needed much bailing out before taking on its cargo of fresh and smoked fish, the former carried loose, the latter packed in sheets of tough black plastic, each huge circular bundle (like a mammoth cheese) securely bound with stout grass ropes. A few dozen ragged islanders milled about, shouting, laughing, arguing dramatically, changing plans, yet finally deferring to the small, grey-haired, taciturn 'captain' – according to Michael a Big Man, but *honest*. The juxtaposition of power and honesty always surprises Africans.

Here I enjoyed my most satisfying Bugala swim, in deep water off the jetty. Then, to my relief, a fleet of dark clouds came sailing over the island's wooded crest. Recalling a gruelling week-long cruise in an open boat through the Galapagos Islands – also on the Equator – I had been dreading this day's exposure to the water-reflected sun. By the time we left, soon after 8 a.m., a strong south-easterly wind was troubling the lake and sheets of *cold* squally rain restricted visibility for the first hour or so. As this was a deep vessel I sat on the gunwale, shivering beneath my rain-cape because propriety had required me to swim in my underwear. Then the clouds lifted, without dispersing, and a strange, suffused, silvery light shimmered on the jade water. We passed close to several lonely islets; high, dark, cave-pitted cliffs were visible through a tropical tangle, rising from narrow fringes of golden sand.

The slightly larger and less precipitous islets were inhabited and from each of these came a tiny dug-out to add its quota to our cargo – one or two Nile perch, weighing fifty to sixty kilos and caught during the night in cast-nets. Presumably these fish are stunned before being dragged aboard; two of the canoes were crewed only by two 12- or 13-year-old boys who could not possibly (even allowing for African strength) have overcome struggling 100-pounders in a net. Other canoes delivered bundles of smaller perch – a mere ten or twelve kilos – tied together through the gills with grass or vines or a weed, the choice denoting ownership in a sort of botanical code. The individual giant catches were branded near the gills with one or two initials the moment they came aboard. I averted my eyes from that operation as the wretched fish, in their long-drawn-out death throes, too obviously suffered from these deep incisions with a sharp knife expertly wielded by the captain's youthful assistant. It was, however, hard to ignore all these creatures heaving and gasping for hour after hour in a bloody welter below my feet. I had had no idea that fish could live so long once out of their element.

Apart from these mid-lake rendezvous, we called at five largeish islands, half-running ashore up sandy beaches to take on many more circular bundles of dried fish. Loading took a long time as most bundles were ridiculously heavy, even for five strong young men standing waist-deep in the water and straining every muscle while two others in the boat pulled and heaved. Why, I wondered, were these loads not divided into two or even three?

The accounting system made me realise the importance of the captain's honesty. Throughout the voyage he sat in the stern, carefully noting down in an exercise-book the name of each fish-owner and the distinguishing mark of his catch. In Kasenyi, I tarried to watch him supervising the weighing of the catches on standing-scales near an ice-truck, the worth of each being given by a pocket-calculator and meticulously entered in the exercise-book – before wads of money were received from the truck-driver.

When we left the last island our clearance was scarcely six inches; passengers as well as cargo had been taken on at each stop, the gunwales were now crowded and the captain warned us all not to move lest the worst happen. As we approached the busy fishing-port-cum-market-centre of Kasenyi, soon after 2.30, a mob of ragged youths rushed into the water, yelling one another down, desperate for porterage jobs and looking as if they would not be above other ways of subsisting. The knapsack I had borrowed from Joy lay buried beneath the piscine cargo and as I bent forward to disinter it my cycling-cape, on which I had been sitting, disappeared: a grievous loss, at the beginning of the rainy season. (The spare shower-curtain subsequently provided by Joy helped during major rainstorms; but one couldn't cycle while wrapped in it.) To my embarrassment the *mzungus* were all carried ashore on the shoulders of stalwart young men: evidently a local custom, which made me feel vaguely like an early explorer.

Waiting for a matatu to Entebbe, I observed several prominent notices, in English, instructing the locals about the beautiful but deadly water hyacinth – now a major threat to Lake Victoria's fish-stocks, to the sewage-pipe system (such as it is) and to the well-being of steamers. People were warned never to cultivate it as a domestic plant, always to pull it up as they passed in their little boats, and not to throw it away but to bring it home and burn it. The cause of its recent spectacular proliferation seems to be unknown.

Cycling into Kampala early next morning, my journey – not only in Africa but on this earth – was nearly ended. Light traffic tempted me to freewheel recklessly down long steep hills and I must have reached thirty m.p.h. when a matatu coming from Kampala decided to return there and swung across the road without warning. My escape was as narrow as that young man's on our way to Masaka.

Geraldine, an Irish kindred spirit earlier discovered working in a Kampala mission hospital, had invited me to stay in her two-roomed bungalow if I didn't mind sharing a room with Egon, whose business in any case took him out from bedtime until dawn. He was a very young owl, his soft abundance of light brown plumage giving him a deceptively substantial appearance; when he perched on my hand, rolling his jewel-like amber eyes in a weirdly engaging way, I realised that he weighed only a few ounces. Geraldine was his mother-figure and each sunrise found him anxiously waiting on the clothes-line for readmission. Lear's saddle appealed to him as a perch; he represented my closest encounter with Africa's wildlife.

Kampala could grow on one. Visually it has little to recommend it, apart from views of the surrounding countryside, but the feeling is of a friendly provincial town rather than a bustling capital. In March 1992 the shops were not much better stocked than Rumania's in January 1990 and the traffic, being light by urban standards, had speeding-space enough to threaten life at every pedestrian crossing. Many of the street names bespeak a residual affection for the British: Queen Mary's Gardens, Burton Street, Philip Road, Wilson Road, William Street, Windsor Crescent. Neighbouring streets pay homage to African heroes: Said Barre Avenue, Nkrumah Road, Nasser Road, Lumumba Road. The rich district, Nakasero Hill, boasts substantial residences lining wide, amply shaded streets. On the hilltop swaggers a Sheraton Hotel, its sweeping lawns patrolled by security guards to keep the poor at bay. These askari looked at me uneasily when I encroached on the territory of the privileged, desperately searching for a bookshop; but most Ugandans give Whites the benefit of the doubt. There was no bookshop, only a few shelves of fat and unreadable paperback novels. Later, while seeking a battery for Lear's lamp, I came on a small pile of second-hand books in an electrician's duka and – almost swooning with relief – bought a stout volume (*The State and Agriculture in Africa*) for 50 pence. Not as relaxing as Nancy Mitford but a considerable improvement on Jeffrey Archer.

One of Kampala's most conspicuous landmarks is a recently

restored Hindu temple, high on a hillside. From a distance it looks quite convincing, inside it is tragi-comic. Painted baby blue and shell pink, with gilt flourishes here and there, it houses a few Hindu gods lurking in niches like refugees in an alien land; it felt totally unlinked to India, where most East African Hindus have never been. (Nor have they made much effort to integrate in Africa.) This vulgar parody of a temple seemed to mark the loss of an ancestral source of spiritual sustenance for which no substitute has been sought.

A group of rather foppish young Indians watched me replacing my shoes in the forecourt; they had the air of people who get by nicely without working too hard. Kampala's Hindu community, one told me, had been reduced to 1,500 but many thousands were expected back soon. 'These Africans need us, *they'll* never get industry and commerce going again!'

His friend added, 'And they've no connections with the money world outside, so they can't attract capital. Who'd trust an *African* with an investment? If we're not here, they'll be left in the ditch.'

'How racist can you get!' I thought to myself as I continued towards the commercial district. In two of the major banks I couldn't change sterling; both had run out of Ugandan shillings. In the third I had to queue for fifty minutes. Behind me stood a gorgeously robed Nigerian from Kano, clutching a thick wad of US dollar bills which he recounted at intervals. Had he not been Black his comments about the Ugandans might also have been described as 'racist'.

I spent one afternoon with Martha, a charming and elegant secondary-school teacher and a Charismatic Christian who ran a 'support group' for destitute AIDS patients. We went from hovel to hovel in an overcrowded shantytown where narrow, dusty, child-filled laneways twisted between suffocatingly hot tin-roofed shacks. Every face lit up when Martha appeared. As we sat beside the dying, holding their hands, Martha emphasised (and seemed herself to believe) that 'Jesus has a special love for all you people with AIDS'. Then she prayed and sang hymns at length and emotionally, the patients' eyes fixed humbly and gratefully on her ecstatic face. This was not my scene; in any environment, Charismatic Christianity switches me off. I caught myself going all ethnocentric and austerely deploring the mawkish humbug involved in claiming that Jesus has a special love for AIDS victims. Then I felt ashamed. Martha was *comforting* these most desolate of people, the majority rejected by their families. And in this case the end surely justified the means.

One 20-year-old mother of two was lying on a straw mat, her naked baby sitting beside her playing with an empty sardine tin. Straw mats were the only furnishing in her sister's two-roomed mud hovel, its walls so cracked and askew one wondered how much longer it could last. In many AIDS cases, one of the most distressing symptoms requires attentive nursing and ample washing-water; here no such relief was available. The 3-year-old was uninfected, the baby HIV+. Their mother was unmarried; her 24-year-old widowed sister was also a prostitute – or 'sex-worker', as the profession is now designated in the best academic and humanitarian circles. The girls had come to Kampala from a Luwero triangle village, in their early teens, to seek *respectable* jobs. Finding none, they settled for the only alternative. 'You can't blame them,' said Martha. 'Their families were starving, everything destroyed in the war – huts and crops burned, cattle shot, normal life finished, no marriages being arranged. There was nothing to go back to and now they can't contact their parents. Families soon lose touch if nobody can read or write and there's no money for bus fares.'

'So what will happen to these children?'

'We must try to give them to the grandparents, if we can find them, somehow. If not – well, we must try to make their aunt care for them. She has none of her own because of her venereal disease. She's almost certainly HIV+ but she won't have the test. If she goes sick – I don't know, there are too many AIDS orphans in Kampala, in my family we are looking after four, we can take no more . . .'

Martha was an active 'behaviour change' campaigner. Everyone agrees that behaviour change (by which is meant one partner, for life) is essential to halt the spread of AIDS. However, few can imagine African behaviour changing to any significant extent in the foreseeable future; so the pragmatic pro-condom campaigners want to preach their gospel to all and sundry, starting pre-puberty. This appalls Martha and her like who see the one-partner gospel being sabotaged by propaganda that implicitly accepts promiscuity as inevitable, however unwise. Even for married couples, Martha insisted, condoms offer no protection in a culture requiring numerous children.

'But,' I argued, 'surely a husband who uses condoms with his extra-marital partners will be less likely to infect his wife during procreation?'

Martha laughed at my naïvety. 'I speak as an African wife – most men bungle condoms, so they'll imagine they're safe when they're not.' In her view the fear of AIDS, to the extent that it exists, should be used to encourage behaviour change, not assuaged by the propagation of condoms.

This controversy pushes people towards fanaticism. In Kampala's bazaar I talked with a young woman pharmacist whose education had been sponsored by an Irish missionary priest and who condemned pro-condom campaigners as auxiliaries of the devil. Her conviction that it was her duty to impose her own views on others reminded me of Ireland's Pro-Life campaigners and the influence of Irish Catholicism was apparent even in her phraseology. Many of her Irish contemporaries would disagree with her, which perhaps explains frequent clerical references to the future of the Catholic Church being in Africa.

I dined that evening with Mike, an Irish doctor on the eve of retirement after thirty years in Uganda. Although widowed in 1990, he was not returning to Ireland; 'home' was his modest colonial bungalow on a hillside overlooking Lake Victoria – quite an isolated dwelling, surrounded by towering forest trees, fragrant in the dusk. Stout iron grilles fortified every door and window; Mike had lived here throughout the Terror but, like the Ugandans themselves, preferred not to talk about that period. He was tall, lean, slightly stooped – physically worn, yet radiating a sort of spiritual energy. As we talked – until midnight – I wished I could see his face more clearly. But that book-lined, comfortably shabby sitting-room was lit only by a feeble oil-lamp; Uganda's electricity supply had failed again.

We discussed the difficulty of explaining Africa's AIDS epidemic through the Irish media without shocking the puritanical and sounding racialist to everyone. 'I've tried to explain', said Mike, 'that many men regard even short-term celibacy as a physiological impossibility, like not peeing. But even in the '90s that concept doesn't go down a treat back home. It's true, though – when separated from their wives, having another woman seems inevitable. Not really a personal decision, not a matter for self-control or will-power. Others believe celibacy is actually *dangerous* – your willy will fall off or your balls wither away. You may smile, but I'm not joking! Nowadays you get worried youths writing to newspaper agony aunts asking if these traditional beliefs are true. And girls writing to ask if their vaginas will be blocked forever if they don't have regular intercourse from puberty on. I wish I were a billionaire! All sub-Saharan schools need a programme to get rid of these fears. It's no good yapping on about chastity and fidelity if kids are convinced celibacy means willies falling off and vaginas seizing up. But it's hard work to get all this across to Westerners without seeming to be accusing Africans of a brutal sort of sex life – plus gross superstition. It's only when you've lived here more than half a lifetime, speaking the languages, that you can *understand* without even secretly condemning. Those who sneer at "the randy Blacks" are missing the point. We've got a cultural problem, not a genetic one. Look at the West since the '60s – as soon as the Pill was invented and the cultural climate changed, randiness set in.'

Mike had little time for the behaviour change campaigners. 'Of course they make sense, if you focus only on the fact that life expectancy for a large percentage of the population has been lowered to the twenties and thirties. And maybe in the next generation their campaign will be realistic. Now it's an irrelevant ideal, confusing the immediate task. Most activists are devout Christians, usually female, who'd always have condemned extra-marital sex. They use the epidemic to proselytise, it seems to justify their compulsion to make everyone else live their way. They refuse to confront the crisis *as it is*. Healthy people can go on enjoying a free and easy sex life for years after they've been diagnosed HIV + – they're feeling fine, they don't *want* to see any reason for behaviour change. Many convince themselves doctors are being alarmist and *they'll* never fall sick. I'm weary of this futile controversy – and it's raging all over Africa. Most Africans can't afford condoms, or wouldn't under any circumstances use them, or have never heard of them. Only nutters would deny them to the minority who *can* be persuaded to use them – and you may quote me on that!'

I asked Mike then if the AIDS death-rate was highest in the slums.

'Quite the contrary – the educated élite, proportionately, are worst affected. And you'll find this in all the cities on your route. Rich men can afford a greater variety of partners and they travel more – often *without* wives – to other sources of infection, through- out Africa. That's why the rate of infection is usually higher in cities, where the élite are concentrated. In Kampala by now at least 35 per cent of the population is HIV +, maybe much more. The death-rate is disrupting everyday life, office and factory staff need so much time off to attend funerals. And medical workers are being presented with dilemmas Hippocrates never dreamed of – like what to do if you incidentally discover a teenager, being treated for some minor com- plaint, is HIV + . . . Which quite often happens, when a given group is being screened as part of some survey. Well, what would *you* do? Would you tell him or her, though they hadn't sought a test or even known they were being tested? Or would you let them enjoy the next four or six or even eight years of their youth? And remember, telling them carries quite a high suicide risk. Teenagers sometimes rush out and hang themselves or overdose on chloroquin. We don't have enough counselling teams to lessen that risk – counselling is labour-intensive.'

I was silent for more than a moment. Then I said, 'If you don't tell them they will almost certainly infect others. If you do tell them there's absolutely no guarantee they won't infect others but they will be shattered, for sure, and their youth ruined – and maybe their families shattered, too, if they find out. It's a nightmare decision to have to make, I couldn't possibly handle it – what do *you* do?'

'We can only follow our individual consciences. I'm inclined not to tell, unless I've good reason to believe responsible behaviour will be the main reaction. You could say that's paternalistic, even arrogant. Why should I decide who may or may not be responsible? And why should I deny anyone the opportunity to make their own moral choices? But in Africa, somewhere along the line, those nuances get blunted. What counts most with me is sheer survival, my patients' survival. And there's the possibility that the demora- lisation of knowing – the tension and acute anxiety – could hasten the development of AIDS. In all cultures this is a possibility, here it's almost a probability – Africans do still lie down and die, for no physical reason, if told they're bewitched. That's not an old mis- sionary wives' tale, it's a *fact*. And the slim disease and bewitchment are still closely associated in many minds. When Museveni's

89

government first publicised AIDS in '87 it wasn't really taken seriously as a medical threat. In the worst-affected areas they blamed Tanzanian witchcraft being used to punish cheating smugglers on our side of the border. Does it surprise you that this association remains strong? Don't we all feel there's something eerie about AIDS? And now the West's failure to find a cure is reinforcing the witchcraft theory.'

Next morning, while sharing breakfast with Egon, I admitted to myself that a disease – with all its social, economic, emotional and ethical complexities – had come, most improbably, to dominate my journey. I briefly considered backing away and concentrating on the landscape *en route* to Zimbabwe, dodging the AIDS issue whenever it arose. But that strategy would have required me to keep my head in the sand, where I don't like it to be.

As this was my last day in Kampala, and Geraldine's weekly day off, she put her quirky Volkswagen at my disposal. After two decades in daily combat with Uganda's war-pocked roads, it had lost all but its most vital organs and contrasted pleasingly with aid-worker vehicles. Its plethora of afflictions required frequent attention but luckily garage mechanics abound in and around the capital; without them, only the élite would be mobile.

We drove first to the Kabakas' Tombs on Kasubi Hill, now a crowded rural suburb – if that is not a contradiction in terms. Small fertile shambas alternated with patches of waste ground and lines of dukas selling gaudy plastic utensils, equally gaudy 'sodas', American cast-offs, scrap iron and those mass-produced trinkets that flood every 'undeveloped' country. On their verandas worked tailors, smiths, butchers and cobblers, while barefooted cyclists in tattered garments pedalled wobbling loads of charcoal towards the city.

On 9 February 1862 this same road was thronged with welcoming Baganda, eager for their first glimpse of a European, and Speke recorded:

They wore neat bark cloaks resembling the best yellow corduroy cloth, crimp and well set, as if stiffened with starch, and over that, as upper cloaks, a patchwork of small antelope skins, which I observed were sewn together as well as any English glovers could have pierced them; while their head-dresses, generally, were abrus turbans, set off with highly-polished boar-tusks, stick-charms, seeds, beads or shells . . . The whole brow and sides of the hill on which we stood were covered with gigantic grass huts, thatched as neatly as so many heads dressed by a London barber, and fenced all round with tall yellow reeds. Within the enclosure the lines of huts were joined together, or partitioned off into courts, with walls of the same grass. It is here that most of Mutesa's three or four hundred women are kept, the rest being quartered chiefly with his mother . . . The palace or entrance quite surprised me by its extraordinary dimensions and the neatness with which it is kept.

The reed and barkcloth palace, on the roadside, still surprises by its extraordinary dimensions and neatness. But now the royal compound within is bare and feels abandoned – even by the ghosts of the courtiers, the chiefs from all over Buganda, the page-boys in training for high government posts, the hundreds of wives. At the far side stands the gigantic tomb hut, containing the graves of Mutesa I, his unstable son Mwanga, Sir Daudi Chwa and his deplorable son Edward Mutesa II – the last of the Kabakas, deposed by Amin in 1966. (Three years later he died unlamented in London.) Day and night, female descendants of the Kabakas attend the royal bones; the number of Mutesa I's wives ensures that this task is not too onerous for any individual. When we entered the twilit hut – respectfully barefooted – the five women sitting silently on the mat-covered floor ignored us. This hut, too, has the non-atmosphere of a place neutered by history. It seemed to me both sad and phoney, the simple graves and pompous portraits illustrating the *muddle* bequeathed by colonialism. These women were continuing a now meaningless tradition, its meaninglessness emphasised by the British decorations on the chests of the last two Kabakas. Here two worlds had met but had not fruitfully merged.

Our next stop – Namugongo, where the Ugandan Martyrs were burned alive in 1886 – is loaded with significance for reasons explained by the Ugandan historian, Professor S.R. Karugire, Museveni's Deputy Minister for Foreign Affairs.

In Uganda, to a much greater extent than in her two neighbours, the missionaries were the most important arm of colonialism. In mainland Tanzania missionaries and their activities hardly became a national issue at all. In Kenya it took the Africans, especially in the Central Province, only a few years to realise that there was no difference between a White settler and the missionary. But in Uganda the most effective agency of transition from the traditional way of life to colonialism was the missionary and the issues of religion have dominated public life in Uganda to the present day.

In 1886 the mad Mwanga had for some time been brooding on the political threat inherent in missionary activity. He was finally driven over the edge when his Christian pages refused to co-operate in what the missionaries described as 'unmentionable abominations'. (Sodomy had quite recently been introduced to Black Africa by Arab-Swahili traders.) All the Christian 'readers' at court were removed forthwith, on 25 May, the lucky ones to be castrated, the rest chopped up and thrown to the vultures. Then, on 3 June, twenty-four young men (thirteen Catholics and eleven Protestants, aged between 17 and 25) were offered a choice: recantation or incineration. The missionaries had presented them with such a vivid picture of everlasting heavenly bliss that they chose martyrdom. It took a week to collect the necessary colossal pile of wood. The four youngest were clubbed to death, to lessen their suffering, before being thrown on that pile; the others were tightly bound and wrapped in reed mats. Onlookers were baffled to hear them singing on the pyre in praise of their newfound God, the White man's God! Their executioner, Mukajanga, was so moved by the young men's courage that he wept after lighting the fire. Uganda also has its incinerated Muslim martyrs, created by Mwanga's father, Mutesa I, whose converted Muslim pages were given not one but numerous opportunities to recant.

To Mwanga's fury, the Namugongo Martyrs proved stronger in death than in life. Their fate drew converts to both Churches in unprecedented numbers and prompted the missionaries to change their tactics and intervene much more directly in domestic politics.

In 1969, Pope Paul VI consecrated Namugongo's pretentious and ungainly Martyrs' Memorial church. Unfortunately Africa's spate of post-Independence church-building took place during the decade when many architects were vying to design the ugliest edifice in the world. Namugongo's circular specimen is redeemed only by a series of magnificent wood carvings representing the martyrs. Stupidly, I forgot to note down the local artist's name.

Leaving the church, we met a septuagenarian Ugandan nun who had spent ten years in an American convent without shedding any of her homegrown bigotry. The history lesson she gave me, about the arrival of Christianity in Buganda, recalled Paisleyite history lessons about the role of the Vatican in world affairs. Having made all allowances for the *Zeitgeist*, it is hard to forgive Christianity's contribution to Ugandan faction-fighting. The pioneering British and French missionaries (manipulated by their respective governments when that suited the politicians, ignored by them when it didn't) poured the petrol of White sectarianism on to an area already smouldering with tribal animosities. Then the politicians found it expedient to strike a match and a century later the embers are still warm.

Throughout the Protectorate period the administration favoured Protestants and as Independence approached Milton Obote formed a Protestant and Muslim coalition, the Ugandan Peoples' Congress, in which the Muslims were junior partners. Then the Catholics, led by Benedicto Kiwanuka, a lawyer trained in London, formed the Democratic Party. Kiwanuka reminded everyone that 'For a period of over seventy years, religion became the springboard to power, privilege and influence in Uganda. All hereditary rulers, all Secretaries-General, all District Heads, all District Chief Ministers were Protestant.' This was no exaggeration and it explains why so many Ugandans are as keen as the Northern Irish to find out which foot you dig with – a significant difference being that the Ugandans ask straight out, 'Are you Catholic or Protestant?' And when you say you don't dig with either foot they are very worried; they would prefer you to dig with the wrong foot than to be Godless.

Kampala's sights being limited, we had time to drive around the once-beautiful Luwero triangle, north-west of the city, where in the mid-1980s Milton Obote's soldiers reduced a population of 6,000 families to 500. Having looted everything movable, including roofs and window-frames, they burned the rest. Nature quickly reclaimed the lush, abandoned land and, though much rebuilding has been done, there is sickening evidence on every side of these Nilotic soldiers' uncontrollable lust for destruction.

Geraldine and I wondered why Uganda was so ludicrously known as a 'Protectorate'. During the Scramble, it will be remembered, the Nile-obsessed Lord Salisbury only reluctantly took over – for imaginary strategic reasons – the disparate areas that were to become Uganda. Therefore benefits had to accrue as soon as possible and within a few years it had been proved that this territory could produce an abundance of cotton, as well as plantation rubber, cocoa and coffee. The Protectorate was deemed 'self-sufficient' in 1915, when the Treasury's grants-in-aid were stopped. By the early 1920s, Uganda had been divided into two zones, crop-producing and labour-producing – a division that still oozes poison. To the fertile and comparatively accessible regions, Buganda and the Eastern province, came migrant workers from the rest of the country; men disinclined to leave home were induced to do so by the imposition of hut-taxes which could be paid only with cash earned on the plantations. The productive zone was developed, while the non-productive zone regressed because of the forced migration of most healthy males. In 1925, when a humane Director of Agriculture began to encourage cotton-growing in the remote West Nile district, he was reprimanded by the Chief Secretary in Entebbe:

> The policy of the government is at present to refrain from actively stimulating the production of cotton or other economic crops in outlying districts on which it is dependent for a supply of labour for the carrying out of essential services in the central producing districts.

By 1929, cotton made up 80 per cent of all Uganda's exports but no Ugandan was allowed to gin the cotton he had grown, just as in Kenya, for many years, no Kenyan was allowed to grow coffee as a cash crop.

In 1925, the Ormsby-Gore Commission had noted prophetically in its report on East Africa:

> When among such people as the Baganda and Basoga, labourers were introduced who came from tribes considered inferior and who worked under conditions which the Baganda and the Basoga could not themselves accept, the latter tended

94

to feel that unskilled manual labour was a form of employment suitable only for inferior tribes. There was even a danger that the question might in time become one of 'caste'.

Post-Independence, a responsible Ugandan government would at once have tried to correct this economic imbalance. Instead, the gulf was allowed – even encouraged – to widen. Hence the Nilotic troops' frenzied destruction of people and property throughout 'the productive zone' and especially in the rich Luwero triangle.

Back in Kampala, we supped at a pavement table outside the Telex Bar in the affluent residential suburb of Kabalagala. Here, the week before, three customers had been shot dead for no reason by a drunken soldier – Corporal Anthony Semugooma, aged 21, who at the time of the crime was supposed to be guarding the home of a Libyan diplomat. Commenting on this event, the *New Vision* leader-writer complained:

A profound fear is that some of our soldiers and policemen on duty are permanently under the influence of alcohol and possibly narcotic drugs. Both NRA and police commanders should therefore take keen interest in those being armed to keep the peace in the city to ensure that they are sober and disciplined while on duty. As long as drunken soldiers and policemen are allowed to keep patrolling our streets, acts of lawlessness are bound to increase, when politically motivated violence has ended. The measure of security and stability in any city or country is the level of activity and freedom of movement at night.

5

Other Kingdoms

Kampala to Fort Portal

As I left Kampala private enterprise was on the move. The traffic (all two-wheeled) flowed against me: hundreds of cyclists bearing bundles of sugar-cane, sacks of charcoal and maize, stalks of matoke, gleaming churns of milk, jerry-cans of village beer corked with cane, wooden planks wavering perilously on either side of carriers. Along the red earth verges streamed laden women wearing long full gowns that seemed to reflect the transient glory of sunrise – indigo, coral pink, violet, dove grey, saffron. Tall plantains crowded the wayside shambas, their dark green fronds drooping raggedly against the pale blue sky. Then the market-goers dwindled as the tarred road climbed gradually into the mountains of Mubende district.

Beyond the market-centre of Busanju, thirty miles from Kampala, a tolerable dirt track undulated for forty-five miles along one side of a narrow, grassy valley. The high, steep, partially wooded hills were strewn with vast rounded boulders and on my left, in a deep cultivated ravine, a river raced noisily amidst dense trees and crimson-blossomed shrubs. High on the slopes numerous small shambas surrounded thatched huts but there were no market-centres. This was an enchanting region, cooled by a steady breeze, traffic-free and tranquil, its war-scars healed. The day's meagre rain-ration, a brief mid-afternoon downpour, served to lay the dust but can't have done much for growth. Two passing locals were hugely amused to see Lear and me huddled by the wayside under Joy's sky-blue shower-curtain: yet another example of *mzungu* eccentricity.

Apart from an imposing new hospital, the long, one-storeyed town of Kiboga is shabby and lethargic – an extremely unlikely setting for a meeting with Sarah and James. I arrived at sunset and the dark guest-house bar seemed empty until James stood up behind the counter; he had been lighting a lamp. Like Albert in Sotik, he might have strayed from some university campus. Why was he running a mud-brick doss-house in the back of beyond? I didn't ask. Many Ugandan lives have been painfully deformed by outside events.

Sarah arrived then from Kampala; I had passed her bus when it was receiving first-aid.

'We saw you pedalling!' she exclaimed. 'Everyone else thought you must be a man but I said no, that's a liberated European woman!' Sarah did work on a university campus, lecturing thrice a week in Kampala where the middle three of seven children were at school. The first-born, a daughter, was on a teacher-training course in London. 'She's a clever girl, 'said Sarah, 'and a *good* girl. She's coming back to work in the bush. She's not getting a London training to become rich.'

While I devoured matoke and beef stew the juniors – two sons – crept in to sit by their elderly father, looking from me to Lear with bewildered fascination. 'You eat nicely with your fingers,' complimented James. My not expecting cutlery always pleased people. Speke presented King Mutesa of Buganda with (among other things) 'one set of table knives, spoons and forks' but most Africans still disdain implements. Several told me, 'I don't feel I've eaten if I haven't handled the food.' And one man remarked, 'Spoons and forks for me are like condoms – I feel I've been cheated!'

Sarah described herself as 'a feminist sociologist' and was dedicated to raising her female neighbours' self-esteem. 'This is slow, hard work and you have to be stubborn not to give up when you seem to be getting nowhere. You have to remind yourself that some of their grandmothers can remember tribal raiding when the prizes were cattle, women and grain, in that order. It will take time to make them value their daughters as much as their sons, to make them see it's their *right* to have a fifty-fifty say in family decisions. Most important is to encourage literacy, among the younger women. With access to information they can make up their own minds and have more confidence to argue with their husbands – not passively accepting that what the man says is true.'

James agreed. 'When only men can read, this gives them too

much extra power. Almost magic power, the way women see it. Here in the bush reading and writing is still White man's magic.'

To be with a couple who were so clearly intellectual companions was a rare enough experience in Africa and we talked until midnight. Sarah had specialized in 'traditional education' and volunteered so much information that I broke a rule and took notes as we talked. In rural communities, she explained, children see little of their parents while growing up. Having been abruptly weaned (often traumatically abruptly, by our standards) at the age of about 2, their time is spent among their own age-group, supervised by that directly above. They may move to live for a few years with grandparents or an uncle; sometimes, at the age of 7 or 8, boys build their own mini-huts in a compound and live independently, fetching their own firewood, finding and cooking their own food. Girls of course must always remain under the watchful eyes of female relatives, learning by observation and imitation how to be good wives and being given a share of the daily chores. Commonly a 5-year-old is left in charge of a 2-year-old all day, taking full responsibility for its safety and appreciating the trust. Sarah chuckled and added, 'Western mothers who did that would have their children put into care!'

In communities uninfluenced by the West, an African child's development is dominated by his or her age-group. Education means conditioning the young to behave in ways conducive to the well-being of their *group*. Signs of burgeoning individuality are promptly dealt with as a serious flaw; strong one-to-one emotional ties with contemporaries (apart from siblings) are rare; the group is the focus of affection and loyalty. Close ties may unite some grandparents and grandchildren, mothers and adolescent daughters, uncles and adolescent nephews; but there is no concentrated emotional dependence on parents. Within an extended family, children have many more important adults in their lives than the average Western child and from an early age the obligation to provide mutual help of every sort is understood to be paramount.

Reading press-cuttings sent from London, Sarah and James had noticed much journalistic puzzlement about the Ugandans' stoical reactions to bereavement. James said, 'Some think we're very brave, some think we're unnaturally fatalistic, others think we're callous – and hint maybe that's to do with being "primitive"!

Which is correct, if you like to call our traditional society more primitive than yours. The various tribal initiation ceremonies were partly endurance tests and very severe. From earliest childhood everyone was trained in all forms of self-control, not just to do with physical courage. Even now good manners mean not showing emotion, whatever stress you're under.'

I admitted then that I, too, had been puzzled on a few occasions, especially when accompanying Geraldine on her midday ward-round in the paediatric unit of a Kampala hospital. In those wards a mother – sometimes both parents – stood beside most cots: statuesque, expressionless, not urgently seeking information from the doctor about their offspring's condition or prognosis. For me that two-hour ordeal was gruelling and confusing, as I transferred to the mothers what my own feelings would have been – while simultaneously their lack of communication with dreadfully suffering children baffled me. Even when one little boy was being given a massive injection, and became hysterical with terror as the needle approached, his mother didn't react – just stood aside and watched, impassively, her eyes glazed, instead of holding him in her arms. Presumably a parental presence, however unresponsive, was reassuring for all these patients. But why (I had wondered, peering across this culture chasm), why were there no caresses and murmured endearments, none of the outward signs of loving sympathy that we would lavish on a sick child? These parents were of course going through hell, but by a route I didn't recognise.

'There's no mystery,' smiled Sarah. 'It's as James said, you were seeing our sort of self-control working. Traditionally, even when giving birth, a woman was encouraged to pretend she felt nothing. That was supposed to toughen her child, make it brave – extra-important if it turned out to be a son. It's not polite to show affection or distress – except when someone dies. Then women must go through a sort of ritual mourning collapse, screaming and wailing and rolling on the ground – even if they're not really distressed but delighted to be rid of some horrible husband!'

Reflectively James said, 'I believe there couldn't have been an AIDS epidemic in times past. People weren't repressed, in the puritanical European way, but such emphasis on self-control kept the brakes on promiscuity. The missionaries had no idea what damage they were doing when they demolished traditional education.'

99

'But they meant well,' Sarah added hastily, perhaps imagining me to be a Christian. 'They hated the "obscene heathen rites" of initiation ceremonies. They didn't think that was any way to prepare young people for adult life, they sincerely believed they could do it better – otherwise they wouldn't have been here! If anyone told them initiations were *religious* experiences, needed to make young men stable members of their community, they didn't listen – that seemed like blasphemy. Yet it was true. And they haven't been able to replace what they destroyed. Now most Black Africans grow up without either a traditional education – only shreds survive – or a worthwhile Western education.'

James opened my nightcap beer and said, 'In a way *all* Africans have been messed up. I'm the third well-educated, Westernised generation and no one ever tried to squash my individuality but I still have a foot in both camps. I could be scared by things that would make you laugh if I confessed . . . Any African who tells you he has both feet in the Western camp is lying.'

Not far beyond Kiboga came a long descent into the old kingdom of Bunyoro which resisted the European take-over, as Buganda did not, and was penalised for its unwelcoming attitude by Britain's annexing this area at the turn of the century. Ahead of me, as I jolted down a deteriorating track, stretched an immense, grey-brown, almost waterless expanse; from the unpeopled bush rose solitary, bare, conical hills long since deforested. Bunyoro was the scene of much fighting throughout the nineteenth century, before ever the Whites arrived. When Hoima was King Kabarega's capital this arch-enemy of King Mutesa gained a reputation as one of the most brilliant guerrilla fighters of his day, on any continent.

For two hours Hoima is visible across this plain, sprawling high on its hills; the Bunyoro capital looks at its best from a distance – glints of tin between mighty blue gums, their girths oak-like. By mid-afternoon I was very slowly pushing Lear up a steep incline under low dark clouds. From the oppressive stillness everyone gloomily deduced 'No rain!' Present-day Hoima is a European creation, scattered over two shapely mountains; when well-maintained it must have been attractive. Terror-time military traffic ravaged the colonial tarmac and the pot-holes between the remaining fragments are so numerous, wide and deep that I continued to wheel Lear

100

across a level ridge-top through the old cantonment area. Here, amidst grassy spaciousness, government offices and a scattering of bwanas' bungalows are decaying quietly in colourful, goatful gardens. Downhill, the unlovely commercial centre occupies a broad ledge overlooking a dramatic ravine. Halfway up the opposite mountain substantial buildings, including a handsome church, peep through tall protecting trees. That looked like the best bit of Hoima but by then the heat had atrophied my exploratory instinct.

I booked into the first available guest-house, enormous and ugly, its two long rows of high-ceilinged rooms haunted, after sunset, by a forlorn little group of sex-workers. My room was much bigger than usual with two beds and a table and chair. Most of the register's entries were in the same hand. 'Our truck-drivers are not educated, I must write for them,' explained Frank, the owner. Sitting in the huge foyer, open on two sides to the breeze (had there been any), I begged Frank to find me a beer. It came, warm and flat, ten minutes later. 'We have no refrigerators,' said Frank. 'We are not an important town.' The foyer had unpainted concrete walls and a dozen uncushioned easy chairs – peculiarly uncomfortable, the rough-hewn wooden bars biting into one's buttocks.

Frank was a melancholy character, thrice married but childless. 'It's God's decision, the good Lord made all my wives barren. I am keeping the last one, I can't afford any more. The others I sent back to their villages.'

It seemed unlikely that Frank had married *three* barren women; but in Africa it's always the wife's fault. Although childlessness is not thought of as an African problem, the proportion of childless couples, made infertile by sexually transmitted diseases (STDs), is far higher than in the West. New strains of bacteria occur regularly and are resistant to all but the latest and most expensive antibiotics: the sort that never get to the Third World. Some doctors see the indiscriminate use of self-prescribed standard antibiotics – on sale in the remotest bush, having been stolen from hospitals or clinics – as one reason for Africa's out-of-control STDs. Another reason is the lack of any treatment for the poorest – all of which helps to explain the rapid spread of AIDS, STDs having left so many extra-vulnerable to the virus.

My food quest took me through four long, straight, wide streets lined with newish one-or two-storeyed shops, some abandoned when

half-built, the rest closed becuase it was Sunday. The detritus of construction work, sporting a stubble of drought-resistant weeds, lay
piled between riven pavements and shop entrances. The electricity
poles seemed to be lurching home from a drunken orgy; their
tangled wires drooped low; no one could remember when electricity
had last been available. By then the clouds had settled, immobile,
above Hoima, forming a dark lid beneath which the heat felt like
a sticky substance, impeding progress. The few visible locals were
mostly young, male, not entirely sober and potentially hostile. But
it is unfair to judge a town by its Sabbath persona; Hoima may be
much more agreeable on weekdays. I didn't, however, feel any
irresistible urge to test that hypothesis.

In a small airless restaurant, smelling of singed feathers and stale
urine, I was the only customer. My mountain of matoke was
enlivened by the leg of a geriatric hen who had died of malnutrition.
Matoke looks and feels rather like mashed parsnip but is less strongly
flavoured: the critical say flavourless. For the *mzungu* it is suitable
only as an evening meal; it immobilises one, physically and mentally, for the several hours it takes to digest. According to some
historians the Baganda, though powerful, rich and well-organised,
failed to realise their pre-colonial expansionist ambitions because
they couldn't function beyond matoke-growing regions. I know not
how nutritionists rate this food, but most of the people whose staple
diet it is have fine physiques.

Opposite me sat the restaurant owner, talking animatedly. A
handsome and pleasingly assertive woman (it always pleases when
African women assert themselves), she urged me to take 10-year-old
Luke, her first-born, to Ireland and there educate him. She spoke
in earnest; *mzungus* are scarce in Hoima and she meant to make the
most of her opportunity. In times past missionaries sometimes
sponsored promising students and I was the next best thing. She had
seen to it that Luke spoke adequate English. 'My family all had good
mission educations so we know English is important. Now the missions can't give good educations, they use *African* teachers, I think
because young people in the West have lost religion. In Ireland my
son would be a good student, clever and obedient.'

These constant demands on the *mzungu* become wearing, even
irritating, at the end of a long hot day. They betray both a worrying
dependency on the revered yet resented West and a total incom-

prehension of Western realities. (Our incomprehension of African realities is no less extreme but doesn't matter – to us.) Unawareness of how the White half lives is illustrated daily by the letter-writing obsession: 'Give me your address, here is my address, we will write letters when you go home.' That seems to be a pathetically important fantasy and feebly one goes along with it instead of saying, 'I write books, I don't have time to write to my closest friends never mind to acquaintances all over the world.' Demands for sponsorship (on behalf of sons or brothers, never daughters or sisters) are easier to deal with bluntly: 'I'm an ordinary citizen, not rich, not representing an organisation, not able to sponsor anyone.' Such bluntness can draw reproving stares or sullen mutterings – because of course I'm rich, otherwise I couldn't be travelling through Africa, even by bicycle. And see how different and expensive-looking that bicycle is! An African touring Europe for months would have to be either personally rich or sufficiently well-connected to help others if he or she wished to help . . .

As compensation for not educating Luke, who longed to see a mountain-bike, I invited him to my room and we were accompanied by an assortment of his siblings. Then I spent an hour in the foyer with the unemployed sex-workers. The only English-speaker was proud to interpret; her father, killed during the Terror, had been a local doctor. All five girls assured me they had been driven to prostitution by sheer poverty and I believed them. None saw AIDS as a *problem*; it was just another disease. They wouldn't even consider asking men to use condoms; there was too much competition in Hoima, you couldn't afford to deter clients. I dutifully 'gave information' and preached the condom gospel. An hour was enough. Lying dripping on my bed in an oven-hot room I was glad to escape into *The State and Agriculture in Africa* where I learned that in Tanzania:

In an attempt to eliminate the middleman so that farmers can realise more from their farm produce, the government in 1962 established the National Agricultural Products Board (NAPB). The Board was given the responsibility of controlling and regulating the price of maize and later maize flour, paddy and rice. In 1973 the activities of the NAPB were taken over by the National Milling Corporation (NMC). As from July 1984,

NMC has been buyer of last resort and deals more with the enlargement of the Strategic Grain Reserve (SGR).

As escapist literature, this fell far short of my Nancy Mitford Omnibus.

Soon a gale sprang up and the tin roof quivered and rattled; but still it didn't rain. The noise was remarkable; I expected a section of the ceiling to sail away at any moment. Happily *The State and Agriculture in Africa* acted like double dose of sleeping pills.

The track from Hoima to Kyenjojo (only theoretically a road) crosses a magnificent remoteness of high jungly mountains overlooking a smooth carpet of forest, far below, reaching greenly to the western horizon. This was Uganda as I had imagined it: a hidden Paradise of luxuriant unfamiliar vegetation exhaling tropical fragrances – pungent, or acrid, or delicate – the silence broken only by bird-calls, or the whisper of little streams in damp shadowy valleys, or the swishing of foliage as monkeys (including many colobus) fled into their own impenetrable world. Flat summits allowed views over vast spaces, the low distant hills a subdued yet glowing blue, the nearer slopes occasionally mottled with patches of cultivation beside grey huts set in circles of bare red earth. But this region is sparsely populated, because of the Terror as well as the terrain. Its hamlets still bore the marks of arson and shelling and several isolated shambas had been abandoned, the dwellings burned, the rich soil lying fallow.

Those ninety miles took two days; on Day One I had to walk twenty miles, on Day Two twenty-five. The manufacturers of mountain-bikes would have us believe that these can be pedalled across any sort of surface. Not so. Even an aristocratic Dawes Ascent is quite often defeated by African roads. Normally I enjoy walking as much as cycling but 'walking' hardly describes the pushing of a laden Lear up near-vertical hills through slithery mud or skiddy deep gravel, or dragging him over rocky outcrops and four-foot-deep erosion channels. (Luckily the local mud was not adhesive, as in Kenya.) These gradients were incomparable; on mountains that in more effete countries would be furnished with several hairpin bends the track went straight up and down. Freewheeling on such slopes and surfaces was impossible and on arrival in Kyenjojo the brake-muscles in my thighs were throbbing. Traffic, however, was not a problem. On Day One I met two vehicles, on Day Two three. All were overladen truck-buses travelling at about twelve miles an hour. Astonished excitement caused the passengers around the edges almost to fall off when they saw me.

At noon on Day One I stopped for a Pepsi where three kennel-size dukas occupied a ledge above the track. On a bench outside sat three plump teenage girls attending to each other's coiffeurs – nit-picking, that is. Understandably the Pepsi cost 450 shillings instead of 300 shillings as in Kampala. Six men came running from their compounds to meet the *mzungu* – and, if possible, batten off her. Did my government pay for my journey? No? A pity! If it did I could afford to buy Pepsis all round. The aid-workers who passed now and then always bought Pepsis for everyone and gave money, and sweets from Europe, to the children. Did I have any sweets from Europe in my luggage? No? A pity!

The most fluent English-speaker asked my religion, then was puzzled. 'If you are not a Christian, how can you have *two* names? I don't understand!' Discarding that enigma, he continued, 'I have fifteen children from one wife' – and then looked at me, almost defiantly, as though challenging some White plot to make the Black race dwindle away. 'Is it true in Europe it's good to have no children? For us this is the *greatest* misfortune! And it happens more often, we think because of the slim disease. Here it is very bad, I have lost many friends in three years. Now we say how they died, before we said it was something else. Does your government have a cure?'

A worn-looking woman appeared then, from behind the dukas, and muttered something in his ear. Turning back to me he said, 'This person needs money for her son's school fees – you can give?' Pretending not to hear, I stood up, shook hands with everyone and went on my way feeling callous and mean. That woman's eyes were pools of sorrow.

Approaching Mabale village, towards sunset, the jungle was replaced by prosperous-looking shambas covering every slope. Here the track, though precipitous as ever, permitted cautious cycling. As Monday is Mabale's market-day, a stream of colourful figures poured towards me down the opposite hill. The pedestrians carried little – many attend their weekly market just for the craic – but the scores of cyclists, going at full speed, were improbably laden. Young wives rode side-saddle on carriers, clutching infants to their bosoms or, in a few cases, wearing infants on their backs and clutching toddlers on their laps. Possibly a sexagenarian cyclist, who has already broken an interesting variety of bones, tends to be over-cautious. Yet most observers would surely have deemed those young men under-cautious. However, I found this daredevilry so exciting that I paused at the base of one hill to watch the performers hurtling down that near-precipice with dependants on carriers and unwieldy loads balanced on cross-bars. To us degenerate Westerners the Africans' physical self-confidence is both enviable and thrilling. Studying these cyclists with a cyclist's eye, I could appreciate their reckless skill as they sped between large stones and deep holes that might have killed a family if not avoided. How could they not think of the consequences should they make the slightest error of judgement? Interesting, too, were the young wives' expressions; clearly they relished every moment of these Wall of Death experiences.

Mabale is draped over a ridge-top and as I pushed Lear up the last lap I noticed that many of the pedestrians, including some women, were reeking of home-distilled banana spirits; had a match been lit in their vicinity they might well have exploded. Several men stopped to demand drunkenly, 'Give money!' I wouldn't care to have met those particular characters on a deserted stretch of road.

Uganda's rains, I was learning, are very localised. Although it had been blessedly overcast and coolish all day I had met only one shower, whereas Mabale had received a three-hour downpour and the 'main street' was a river as I sloshed upwards. My lodging enquiries stimulated unhelpfulness; the adults stared, then turned away, their expressions indicating that they would prefer not to get involved. But dozens of small boys pursued me yelling 'Give money! Give money!' At last an elderly woman pointed to a duka, said 'Sleep!' and hastened away. I would never have guessed; there was no sign.

My host and hostess were friendly enough, though joyless and incurious. The young wife led me to a back entrance suitable for Lear and across a small smelly yard through ankle-deep muddy brown water. Six tiny windowless cells led off this yard; mine looked like the original home of the bed-bug – filthy smeared walls, a grass roof-ceiling, an ancient wooden bed, grubby bedding, no light. But one can't judge by appearance and I slept undisturbed.

I spent the last half-hour of daylight surveying the remnants of the market. Women still sat damply at their little stalls – there were scores, all under low grass 'umbrellas' – hoping for more trade before darkness; heavy rain is bad for business. As my doss-house provided no meals I hungrily bought a dozen buns which looked good but were menacingly sour and mysteriously tough – made of God knows what, God knows when. As I carried them away in a plantain-leaf parcel young men followed me, pointing at the parcel and jeering. I then wandered up and down the village street, peering into dukas in search of more food (there wasn't any) and hoping to meet an English-speaker; but none came my way. Generally the *mzungu* was regarded with – with *what*? I wasn't sure: not hostility, exactly, but a mixture of derision and suspicion. Most of the adult males were at some stage of intoxication, from mild to footless – perhaps a market-day phenomenon. No doubt when friends come from the bush everyone waxes convivial. The adolescents, male and female, sniggered as I passed and occasionally shouted, 'Where from?' or 'Where to?'. But when I stopped to answer they ran away, laughing as they skidded through the mud.

I was beginning to identify as 'demoralised' the feel of rural Uganda. (Jinja, Kampala and Entebbe are different: the yeast of hope is discernible.) Since crossing the border I had been aware of disquieting vibes and from Kampala onwards these became increasingly apparent. It is hard to articulate such traveller's reactions. An atmosphere of gaiety or depression, triumph or fear, is easily enough described. Demoralisation is different: something under the surface, without tangible manifestations yet palpable when one is there, on the spot.

Every weekday, throughout Uganda, between 7 and 8 a.m., I passed hundreds of schoolchildren – yes, hundreds, however apparently remote the area – thronging brightly towards their primary schools. (Many were in their mid- or late teens; the Terror disrupted Uganda's educational system – such as it is.) Each group wore identical immaculately laundered uniforms: pink, green, maroon, yellow, scarlet, orange. They made a memorable picture, seen on glowing red roads – or coming through plantations of coffee, matoke, maize – or descending broad sloping pastures from distant shambas – or glimpsed kaleidoscopically amidst dense drab bush like flitting tropical birds. But this impractical adherence to a colonial tradition bothered me. These uniforms are expensive: for girls a skirt or gym-tunic and blouse, for boys shorts and shirts. Repeatedly parents complained that even if they could somehow scrape together the fees, there would then be nothing over to buy uniforms. Thus the poorest are tethered to poverty, however intelligent their offspring. Yet most teachers support this tradition; they spoke to me as though well-turned-out pupils exalted their own status and compensated for the lack of books and equipment. Many of these children, having contrived to meet archaic 'grammar-school' sartorial requirements, spend the day in deskless schools where the cracked blackboard is only useful while the term's meagre chalk-ration lasts and teachers frequently go AWOL to supplement their equally meagre pay.

Slowly coasting down from Mabale (hereabouts the surface was cycleable, with care) I saw the comparatively fortunate making their way to school while the ragged rest were already working in the shambas – boys and girls, aged no more than 6 or 7, expertly wielding child-sized hoes. Then I wondered if this inequality mattered; in rural Africa, education's main benefit may be the postponement of hard labour.

The weather was being kind. Again, a procession of high, broken, slow-moving clouds protected me all day; yet the rain held off until I was within a mile of Kyenjojo. Here the landscape had changed to a blue-green panorama of low, rounded, wooded hills and shallow valleys dominated by plantains – in whose leaves everything is wrapped, from school lunches to prayer-books. Then suddenly a wild wind arose and away to the west I could see the advancing deluge, a hastening greyness of blinding horizontal rain, loud on the maize leaves before it reached me. I arrived in Kyenjojo, on the main Kampala–Fort Portal road, soaked through and chilled; that unforgettable track had taken me to 5,500 feet.

Kyenjojo is merely a row of colonnaded dukas, with a dilapidated health-centre across the road, a small minaretless mosque and an abandoned tea-packaging factory. Beneath the colonnade dozens were sheltering as water cascaded off the tin roofs and surged over the street from flooded gutters. Everyone was damp and looked relieved. In this region real hunger had followed the failure of the

108

previous rains: not a famine but literally a tightening of belts. Another failure would have been catastrophic. Although coming from a blessed land where rain is taken for granted, I shared in the general jubilation.

Ali's duka had beer-crates piled outside. Inside, I sat on the sharp edge of a box full of plastic plates and shivered as I drank. Ali – tall, handsome, welcoming – wore a thick sweater and viewed my thin sodden shirt sympathetically. 'You have no hot clothes? You will get a sickness – here is very cold in the rains.'

'I like it,' I reassured him. 'It's better to be chilled than fried!'

Kyenjojo's population seemed to be half Muslim, judging by the visible inhabitants – old men with narrow faces, wispy beards and embroidered skullcaps, young women carefully scarved, children protected by Islamic amulets, old women with hennaed palms wearing long black gowns. Ali said, 'In this town we have no problems, we don't listen to outsiders making trouble. We like to live in peace. Muslim and Christian – why should we fight? One is born one way, one is born another way, it's not important . . .'

An attentive crowd had gathered around the door to listen to our exchanges. Their view of my journey was typical: 'No African could do this!' How often I heard that comment – with increasing irritation. When I argued the point most people conceded that maybe Africans could do it, physically, given such a fine bicycle, but they would be afraid to travel alone, in unknown countries, cut off from all relatives and friends.

'You have an accident, what happens?' challenged Ali, as though playing a trump card. 'Or you get a fever alone in the bush, who helps?'

Someone by the door added, 'You die, who buries you?'

'If I'm dead,' I retorted, 'that's not my problem.' To Ali I replied, 'When we have less drastic misfortunes, we cope as best we can. But we don't worry about them before they happen.'

'Why don't you fear wild animals?' asked someone else by the door. 'You have a gun?' He poked Lear's panniers, then was reprimanded by Ali for doing so. That was another widespread obsession; there being no wild animals left, in most areas, has not yet exorcised inherited fears. I said that I did not have a gun, my plan being to avoid wild animals' territory. Then I switched the conversation to bicycles.

109

'Only rich people own good bicycles,' said Ali. All East Africa's bicycles come from India or China and in Uganda cost the equivalent of £45 each: a prohibitive sum when the average wage is £1.50 a month. About one-third of the bicycle population is crippled, without pedals or brakes or saddles, or with ingeniously homemade handlebars welded to antique frames. Yet one sees many ragged and barefooted men transporting loads on sound bicycles. Those poor cyclists, Ali explained, were not bicycle owners but the servants of rich men. At the end of the day's work they would have to walk home.

When the rain had dwindled to a drizzle I found lodgings behind the dukas, up the rushing torrent of a laneway. In my 50p cell a defective oil candle filled my nostrils with blackness in the brief time it took to change. The elderly proprietress was small, bony, ill-tempered and suspicious; she made a fuss about being paid at once, though I had no small change and was leaving Lear as hostage. In a minuscule hoteli I ate hugely: 95 per cent matoke, 5 per cent rubbery beef. That night I dreamed I was eating ripe Stilton and my own homemade bread – which may not have been a coincidence.

Beyond Kyenjojo a wide straight dirt road undulated gently between low grassy embankments or clumps of fubsy Christmas-tree con-ifers. The first light revealed the shape but not the colour of a wide humpy landscape, bare and uninhabited, its scattering of isolated trees so often plundered for firewood that they had lost their figures. The eastern sky was clear and faintly blue below a thin length of cloud – raw silk fringed with silver. Then the road rose to a hilltop and what I saw was unreal, magical: a long snowy ridge, the highest of a series of ridges filling the south-western horizon.

To me these were the Mountains of the Moon, rather than the Ruwenzori; in childhood that lilting phrase seemed to contain all the inaccessibility and wonder of Africa. And now there those gleaming mountains were, aloof beyond many miles of green hilly lushness, withdrawn from and contradicting all that lay about them. I stopped and sat and looked.

Then on and steeply up towards Fort Portal, through miles of tea-gardens. Pre-Terror, a chatty fellow-cyclist boasted, this was one of 'the biggest tea estates in the world' – perhaps an overstatement but it didn't look like one. However, the estate had to be deserted during the Terror and has been only partially reclaimed. On my right all was restored to productive trimness; on my left overgrown tea bushes were locked in deadly combat with the native vegetation. The workers' quarters – long dreary lines of tin-roofed mud huts – stood out against the sky on a high ridge-top, above the company-provided school. There were a number of unusually fair-skinned young adults among the local population.

In India, Fort Portal would be described as a hill-station. It faintly echoes Simla, with many little roads twisting around wooded hills, and stolid churches guarding the graves of those who died young that the Empire might expand, and well-proportioned government offices with crumbling façades in shrub-filled grounds and architecturally frolicsome villas poised above shack-filled chasms. Yet the echo is very faint. Britain and India coalesced as Britain and Africa did not – could not. Simla in independent India is still Simla, changed but affectionately valued as one more tiny piece of India's immense and ancient cultural mosaic. Fort Portal now is a battered, slovenly symbol of failed paternalism.

English-speakers rarely use cheap lodgings so I chose a moderately expensive hotel: £3.75 per night. Luckily I felt no craving for extra comfort; my bathroom was waterless and the electricity generator had 'lost a piece'. A tall young woman with weight-lifter's biceps carried ten gallons of water up two flights of stairs and was not out of breath when she carefully lowered it from her head into the bath. I used nine gallons in an effort to destink the lavatory; in this important respect cheap lodgings are preferable to malfunctioning up-market hotels – one's cell is always far from the latrine.

Evidently this hotel once cherished dreams of an expanding tourist industry. Above the receptionist's small table – its drawer containing the room keys – hung wan posters urging guests to 'See the Pygmies!' and giving obsolete advice about transport to the Semliki Valley and Toro Game Reserve. The beaming young receptionist, bouncy and broad-faced, had grimly straightened hair and an ominously flawed complexion; skin-lightening creams and soaps, on sale in most villages, add another serious health hazard to African daily life. Eva supposed I wanted to see the pygmies; on the morrow she could arrange transport. Firmly I disabused her. Pygmies are human, too.

On another wall flapped two new anti-AIDS posters, in English

and Luganda. 'Do You Want *Your* Children To Be AIDS Orphans?'
And: 'One Partner Only – So *We* Kill AIDS! More Than One Partner, AIDS Kills *Us*!' Two youngish women sat chatting under the
posters and watched me jotting down the slogans. As they made
room for me to join them one stated flatly, 'No Ugandan child will
reach the age of 60.'

I demurred: this was over-reacting, surely?

'You think? OK, I'm too pessimistic, but that's how I *feel*. My
mother had fifteen kids, I've stopped at two. I told my husband,
"Enough! Why have more to die of AIDS?" He's left me now but
I don't care. He's a government agricultural inspector, always on
the move. You know what that means! I couldn't trust him, he was
a risk. For sex I can choose educated men who'll make it safe, not
looking for more children from me.'

The other young woman said sombrely, 'Three of my friends
have gone in one year.'

It was notable that while the loss of friends was freely mentioned,
few admitted to having lost relatives, at least in conversation with
the *mzungu*. Yet the Ugandans were said to be over the shame hump,
AIDS having bereaved so many. Such generalisations are of course
absurd. There must be as many subtly differing responses to the
epidemic as there are Ugandans.

The hotel's long, low-ceilinged bar-cum-restaurant was a restful
study in red brick and natural brown wood. Between the arched windows and alcoves hung dim photographs of jolly colonial officers in
shorts being matey with smug-looking chiefs in tribal attire. As I
mused over these imperial alliances the barman asked, 'You like our
pictures? The British brought us civilisation. Now most Ugandans
are Christian. Are you Catholic or Protestant?'

Later, as I dined, that AIDS conversation in the foyer had a
sequel. I was sharing a table with the only other guest, a senior army
officer. Nathan was unusually well-informed about distant political
problems, including Northern Ireland. When I remarked on his
understanding of that conflict he replied, 'I've followed it quite
closely, these sectarian tensions interest me as a Baganda. Years ago
an English friend sent me a good book about the details – *A Place
Apart* was the title, the author I've forgotten. Do you know it?'

I hesitated, then decided it would be unfair to dissemble. After
that Nathan said, 'Now we must talk frankly if you are going to write

about Uganda. Earlier, sitting in here, I heard you out there talking to those women about AIDS and I was ashamed. That woman talking about choosing men . . . Such vulgarity is new, a result of AIDS. People are being encouraged to discuss sex – before, it was completely taboo. Husbands and wives would not discuss it together yet now we have women shameless in public . . . Maybe you think this is good, I know how things are in the West. To me it is a tragedy, our culture being eroded – I wouldn't like you to think this is normal behaviour in Uganda.'

I defended the young woman. 'Her standards may not be yours or mine, but she's confronting the AIDS threat as it must be confronted. No taboo will restrain her from discussing sex, in detail, with her children. She knows that's essential, to protect them. And she also knows it's essential for African women to become more assertive – immediately. Are you sure your real worry is cultural erosion? Could it be more to do with men losing control of their women?'

Nathan looked startled, then transferred his attention to his plate, deftly rolling a ball of matoke while changing the subject to cattle. His father owned 200, his father-in-law 700 – 'which is too many'. Cows on good pasture can yield five litres a day but it costs so much to keep herds tick-free that milk production, at 100 shillings a litre, doesn't pay. In a modern economy, Nathan argued, the 'cattle fixation' of so many African tribes should be penalised. Some families, when it comes to buying medicines, give priority to bovine patients. 'It's cheaper', Nathan noted dryly, 'to replace a baby than a cow.'

Fort Portal is named to honour Sir Gerald Portal, the Consul in Zanzibar who in 1892 was persuaded by Frederick Lugard that a British withdrawal from Uganda, which had just been ordered by Gladstone, 'must *inevitably* result in a massacre of Christians such as the history of this century cannot show'. For this exaggeration Lugard had reasons unconnected with protecting Christians, but he knew which button to press in relation to British public opinion; it was only six years since Mwanga's creation of martyrs. Once Portal and Lord Rosebery had succeeded in postponing a decision on withdrawal, until 30 September 1893, Lugard returned to England to lead a 'Keep Uganda' crusade and argued eloquently:

It is well to realise that it is for our *advantage* – and not alone at the dictates of duty – that we have undertaken responsibilities in East Africa. It is in order to foster the growth of the trade of this country, and to find an outlet for our manufactures and our surplus energy, that our farseeing statesmen and our commercial men advocate colonial expansion. There are some who say we have no *right* in Africa at all, that it 'belongs to the natives'. I hold that our right is the necessity that is upon us to provide for our ever-growing population – either by opening new fields of emigration, or by providing work and employment which the development of overseas extension entails – and to stimulate trade by finding new markets, since we know what misery trade depression brings at home.

At the end of November 1892 Gerald Portal was appointed as Commissioner to Uganda and his pro-expansionist report was a major factor in the government's decision to take over the territory from the wobbly Imperial British East Africa Company which had been in charge since 1888. The IBEA resembled the British East India Company in design but not in wealth or efficiency. It had nevertheless been controlling Uganda for four years – though not making money for its shareholders – and in Lord Rosebery's view, 'As a rather one-horse company has been able to administer Uganda I suppose the Empire will be equal to it.'

Fort Portal's most conspicuous edifice is unfortunate. Standing on the highest of the surrounding hills, it dominates the town and looks like a ruined concrete water-tower. In fact it is a ruined concrete palace which must have looked equally ugly, in a different way, before it was shelled and burned during the Terror. I had asked Nathan whose palace it was and who attacked it. In reply he went into some detail about its having been designed by a British architect and built by a British company, then suddenly he switched to another subject. I was by then getting used to these Ugandan evasions.

The palace hilltop grants a superb view of the Mountains of the Moon – and many lesser mountains in every other direction. The circular ruin, roofless and scorched, is small as palaces go and prompts thoughts about our deprived descendants. A stone ruin is a thing of beauty; a concrete ruin, with jagged bits of rusty metal sticking out at all angles, seems the apotheosis of ugliness. Another sort of ugliness covers every accessible interior wall – graphic graffiti, much of it obscene, all of it violent. Guns and penises are frequently equated. The artistic skill in evidence might, I reflected, have been better deployed.

Not far from the foot of the palace hill is the Toro Babies' Home, founded long ago to care for motherless babies who were given back to their remarried fathers at the age of 3 or so. Now, after three years, there is often no father to reclaim them and the home, designed and equipped to care for thirty, was caring for sixty in April 1992. The staff seemed to be coping heroically but the matron – she combined hard-headed efficiency with soft-hearted imaginativeness – admitted to being at her wit's end. What to *do* with 4- and 5-year-olds who have nowhere to go? Under the impact of AIDS the extended family support system is collapsing, especially in towns. A common pattern, the matron explained, is for husbands to infect their wives who develop AIDS first, probably as a result of malnourishment during pregnancy, and die in childbirth or soon after. Infants then taken to the Home sometimes themselves develop AIDS and die at about the same time as their fathers; but more than 50 per cent are uninfected.

My arrival was unexpected and before anyone noticed me I had glimpsed teenage girls mothering the orphans, 5-year-olds carrying infants, toddlers playing on the veranda with homemade wooden toys. The atmosphere was affectionate, not institutional. But it was also desperate. The chaplain came to the matron's office and demanded, 'Why so much *studying* AIDS in Uganda, so much research and so little *support*.' He stressed that the staff were 'devout Christians'; if brought up as 'pagans' they would feel no obligation to help anyone outside their own clan. Very likely this is true. In other countries other Africans, not necessarily 'devout Christians', made the same observation.

A shy neatly dressed girl, who spoke no English, showed me around the Home. Despite Fort Portal's acute water shortage the cooking vessels and bowls were spotless, every child wore clean clothes, every cot was well-tended – even those occupied by toddlers dying of AIDS, with all that that implies. In Africa it isn't easy sensibly to dispose of 'surplus wealth' but beyond doubt the Toro Babies' Home, as run by that matron, was a worthy cause. (A change

115

of staff could of course quickly lead to unworthiness; this is what makes donating so chancy.)

From the Home a grassy path leads uphill, between soaring blue gums and pines, to the Church of Uganda cathedral, an elegantly simple building of mellow brick completed some sixty years ago. Wandering among the graves (many vandalised), I again pondered the value of White intervention in Africa. My misgivings were strengthened in the Bishop's Palace, a rambling bungalow half-smothered by bougainvillaea and jacaranda. Here a worried white-haired clergyman took up where the Home's chaplain had left off. He deplored various ill-judged Western projects to help AIDS victims' families, particularly the funding of orphans' schooling. This, he said, involved providing fees, books, uniforms and a weekly food allowance. It seems such projects can provoke serious dissension. Many orphans, had their parents been alive, could never have gone to school – so why should they now be given a privileged status? How could schooling compensate for the loss of parents? The system might even make life harder for them if they lost the support of their envious age-group, which they needed more than schooling. Some children, with both parents alive and well, were leaving home – egged on by their families – and presenting themselves elsewhere as 'orphans'. Would it not make more sense to fund the expansion of refuges like the Toro Babies' Home? A Ugandan-run institution could be more effective because those in charge were aware of all the cultural nuances. It was hard to disagree with that angry old man.

Later, in Fort Portal's astonishingly well-stocked public library, an angry young man voiced even stronger views. Having acknowledged Britain's annual contribution of £4,000 worth of books, he got his teeth into the exploitative West. 'Rich countries have organisations to help poor countries, OK? They need money to keep going and give wages and run four-wheel-drives, OK? They make publicity about something like AIDS in Uganda and that's good for getting money, OK?' (I clenched my fists; one more 'OK?' might goad me into hitting him over the head with a volume of the *Encyclopaedia Britannica*.) 'So they make projects that sound good if you know nothing about Uganda, OK? Then they send their people out to nice jobs and want us to say "Thanks" – but I say "Go home!"'

116

Dining again with Nathan, I repeated that diatribe. He chuckled and said, 'Didn't he have a point? If you weren't so irritated by his OKs you might have seen it!'

Nathan's mission in Fort Portal, he now confided, was a delicate one. A week before, two soldiers from the local Muhote barracks had been attacked in a neighbouring village; one died of his injuries on the spot, the other was not expected to recover. When law-abiding villagers reported this incident to the barracks they were arrested and beaten up by the dead man's comrades. Next day the District Administrator directed the army commander to hand over the imprisoned civilians to the police. The major complied, where-upon all the soldiers attacked the village, firing indiscriminately. Many families fled to Fort Portal police station and camped there until the troops withdrew. The police who escorted them home found two corpses in the bush, severely bludgeoned and slashed and minus tongues and eyes. The following day the army commander told a public meeting, convened in the local school by the DA, that his men had mutinied before leaving the barracks to attack the village. They had also wanted to raid Fort Portal town centre but he had restrained them; Nathan didn't reveal how this had been achieved.

Nathan was then sent from Jinja to sort it all out. This was how Amin's army, Obote's army, Okello's army behaved; it is how Museveni's army is alleged not to behave. Nathan's task was to discover the motive for the original attack on the soldiers – had they provoked it or not? And why had the mutinous troops had access to their weapons while off duty? An unenviable task, I reckoned, but no better man for it were a cover-up to be avoided.

This little local difficulty prompted me to consult Nathan on a matter of dress. In Jinja Peter had warned me that my jungle trousers were dangerously inappropriate for Uganda. These were a bargain buy in Belfast, drab green and vaguely military-looking, made of some tough material with the thigh-pockets convenient for a cyclist's maps. Anxiously Peter had foretold, 'In the bush they will think you are a foreign mercenary! For that they could kill you. Our village people are very frightened of soldiers – even if they don't kill you they won't be friendly, they'll be uneasy. They won't believe you're a woman. No Ugandan woman cycles, we don't think it's nice.'

117

At the time I laughed; the notion of my being mistaken for a mercenary (paid by whom?) seemed too absurd. But one should never laugh at local advice. Those trousers did provoke suspicion and on more than one occasion verbal aggression. Repeatedly I was asked, 'Are you a soldier from Europe or America?' Or, 'Why has your army sent you to Uganda?' Or, 'Why do you pretend to be a tourist when we can *see* you are a soldier?'

To that last I replied, 'If I were pretending, would I be wearing what you call army uniform?' But logic doesn't get you far in the bush where people tend to seize hold of an idea and not let go, however irrational and bizarre it may be.

Now Nathan agreed emphatically with Peter and suggested my wearing a bosom-revealing blouse instead of a loose shirt. While in Uganda I acted on this suggestion and there were no more awkward confrontations.

6

Feminism Rampant

Fort Portal to Kyotera

The first hour out of Fort Portal was wondrously beautiful. Ahead marched the vanguard of the Mountains of the Moon: sheer, smooth-crested and inky blue in the early light. Being only a few miles away, this mighty wall concealed the higher snowy summits. On my left, far below the road, lay a fairyland loveliness of translucent cloud – white vapour coiling through the depths with the wraiths of trees just discernible on a long ridge beyond the deep cleft. Then swiftly the sun drew those clouds across the road, enveloping me in damp chilliness, and wrapped them closely around the mountains.

By 11 a.m., after a forty-mile descent, I had lost 1,500 feet. Ahead stretched a colourless plain, reduced by drought and over-grazing to stark desiccation. The sky was cloudless, the heat threatening, the possibility of finding shade minimal. I took refuge in Kasese, a smallish town tucked into the arid foothills of the Ruwenzori and more important than it looks. A large copper mine inspired a rail link with Kampala and the place has recently become a backpackers' base for the Ruwenzori climb or for finding transport into nearby Zaire.

I was about to go on my way, at 3 p.m., when the rain came: a standard three-hour torrent. The evening was misspent drinking reprehensible quantities of Nile beer with a group of ex-Bugala Lonely Planeteers – including Ian – just down from their Ruwenzori climb and looking predictably gaunt and pallid. This three-day forced march through swamps, ice and snow, to an altitude of 15,300 feet, with local guides but without adequate gear, does no one any good.

As I left Kasese before dawn something sinister and witch-like

119

floated blackly through the starlight close above my throbbing head. Something silent and very large – perhaps the equatorial equivalent of pink elephants? No, only a maribou stork going to join its mate on a tree-top.

A brand-new 'donated' road allowed me to speed through the cloudy coolness, only pausing to photograph Lear leaning against the Equator monument, a wheel in each hemisphere. This was a flat, brown-turning-green landscape, low bush interspersed with cotton fields. To the east, for a few miles, Lake George glinted beyond a mile of golden-brown elephant grass above which kites hovered and eagles circled. In a wretched hamlet where only the flies seemed to have any vitality I paused for 'dry' tea – as milkless tea is oddly described by the Ugandans. From a butcher's stall beside the filthy tea-shack came a stench of rotting offal which would have killed my appetite even had food been available.

Downhill from the hamlet an incongruous hi-tech causeway spans the Kazinga Channel linking Lake George and Lake Edward – formerly Lake Idi Amin, but the Ugandans prefer to remember their colonisers. Then for eight hot flat miles I was again on the floor of the Rift Valley, crossing the Queen Elizabeth II National Park. Only thirty years ago this area supported countless elephants, hippos, buffaloes, kobs, topis and even tree-climbing lions. I saw only gazelle and a few eland; almost everything else was slaughtered by Amin's and Okello's soldiers, or by the Tanzanian troops who saw ivory as legitimate loot.

Under a leafless thorn-tree I partook of elevenses – energy-generating groundnuts. In an acacia grove, no more than fifty yards away, an eland nuclear family – parents and child – had settled down for their siesta and were pleasingly unafraid. I wondered then about the genesis of this little-used road. Was its mere existence meant to stimulate efficient industrialisation throughout the region? Or did some European construction company need a big contract? Why must African roads go to extremes? Either this flawless model, with its high, harshly blue motorway signs intruding every few miles, or that Labour of Hercules from Hoima to Kyenjojo. Why cannot *Africans*, independent of foreign money, machines and technicians, maintain adequate earth roads?

Gloomily I viewed the massive escarpment rearing up from the edge of the plain some four miles ahead. At such moments my inefficiency as a traveller stuns me; no even partially sane cyclist would have been *there, then*. Every climb out of the Rift Valley is punishing and none should coincide with the equatorial noon heat.

During the next two hours only the beckoning coolness of the heights above kept me going. Here the invention of the mountain-bike seemed justified; given a donated surface and gradient I was able to pedal, very slowly, all the way up those sun-scourged matoke-clad hills. At the first wayside hamlet I stopped on seeing a bore-hole pump – already a prodigious sweat-loss had occurred. Four little girls were queuing but their elders directed them to make way for the *mzungu*.

Then something scary happened. A truck-bus, packed with brilliantly clad women, halted to water its engine and quickly I took out my camera. This was an act of gross stupidity; I can only plead a sun-scrambled brain. The women were obviously Muslim and brilliantly clad in celebration of Id. As they waved clenched fists and screamed at me I was surrounded by what felt like a hundred (probably twenty) infuriated men shouting and gesticulating, their eyes aflame. When one seized my arm and another tried to grab the camera I forced my way through them and fled – downhill. Uphill would not have served my purpose. A mile away I braked and hid in the matoke, marvelling at my own crassness. I was trembling slightly; one is easily unnerved, in Africa, by the potential for spontaneous mob violence. That is realism rather than racialism. And the combination of Black volatility and Islamic fanaticism is extra-frightening.

When the truck could be heard grinding upwards I continued. Back in that hamlet, two elderly Muslim women beckoned me; they spoke no English but their message was clear. They were apologising and would like me to drink tea – the cup of peace, as it were. I also apologised, sitting on the floor in the comparative cool of their grass-thatched hut, furnished only with mats. A teenage boy was recruited to interpret. 'This womens is not liking you made go back on hill. This womens like *mzungu*. Say only bad men make trouble for you. Say *mzungu* not know camera is bad for us. Islam say no camera, pictures is bad in Koran.'

Then on and up, the Rift Valley no longer visible, all around a jumble of green red-streaked mountains, occasionally parting to reveal dark volcanic lakes. On a high pass there suddenly appeared, far below, an apparent infinity of forest, the trees so tightly packed one fancied one could cycle across their mass. Then steeply down and up, down and up all the way to Bushenyi, only sixty miles from Kasese though it felt further. In this dreary little town one night would be enough, I reckoned; but I was wrong.

Bushenyi's only source of Nile was a standard main-road duka selling bags of coarse salt, bars of toilet soap, Sportsman cigarettes, white loaves and buns (nutritionless but hygienically wrapped in cellophane), two-ounce packets of (probably stale) biscuits, plastic pots of margarine and tinned fish in a foul sauce – inedible, I had long since discovered. Most of these goods came from Kenya; Uganda hadn't yet got its manufacturing act together. A refrigerator behind the counter held beer and 'sodas' and a courteous youth, wearing a Persil-white cotton shirt, was in charge.

However, that standard duka contained two extraordinary phenomena. I noticed Jill first, a Western-dressed, copper-skinned woman in her thirties: tall, well-built, handsome, with an oval face, Nilotic features and great poise. She was reclining in a low chair by the doorway, drinking beer and *smoking*. This was sensational; most respectable Ugandan women don't publicly drink alcohol (at least in rural areas) and even Ugandan prostitutes don't smoke. Jill greeted me warmly in perfect English and I sat on a high stool beside her. As we talked she puzzled me increasingly; her sophisticated conversation and air of natural authority didn't match her humble job in the local post office. I scented a mystery and was curious. But, although she and I spent much time together over the next few days, my curiosity was only satisfied, by an odd little coincidence, after I had left Bushenyi.

Then that duka's second extraordinary phenomenon caught my eye. On the wall above Jill's head was displayed a page from an exercise book, inscribed in printed letters:

THE WOMEN OF AFRICA DO NOT WISH TO DOMINATE THE MEN. THEY WISH TO BE TREATED AS EQUALS WITH THE VALUE OF THEIR CONTRIBUTION TO SOCIETY RECOGNISED.

Jill chuckled. 'You didn't expect to see *that* in Bushenyi! In this shop you have fallen among feminists. Helen wrote it out and put it up and she *means* it. She's gone to the shamba but you'll meet her in a minute.'

Helen owned the duka and was mother to Patrick, the charmer behind the counter, and eight others. She soon arrived, in appearance a typical Ankole woman: very black, short of stature, hugely fat – hereabouts a sign of beauty. Her English was not as correct as Jill's but it was passionately fluent. Since girlhood she had been a latent feminist; AIDS had sent her into action. The arrival of a liberated female Irish cyclist delighted her. She helped herself to a Pepsi from the fridge and declaimed, 'Equality for African women isn't no more only a nice idea, it's to save lives. Women with risky husbands have to say "No!" But they can't, on their own. They're scared, they don't want divorce. OK, so we get together. A husband living risky comes home and sees not only his scared wife, waiting to obey. He sees a *group* of women, all with the same problem, all saying the same thing! This is a revolution. It's bigger than our political revolutions, it's men made to hear women. Our men have gone weak since all the life changed. Before they were important, now there's no warriors, no hunters, just lying around drinking. Then hunting girls to prove they're still *men*! But for us nothing's changed – work and more work, from before dawn till after dark. Our only change is a bad one – more children, when men only have one wife. You understand all I say? You see how is the revolution – men have gone so weak they're frightened of women in *groups*! They can't say we're silly, Ankole has funerals every day – and Rakai district is even worse than here. Now for us it's children first. Mothers want to live for their children. Risky husbands come second.'

Jill wondered, 'Did we need AIDS to make this revolution possible? How heartless I sound! But only a catastrophe would have stirred up ordinary women. Taboos don't go easily in the bush. Then I'm scared, looking over all of Africa. How long will it take the revolution to spread? How many Helens are there?'

Three men arrived then and sat on a bench opposite Jill and me. They were regulars: a doctor, a senior civil servant and an agricultural officer who complained angrily that imported pesticides did as much damage to their illiterate Ugandan users as to the pests.

There followed one of the most improbable evenings of my journey – Nathan would have been horrified. I have, I suppose, led a sheltered life; certainly I have never elsewhere participated in such an explicit discussion of the sexual act – and alternatives. All this

123

was in relation to contraceptive methods and 'safe sex' between partners, one of whom is HIV+. When the embarrassed adolescent
Patrick tried to slope off his mother restrained him – 'You stay and
listen, you need to know!' Jill remained impressively in control of
the debate – three women versus three men. Normally there would
have been a male take-over, a polite but decisive extinction of the
female viewpoint. As a local woman Helen couldn't have held the
fort – nor could I, as an inexplicable oddity who had drifted in from
the decadent and predatory West. Jill, however, cowed those three
intelligent and well-informed but deeply sexist men. She was one
quiet, gracious, logical woman and she left them sounding inco-
herent, self-contradictory and prejudiced to the point of cruelty. Of
course Helen and I did our bit, said our say. But the victory was
Jill's.

As light relief, during the last round of Niles, we considered the
recent pronouncement of a government minister who had calculated
that the average man needs eight condoms a night. The minister had
promised that packs of five, with instructions in Luganda and
English, would be provided at the subsidised price of 200 shillings.
If the minister's estimate of his compatriots' virility were correct,
a responsible man on the average monthly wage of 3,000 shillings
would soon go heavily into debt. We concluded that the minister in
question must be impotent and given to fantasising about potency.

Bushenyi feels like a mistake. Someone somewhere sometime
thought a town here would be a good idea, to service the dense
population of the lavishly fertile surrounding countryside; but then
came the Terror and Bushenyi was aborted. Shoddy buildings line
the steep main-road section; even shoddier buildings, including my
guest-house, line a rough track far below the main road. Many con-
structions are in that half-built-then-abandoned category which I
find peculiarly dispiriting. Most dukas are lock-up shops, their
owners living on distant shambas. Two petrol stations confront,
respectively, Helen's duka and a large church with shattered windows which seems not to have been opened for years. The headquarters of the Regional Electricity Board is a neat semi-detached
dwelling rather like an Irish council house. And then there is the
nearby Rukararwe Rural Development Centre, which kept me in
Bushenyi for three days.

Some Africans suffer from an exasperating mental inflexibility. On my way to the Centre, early next morning, I noticed Bushenyi's little milk depot and rejoiced, fresh milk being my No. 2 addiction (the attentive reader will by now have discerned No. 1). Scores of cyclists were delivering anything from a giant metal churn to a two-litre cooking-oil container. The 'incharge' was a tall earnest-looking young man wearing a peaked cap and a long cotton coat, spotlessly white and impeccably ironed. His eyes popped with horror when I tried to buy a litre. 'This is not pasteurised, I cannot sell, you cannot drink! This has *so* many bacteria, microbes, viruses, parasites – you get very sick from it, you . . .'

I interrupted. 'For a month I've been drinking unpasteurised milk, buying it on the road whenever I could. *You've* done your duty by warning me, if *I* don't mind the risk why not sell?'

The young man rolled his eyes and in agonised tones demanded, 'Why you're trying to make me do this bad thing? My job is to teach and protect people! When they see a *mzungu* drinking this dirty milk they think that's OK and I'm crazy . . .'

'But they won't see me drinking it, I'll take it to my room and drink it secretly – I *promise*.'

'Then you get sick,' said the young man. 'You get very, very sick and it is my fault and I lose my job!'

The Rukararwe Rural Development Centre is a pioneering self-help project started by a local women's group in 1985 in defiance of the Terror, then going through its last ghastly convulsions. Six other groups joined; local farmers donated ten hectares of medium-quality land; Christian Aid in Britain and a similar NGO in Germany provided modest funding – and away went Rukararwe. Soon the local schools became enthusiastically involved, many pupils persuading conservative parents to join. Each weekend seminars are held and outsiders come to learn from Rukararwe how much can be achieved with the minimum of funding augmented by the maximum of hard work and good management.

The tree-planting group replaces those indigenous trees felled during the past few decades to extend grazing lands (now being washed away) and previously replaced only with blue gums – a dirty word in Rukararwe. Another group runs training courses for youths (over 200 at a time) who have failed to find work in the cities and returned home eager to be self-reliant, to learn how to do something

125

new and profitable on the family shamba: for example, growing pineapples and passion-fruit for the Kampala market and 'civilising' forest honey for sale to expatriates at high prices. A third group looks after pregnant teenagers, providing board and lodging for one year and training in a craft. A document has to be signed by the girls' parents stating that they understand their daughters will not be earning. 'Otherwise,' said Janet, who runs this group, 'parents would expect them to contribute to the family budget though they're living free here.' In Ankole an 'early' pregnancy reduces the bride-price but is no bar to marriage if the girl's parents are willing to bring up the baby.

Each group has its own elaborately structured committee and an overall co-ordinating committee occupies a handsome office-hut. The African addiction to bureaucracy alarms me. Committees must have two or three vice-chairpersons, a sub-treasurer, an assistant accountant, an under-secretary – every conceivable sort of titled officer. Irresistibly one is reminded of children playing 'houses'. Happily this addiction has not yet impaired Rukararwe's functioning, though Jill thought the Centre might achieve even more if it held fewer committee meetings.

I walked the three miles to Rukararwe across flower-bright expanses of gently curving pastureland under a sky mobile with high, billowing, silver clouds. There is a pastoral tranquillity about this rolling, generously fertile landscape, studded with groves of blue gums and pines and gleaming freshly green after a rainy night. Everywhere, in the near distance, rise low grassy mountains beribboned by little red paths linking groups of plantain-roofed huts that look from afar like untidy haystacks. Some long wide slopes are heavily cloaked in matoke. As one cycles past these plantations they seem just that; on foot I discovered, concealed within each, numerous tiny scattered huts, dwarfed by their dense surrounding 'jungle'.

The Centre is neatly spread over a wide hillside, all its buildings thatched and constructed of local materials. Janet guided me round – then Carol breathlessly overtook us, eager to show me her project, an enormous nursery where the cherished seedlings of indigenous trees are given individual attention.

In the kitchen two new types of fuel-conserving stove were being tested: mud and brick, lined with tin. Rukararwe emphasises economy and frugality – rare virtues in any African project, the general tendency being to imitate our 'conspicuous spending'. All the spinning-wheels and looms, the potters' and chair-makers' and blacksmiths' equipment were made on the spot. Glazing for the pots was obtained from cowdung and ash, or cowdung and rust; I thought that last the ultimate in frugality and scarce forebore to cheer. In the staff canteen-hut a pleasant surprise awaited me – the only unsweetened tea I drank in Africa, sugar being an unnecessary luxury and bad for the teeth.

'I must leave early today', said Janet, 'to go to my father's brother in Mbarara. Last night he lost his fourth son, aged 35. I didn't know he was ill, he got malaria and that was enough – it often is, when people are HIV +, even if they've seemed fine for years. He's left three children and an HIV + widow. In three years my uncle has lost all his sons. His three daughters are married in Kampala and Masaka. He and my aunt are like parents for me – they brought me up, I was an orphan.' She looked grieved as she spoke, yet had spent a jolly morning with me, to all appearances happy and relaxed.

That evening in the source of Nile Helen presided behind the counter and the regulars were joined by Miriam and Carol, from Rukararwe, and by a shifting population of young men who had heard about the cyclist weirdo and wanted to suss her out.

Stephen – tall, rather flashily dressed, an 'electrical technician' – started an illuminating debate. Aged 22, he longed to marry. But alas! none of the possible brides was going for less than five cows and his father said times were hard and he couldn't afford more than two so his son must wait.

'Wait!' exclaimed Stephen bitterly. 'How can I wait for a woman? Now I must have girls who could infect me. This is a crazy thing! We should marry, like in the West, only for sex, not for cows!'

Miriam, the Rukararwe medical officer, turned towards me. 'This is a very hard problem. When our President Museveni came to power he was honest about AIDS, not hiding the crisis like they do in Kenya. He made a special strong appeal to young people not to have more than one partner, then he begged parents to bring down bride-prices. But most families won't.'

Stephen pointed to the Health Ministry anti-AIDS poster above the refrigerator – LOVE CAREFULLY! STICK TO ONE PARTNER! He demanded, 'Why no poster telling parents how to behave?' Then he glared at me. 'You, madame, what do *you* think?'

'I think the notion of buying a wife, with all that that implies for women's status, is barbarous. The system must be scrapped as stage one in the campaign for equality.' I glanced at Helen, confident of her support – but, disconcertingly, I didn't get it.

'You don't understand,' she said. 'You think a woman feels bad if she's exchanged for cows or money. But if there's no exchange she feels worth nothing. I cost my husband *ten* cows. I had good education from Irish nuns in Mbarara, I speak English and can run a business. My father spent money on me, why give me away for nothing? Our families keep accounts of what girls cost to feed and clothe and educate, that way they can show a daughter is valuable to a young man's family. You want a healthy, educated bride – OK, you pay for it!'

Jill, who had been watching my face, cautioned Helen. 'Our liberated friend can't cope with all this – she thought you too were liberated and now you've gone bush!'

Stephen raised his voice as though addressing a public meeting. 'I only want my own woman, I'm not crazy, I know all about AIDS. With a wife I wouldn't live risky. In the West you get a wife free, why must Africans pay to make women feel better? A wife costs money, you have to keep her. Her family would have to keep her if she didn't marry. Why must I pay to get her so she costs her family no more?'

Jill began to look sorry for me. 'We're getting our cross-cultural lines in such a tangle we'd better talk about something else.'

'That's bad thinking,' said Helen. 'People who want to understand must listen. It's crazy if our friend goes home saying Western Women's Lib is OK for African women's problems. She's so shocked by bride-price she can't see we must feel valued or we can't look for equality. If my husband got me free, like Stephen wants, I couldn't start a revolution. Stephen sounds right to Dervla, saying he should get a free bride. But he talks mixed up, knowing only a little about the West and nothing about Women's Lib. Here a free bride's a slave – no worth, no status, no respect. Everyone knows my bride-price was ten cows. When I talk revolution they listen, with respect.'

Jill asked me, 'Have you got the message? For us Women's Lib has to start from where we're at, not where you're at!'

During the following, Sunday, afternoon sheets of rain fell for three and a half hours, giving Helen's regulars a good excuse for more than one pre-prandial Nile. Then out of the storm came Mr Bongyereirwe, a Kampala construction engineer whose jeep was, he hoped, being mended across the road. He introduced himself to me as the son of a Makerere professor of law and the grandson of a Baganda chief, which didn't seem to impress anyone. He had spent two postgraduate years in the US, where his wife also studied; she was now teaching mathematics at a missionary college. 'We have two daughters and one son, then I told my wife to have a ligation – it is very anti-social to overpopulate the world. This causes many ecological problems.'

Mr Bongyereirwe's comprehension of the West had not been much extended by his postgraduate years; he directed all his conversation to me, ignoring my friends. And he firmly believed AIDS to be the result of American biological warfare experiments in Zaire. 'Then some GIs got accidentally infected and took the virus to San Francisco where it spread among those men with dirty habits.'

When I sought Mr Bongyereirwe's views on the bride-price system he replied, 'I am an educated man, I require no price for my daughters, but I will give permission only for marriages to rich husbands, with good prospects. Among the uneducated it is different, marriage customs are too important to change quickly. At least one hundred guests are common at a poor family's wedding and tons of food, and nowadays money, have to be collected from neighbours. I expected change in the cities, but no – it's worse, more guests invited, more resources squandered.'

All the regulars grinned when Jill intervened. 'But *are* those resources squandered? What you call the uneducated don't have much fun – maybe they deserve a feast and a celebration now and then?'

Jill was sitting behind the counter, hitherto unnoticed by Mr Bongyereirwe. His reaction to her challenge fascinated me. 'Madame,' he said sharply, 'you are too far from home!' At which point a shout from the petrol-station mechanic summoned him. His departure occasioned no dismay. Helen muttered, '*Bad* types became chiefs under the British!'

As the rain eased off we watched a fine Friesian cow, with European-sized udders, being driven up a grassy slope opposite the dukas. Jossy, the agricultural officer, looked upset. 'There's a good cow, only four years old, going to be killed this evening. Her owner had sudden bad money luck and couldn't sell her for milk. We've a local surplus, but beef's scarce.'

'Another distribution problem!' exclaimed Jill impatiently. 'In towns not far from here people pay 600 shillings for a half-litre of Kenyan Long-life – disgusting stuff!'

A new white Samurai stopped for petrol, its job description writ large below the appropriate logo.

FAO/UNFPA
UGA /88/PO8
INTEGRATION OF FAMILY LIFE
EDUCATION IN AGRICULTURAL EXTENSION

For a moment we all stared, my companions' expressions a study – irritated, sceptical, scornful, angry.

'Why', wondered the doctor, 'do expat vehicles always look fresh from the shop?'

I asked, 'What does that inscription *mean*?'

Jill smiled sourly. 'It means teaching extension workers how to encourage peasants to use condoms. It also means a whole new FAO/UNFPA Project, a sub-department with lots more well-paid jobs for the boys – and girls.'

Helen added, 'It's good for extension workers too, they sell those condoms in Mbarara. Only the UN believes Ankole farmers will use them. And why should they change their ways, just because some youngster on a motor-bike says so?'

Suddenly the doctor flared up, banged his fist on the counter and shouted, 'Why do they make *our* tragedy *their* industry?'

The question was rhetorical but Jill responded, 'There's a serious job shortage in the West.'

Every Monday, from villages within a radius of thirty miles or so, traditional healers come in turn to Rukararwe to hold joint clinics with a modern doctor in a specially built hut; the two doctors, until recently natural enemies, sit side by side. It took four years to persuade the medicine men to reveal their secrets; now their income is up and they are happy, though still on guard. Only

130

modern doctors of integrity co-operate in such ventures, people who disdain to profiteer on the Western medical drugs market. The diagnoses are made after scientific tests, then the medicine man prescribes his cure should it seem appropriate. A research project was being efficiently organised to prove which traditional cure really works for what; it would of course be beyond Rukararwe's resources to discover *why* a particular cure works.

At 7.30 a.m. a few dozen patients were already waiting outside the clinic hut and bicycles stood around on the grass. Some were cycle-taxis but most patients had walked and looked alarmingly exhausted. As yet there was no sign of the doctors, or of Miriam, the middle-aged London-trained nurse who assisted with the testing. I sat on the grass near an adjacent hut, from which the traditional cures are dispensed, and observed that entrance to this sanctum was being closely controlled.

An hour later, when the medicine man debarred me from the clinic-hut, Miriam was greatly discomfited; she had urged me to be there that morning, confident that I could sit in on the session. I, however, was pleased. Rukararwe's most valuable feature is its African-ness, only slightly diluted by Western interference. For all the medicine man knew, I might be a potential meddler and his exclusion order seemed prudent.

Jill's comment was interesting: 'Not all of Africa has moved into the age of literacy. Knowledge in the West is public property, freely available in books. Our traditional minds work another way – and a medicine man's knowledge has gone from father to son, in total secrecy, hidden like an *object* sensitive to light. We've myths about knowledge being stolen, run away with as if it was a jewel! I don't mean running away with medicine or charms, but with knowledge itself. The bush doctors' secrets gave them such power they scared everyone, and got very rich. Those men working here have been clever enough to compromise. Diagnosis is their weakness, all guesswork when it isn't something obvious, and they realise they can do better by collaborating with doctors who have the "magic" to get the diagnosis right. Then their cures can be more acceptable than expensive imported drugs. I'd guess this medicine man feared you were spying. We're all afraid of that. Once our team has *proved* A, B and C can cure X, Y and Z it's likely the transnational gangsters will move in. Herbal medicines, scientifically

131

developed in Africa, by Africans, for Africans, would wreck their profits unless they took over the marketing. But in my lifetime we've learned a lot, we're no longer so easily fooled by fancy packaging and mumbo-jumbo leaflets in scientific jargon. It's a big step forward to have those teams working in the bush. Villagers seeing a modern doctor approving of herbal medicines don't feel it's "primitive" to use them. They can believe their own medicine is as good or better "magic" than the White man's – and cheaper, so they don't have to borrow, or get sicker while saving up for a cure.'

In Bushenyi's only restaurant – small, fly-blown, concrete-walled – Jill and I ate our Last Supper (matoke and beef) by candlelight, the electricity having failed during a melodramatic afternoon thunderstorm. (Stephen, we were assured, was fixing it.) Our conversation wasn't flowing as usual and Jill looked pensive – then abruptly said, 'I've a warning for you, please don't laugh at me! It's about your way of answering questions. You're too honest, explaining you've never married, have no religion and so on. Amongst the élite, used to mixing with Whites, that's fine – but it's different in the bush. You don't realise how upset some people can be when you talk like that. They're not used to travelling the world, making allowances for new attitudes. When you give these honest answers – well, forgive me, you're really being a cultural imperialist. You don't mean it, I know, but you can upset even people like Helen. Maybe you think it's educational for African peasants to see how the other half lives, but you're ignoring their religious feelings, offending their whole sense of what's *right*. It's almost as if an African in London was asked his favourite food and said, "People!" No, don't laugh, I'm serious. Here we're deeply religious and spiritual, not necessarily as Christians but as *Africans*. Not marrying is a sort of blasphemy, against all the laws of God and Nature. Then when you say you've no religion you could be seen as not only shocking but dangerous. Especially as you travel around alone, without fear, on a bicycle, at the age of 60. Do you notice most people ask your age? That's why I'm worried about the rest of your journey. Not so much around here but in remote bits of Tanzania, Zambia and so on, where the bush people, to be blunt, can still react in primitive ways. You know what I'm saying?'

Feeling chastened but bewildered, I shook my head.

Jill smiled. 'To you a big area of the African soul is invisible –

Whites can see it only after a lifetime here, speaking some of our languages. So I'll talk plainly. It's possible some villagers could see you as a powerful, very frightening witch, and both Blacks and Whites have occasionally been killed for that reason. Someone panics – and it's all over for the stranger.'

I made an incredulous, protesting noise.

'Don't sound like that! I'm not being alarmist. It's fashionable to pretend the belief in witchcraft has almost died out, but truly it's as widespread as ever and even more *feared*. Traditional religion provided all sorts of safeguards against it, Christianity doesn't – so people feel extra twitchy. In Bushenyi I'm probably the only person who doesn't believe in witchcraft. It's part of everyday life for all sorts – government ministers, university professors, clergymen, diplomats, international football teams – maybe modified, in some cases, but still *very* real. It's the villagers' fear I want to impress on you. Everywhere you'll be asked these questions and your answers could be misinterpreted. Please be cautious, say your husband's dead, say you're some sort of Christian – a Jehovah's Witness, a Christian Scientist, anything you fancy. It's the "no religion" concept that upsets them.'

This was the most *outré* local advice I have ever been given; but I didn't entirely ignore it. Curiously, it was only as we walked to my guest-house by starlight that Jill told me her husband had died three years previously, aged 32, leaving her with a daughter now aged 6 who lived with the maternal grandparents. The cause of death was not specified.

For centuries Ankole was a two-tribe territory, divided between the pastoralist Bahima and the agriculturalist Bairu, the latter in the majority but always ruled by the cattle-rich minority. My seventy-five-mile ride from Bushenyi to Lyantonde took me down from the lush Bairu hills to the stricken aridity of over-grazed Bahima pastures, as shattering a contrast as one could find in any day's cycling. Beyond war-scarred Mbarara – Ankole's capital, where there was nothing to detain me – the sun came out with noontide ferocity and for mile after mile I was pedalling through apparently uninhabited hilly bush. The too-numerous skinny cattle – each accompanied by an escort of egrets – looked sorry for themselves as they plodded towards some distant source of water, their immense

horns seeming too heavy to be comfortably supported. The emaciated yearlings had clearly suffered most from the recent drought
yet all wore glossy coats, perhaps because of their weekly (sometimes
twice-weekly) anti-tick dipping. I paused to watch a few of these
ceremonies through my binoculars – herds being driven into a tin-
roofed tank with much cruelty. Jossy, the Bushenyi agricultural
officer, had told me that the water shortage causes some of these dips
to be repeatedly re-used, fresh chemicals being added weekly, which
seriously endangers the animals' health.

Jossy, a middle-aged man, felt angered by the fate of this area.
He remembered how it was in his youth – with abundant edible wild
fruits, rich pasturage, a variety of wildlife, ample stands of mature,
spreading trees. Today no trees remain and there wasn't even a
rabbit to be seen as I crossed the Lake Mburu Game Reserve. Those
trees were vital to reduce wind erosion, a major consideration here;
all afternoon a strong cross-wind saved me from heat-stroke. Yet
they were sacrificed to branch-fencing – which needs to be renewed
every few months – for kraals and grazing areas. Now 200 cows are
being grazed (or not grazed) on an acreage scarcely adequate for fifty
and the herders' reckless firing of the bush destroys both valuable
vegetation and the soil's nutrients. Most of the seasonal swamps –
and therefore their useful permanent swamp vegetation – have
vanished, as have the valley dams excavated by the British in 1956
on behalf of the cattle. The rainfall has been decreasing annually,
regardless of good or bad rainy seasons elsewhere, from
875–1,000 mm in 1970 to 500–750 mm in 1990. Here, as throughout
Uganda, the two main threats to the environment, apart from the
bovine population explosion, are brick-bakers and charcoal-
burners. The former, Jossy had said vehemently, should be made
to plant four times the number of trees they fell and the latter should
be put out of business by the provision of cheap countrywide electricity. Electricity is so much more expensive than charcoal that even
in towns like Bushenyi which are – more or less – electrified, few
can afford to use it.

This ravaged Bahima territory extends far to the north-west of the
main road and still supplies, every day, some 15,000 litres of milk
and 20,000 kilos of beef to Kampala and other towns. Jossy,
however, foretold that within a decade it would be reduced to true
desert – a famine area, appealing to the West for emergency aid.

Yet even now, he was confident, it could be rescued; he had a long list of practical remedies but these needed the Ministry of Lands, Water and Mineral Resources, the Ministry of Agriculture, Animals and Fisheries, and the Ministry of Environmental Protection to swing into unified action. 'This is not a natural disaster,' Jossy had fumed. 'It is a man-made disaster and man can unmake it. The remedies don't need big money, they don't need hard currency or expats or machinery. They *do* need education about the environment and then responsible behaviour. Look at the Rukararwe tree-planting, with voluntary labour – it costs very little and in a few years will have given health to the country all around. If the *will* is there the damage can be undone. But the Bahima are like all cattle-people – stubborn and jeering at advice. Even when some of their cattle and children are already dying . . .' (Jossy was a Bairu.) 'And the ministries only make long speeches about the crisis – they do *nothing*, though this is our President's homeland!'

The last hour was coolish, with a strikingly complicated skyscape to the north-west – shifting layers of many-hued clouds above the brown eroded hills. All day I had been on the Africa Highway, which carries more truck traffic than I had had to endure since leaving Kampala. The little town of Lyantonde, its tin roofs visible for miles before I arrived, is a long-established truckers' stop and singularly depressing.

At sunset colossal articulated trucks lined the long main street – a dusty (or muddy) deeply rutted track. The countless lodgings had names like Sweet Dreams, Happiness House, Heavenly End. Lyantonde is in Rakai district, reputedly Africa's most AIDS-stricken region. (That reputation is no longer deserved; I was to come upon several other equally stricken regions.) Yet sex-workers swarmed; by now I could identify them at a glance – always comely, well-groomed, well-dressed, well-manicured, never having the 'cheap' aura that we might associate with prostitutes who service truck-drivers. African men are quite obsessional about the cleanliness of their sexual partners; a not uncommon cause of divorce is the 'dirty, smelly wife' who, poor thing, may have neither the energy nor the surplus water to keep herself squeaky clean.

I chose Jane's Paradise Garden which seemed otherwise unpatronised. The drab little bar was decorated only by Museveni's photograph. In one corner Abel sat alone, a frail elderly Presbyterian teacher drinking a soda and looking unhappy. 'This is not my town,' he said defensively. 'It's a bad place but I'm sent here by God. My town is Kabale, very high in the mountains, near the Rwandan border.'

It was coincidence time. 'Kabale!' I exclaimed. 'That's where one of my new friends comes from', and I told him about my days in Bushenyi.

Abel smiled slightly. 'I think your new friend is called Jill?'

'Yes – you know her?'

'Everyone in Kabale knows this family. They are not Ugandan, they are Watutsi from Rwanda – thousands came as refugees in 1960. They are very clever and arrogant and proud. You have heard of them? They ruled for centuries though only 10 per cent of the population! They never worked, the Hutu were their slaves. But that was always Hutu land, the Watutsi came from somewhere far up in the north. That's why they had to run away in the end, when the Hutu killed more than 100,000. Now there's more killing in Rwanda and more refugees coming to us. We've too much killing in Africa. Why don't we talk instead, like Christians? Christ said we should turn the other cheek. I think he meant we should listen to one another instead of killing.'

I agreed that this was an excellent idea but pointed out that Africans are not alone in failing to implement it.

Lyantonde's poverty was extreme. The hordes of unwashed, ragged small boys who gathered around Lear outside Jane's Paradise Garden were pitifully malnourished, their hair rusty, their faces and limbs pocked with open sores. The skinny teenage bar-boy and his apathetic friends – a trio who just hung about, scarcely talking – seemed charmless to the brink of ill-manners. Pre-AIDS Lyantonde, I heard later, was notoriously STD-infected with a tragically high percentage of congenital syphilitics.

There was no running water in the town but the rains had assured plenty of self-service washing water; one fetched it in a basin from one of two large tar-barrels now filled daily from the roof gutters. I had often wondered why so few township tin-roofed homes were equipped with gutters and barrels, a significant labour-saving device during one-third of the year. In Bushenyi I asked and the answer shamed me. Having built a one- or two-roomed shack, there was nothing left over to buy guttering and barrels. The unpoor can be very unimaginative.

136

Abel advised me to eat in a bright tidy little restaurant across the street from Jane's Paradise Garden. I chose matoke and beef instead of rice and stewed chicken; no one (not even myself) cooks rice as badly as the Africans. The proprietress – a fatly handsome fortyish woman with three chins – sat opposite me, threatening the small table's equilibrium as she leaned her vast bulk on it. She bewailed the fact that the slim disease was ruining business. Half the town's sex-workers had moved out, including her own two daughters. These were AIDS widows in their twenties, they had to go into the business to support toddlers. Too many truck-drivers were bypassing Lyantonde, all because of bad publicity about Rakai. My mind boggled. There wasn't room for one more truck on the street, sex-workers adorned every doorway – what must Lyantonde have been like pre-AIDS? But it slightly cheered me to hear that some truck-drivers at least were apprehensive.

I dressed before dawn, by my own candlelight; the room was vibrating as scores of trucks revved up outside. Unrefined diesel fumes almost asphyxiated me as I pushed Lear past the drivers and their passengers who stood around making largely fanciful arrangements to meet again – a feature of such junctions. Several wore T-shirts portraying Saddam Hussein with adulatory slogans, a common phenomenon all along my route. This bias evidently sprang from the realisation that everything the US did in Iraq was done out of ruthless self-interest and virtually everything they said about the conflict was untrue.

Leaving the Africa Highway, I pedalled into Rakai's magnificent mountains and over the next seventy miles met only two vehicles. For an hour or so there was a homeliness about the weather; in Ireland this sort of fine, warm, drifting rain is described as 'A grand soft day, thanks be to God!' A few children were on their way to school – for once, un-uniformed. One little boy, unaware of my presence, stood on the red embankment leading down from his hut very carefully wrapping a thin, tattered book in a brown plantain leaf, tied with tough grass. Putting his satchel on his head he descended to the road where, on seeing me, he genuflected. Most children in rural areas greeted me thus – I hope (and believe) merely because I'm an elder, not because I'm a *mzungu*. Here I saw my most comical bicycle load: four hens and four cocks secured to a long plank laid across a carrier, all looking perfectly composed as the cyclist bounded downhill at speed.

A Martian dropped into Rakai would be puzzled. Why so many fertile but weed-infested shambas, so many derelict huts, so many forlorn-looking elders, so many devitalised, aimless children crouching in groups under the plantains?

For miles the track switchbacked – mostly ascending – through flat-topped, cattle-grooved, red-brown mountains. I thought, 'What a nuisance is ecological awareness!' Aesthetically those mountains, austere in colour and contour, were extremely pleasing under a deep blue sky. Then came a long serious climb on a surface so rough that it constituted another Labour of Hercules.

That high pass overlooked an immense expanse of long blue table-top mountains, deep green valleys and sheer red cliffs rising from narrow glens full of tangled vegetation. An unpeopled landscape, it seemed, until my binoculars revealed many tiny isolated home-steads. Here the wind blew cold; the clouds had returned and were playing with the sun. Then as I nut-munched, a transforming blue light suffused the whole scene giving it the look of a stage-set, a mighty theatre awaiting some eerie drama. But of course the drama has already started . . . All I seek as my traveller's reward was about me: silence, solitude, space – so beautiful and peaceful and satis-fying for the *mzungu*, yet for the inhabitants of those distant home-steads not any more a good place to dwell.

The gradual descent took me past a few destitute-looking Muslim hamlets and below the track lay wave after wave of smooth deforested ridges, separated by inaccessible grassy clefts. In a big T-junction village of ragged unsmiling people I could buy only two cups of weak black tea and two warm maize buns. The track then ran level for twenty miles, through matoke, forest or scrub. In the bush new emerald-bright grass was spangled with carmine flowers, scarcely two inches tall, and under umbrella acacias grew giant orange mushrooms, a foot high. Back in inhabited country – the noon sun brutal in a cloudless sky – there was much more up-and-down with repeated glimpses of Lake Kijanebalola in the near distance: a long, coolly shimmering expanse, its low reedy banks sustaining a wealth of water-birds.

On the map Rakai is a town; in reality it is an impoverished scattered village in a superb setting of wooded hills and cultivated valleys. At 2.30 my most unerring instinct led me to the only and improbable source of Nile: a dressmaker's duka. While I drank, the heavily pregnant dressmaker dressmade and told me this would be her tenth and she hadn't wanted it because the Irish nuns in Masaka – all doctors – warned she might die if she had another but they wouldn't give her the Pill because of her blood-pressure. 'Isn't it wrong', she said, looking up from her work, 'that in Africa the most popular birth-control way must be the most dangerous for women? We must take the Pill because we can do it secretly. If we had love and trust with our husbands we could get something safer. My husband only laughed when I told him what the nuns warned about the blood-pressure and anaemia. He said, "If you can have nine you can have ten and double figures are better!" Look at me now!' – she pulled up her skirt to display gruesomely swollen legs. The nuns, it seemed to me, had not been exaggerating. 'If I die giving him his tenth can he look after them all? He'll get another wife but she won't be a good one – she'll be a bad one that couldn't find anybody else. Good girls don't want a man with the other wife's nine kids. Or maybe ten . . .' She looked down at her belly. 'Maybe this baby will live, only I'll die. From the nuns in Masaka I went to the Family Planning Clinic but they won't give advice unless both partners are present.' (This bit of Western nonsense renders such clinics virtually useless in Africa, except perhaps among the educated élite who need them least.) As we talked a pathetic figure shambled past, an old bent man in torn shirt and trousers with an odd expression: half-frantic, half-cowed. 'The BBC put him on the radio,' remarked my companion. 'The slim disease took all his family, six sons and three daughters. And their wives or husbands are dead or dying. His grandchildren die too. He lost his mind when the little ones started to die.'

Another twenty miles – cruelly hot on a worsening road – took me down to more over-grazed bush. Beyond a mature forest of British-planted blue gums lay the old village of Kyotera where the rains had come too late for the maize and a new crop was going in. The dismal main-road township of Kyotera has been visited by many afflictions: the Tanzanian army, AIDS and, most recently, renewed fighting in nearby Rwanda. This turmoil had stopped all trading and brought much extra hardship to the whole region, including Mbarara.

Within the past four years most Kyotera businesses have changed hands once or twice following their owners' deaths. Outsiders were turning down good jobs in this district, the implication again being that celibacy is impossible and marital fidelity not much easier. Yet in Masaka I had met a young Bairu woman doctor who admitted to having recently married an untested husband: securing a husband and children had to be given priority. Such encounters (not unusual) always deepened my gloom. When the medical profession refuses to take AIDS seriously, what hope is there for the masses?

In the ramshackle compound of Kyotera's Catholic Mission an Irish NGO, Concern, has its fittingly modest base, almost devoid of expatriate luxuries. A four-person team, including two volunteer workers, had recently set up a 'participatory approach' programme to help AIDS victims and their families and here Irish hospitality struck again. My last few days in Uganda were spent participating, as an interested observer, in Concern's various projects.

7

Tanzania Through the Back Door

Kyotera to Shinyanga via Bukoba

At dawn the Concern compound's gnarled trees stood out blackly, like an Arthur Rackham etching, against a greenish sky streaked with slender clouds: smoky blue, old gold, mauve, then suddenly all crimson. Kyotera is a virtual cul-de-sac; the twenty-five miles to the border, on a good gravel road through open rolling country, were traffic-free. To the east shrub-scattered golden grassland stretched all the way to the invisible Lake Victoria and the mountains of Rwanda smudged the south-western horizon. I passed only two wretched hamlets where it bothered me to see World Vision AIDS Advice Centres, an interesting measure of that organisation's thoroughness; 'AIDS Orphans' photographs must delight their fundraisers. As Graham Hancock wrote in *Lords of Poverty*:

> World Vision regularly makes powerful and emotional appeals to our humanitarianism. Operating a survival-of-the-fittest philosophy in a competitive market-place, and apparently defining 'fitness' not in terms of the work it does amongst the poor but in terms of the funds raised, it is not above sabotaging the efforts of other charities to fill its own coffers . . . The onward march of Christianity remains an abiding concern of many voluntary agencies. According to Ted Engstrom, President of World Vision until 30 June 1987, 'We analyse every programme we undertake, to make sure that within that programme evangelism is a significant component. We cannot feed individuals and then let them go to hell.'

The Mutukula border-post has a make-believe air; one feels the intrusion of reality, in the form of a foreign traveller, can't be taken seriously. Here bureaucracy has many overlapping layers, as though Mutukula had deliberately set about burlesquing the whole notion. Nobody's function, as a cog in this hilariously elaborate machine, seems clearly defined – perhaps because so rarely exercised.

Layer One was a teenage policeman found snoozing under a mango tree. Seeing the rifle cradled in his arms I roused him gently, lest he leap to his feet, alarmed, and shoot wildly. He shook hands, asked the usual questions, requested me to unpack. Meekly I did so, assuming him to be also the customs officer. Soon I realised that he was simply curious about the gear needed by a *mzungu* cycling from Kenya to Zimbabwe. Opening my minuscule first-aid box he exclaimed, 'Little medicine! Why so little? In our countries we have many diseases!' Then he seized on my Masta kit and asked, 'What is this? Please, let me see!'

'Sorry, that can't be opened until you need it.'

'Magic!' he muttered, turning his attention to my tent. He didn't believe any tent could be so compact. 'Make it work, let me see!' I made it work and, fascinated, he crawled in, then emerged to say, 'But against lions this is no good!' I explained that tents don't aspire to be lion-proof. Luckily my gear is minimal; otherwise I might have been stuck for the day at Layer One.

Layer Two – a sentry-box-sized hut, opposite the mango tree – contained Stage One of Passport Control. The occupant was a small, thin, elderly man wearing an urban suit complete with neatly tied tie. He glared at the policeman and said, 'Young people are very silly!' Scrutinising my Ugandan visa he frowned, then reproached me. 'You are two days late, you should have left on Saturday.' He looked at me sadly. 'Why are you two days late?'

Truthfully I replied, 'I was enjoying myself in your beautiful country, I wasn't thinking about time.'

The officer sighed. 'You are silly, you could be in prison.' With a leaking ballpoint pen he transcribed all my passport details into a tea-stained exercise-book. Then he applied his rubber stamp. 'I'm happy today because you enjoyed Uganda. I hope you will come back.'

Approaching Layer Three, a hundred yards up the track, I reflected that that had been, according to the mythology of travellers, a classic bribe-seeking situation. Quite likely our expecting the worst often creates bribery demands by injecting hostility into the atmosphere.

Layer Three was unexpected: Stage Two of Passport Control, which I'd fondly imagined was done and finished. A tubby little man rushed out of the shack and said, 'Fill in the form, I go now for my breakfast.' He disappeared around the corner, then reappeared on a bicycle and laboriously pedalled away up a side-track and out of sight.

Three youths were sitting on a bench outside the shack. I appealed to them, '*What* form?' They grinned sympathetically, one entered the shack, there was a grinding noise – a rusted tin trunk being opened – and the youth returned with the document in question. It was unusually rational, not inquisitive about my mother's maiden name, my father's date of baptism or my grandfathers' occupations. When Tubby returned, forty minutes later, I had been informed that the CIA introduced AIDS into Africa so that their compatriots could eventually occupy the depopulated continent – needed because their own was becoming overpopulated.

In the shack I presented my passport and form rather ingratiatingly, hoping Tubby would also be lenient about those two days. He didn't even glance at the visa, he was too riveted by my journey and in his excitement misapplied an 'Entry' stamp while questioning me about Kenya. Were they going to have a civil war? Was Moi as bad as Amin only more clever? Why was I interested in Africa? How could anyone earn a living by writing books? Did I sell mine from a duka in a city? Who read them? Why did they read them? What university paid me to write them? Would I please send him copies of each one; he had an army brother stationed in Karamoja who liked reading books and would be pleased to have them. Briefly I considered asking for an 'Exit' stamp, then decided to leave well enough alone.

I almost overlooked Layer Four, Customs and Currency Control, in a small round hut where a long notice above a wicker desk gave awful warnings about CURRENCY REGULATIONS (1987). Logically, this is where my panniers should have been unpacked. A languid young man in a purple and green track suit blinked on seeing Lear and me, then said 'Yes?'

'You want to look at my luggage?'

He glanced superciliously at Lear. 'No.'

143

'My currency exchange documents?' I suggested, eager to display my law-abiding persona.

He blinked again and said, 'Those are not important.'

I moved on to Layer Five which was Security – a tall young army officer lounging in a wall-less thatch-shelter like a market stall. Severely he demanded, 'You have a camera?'

I confessed.

'On the border it is forbidden to photograph, this is a sensitive area.'

'Of course,' I murmured understandingly, my eyes straying to the tranquil bush, innocent of anything remotely 'sensitive' – such as a telegraph pole.

Then bait was cast. 'In Kampala,' observed the young officer, 'you can get a permit to photograph here. Why did you not ask?' When I involuntarily smiled at this naïvety he looked annoyed, hesitated, then decided I wasn't worth another cast.

Beyond no man's land the Tanzanian border-post stood back a little from the road – not scattered mud huts but one long shed-like edifice, its grim grey concrete preaching Socialism. There seemed to be no one around and I was tempted to pedal on. Then a Masaka-registered matatu appeared, returning from Bukoba and insanely overloaded with jerry-cans, sacks, cartons and passengers: none black, all fawn with dried mud. Their haggard faces puzzled me until I, too, had experienced those fifty miles.

The matatu's engine activated officialdom and its passengers were processed first. Momentarily that irritated me: *I* was at the head of the queue. Then I thought, 'What a stupid *mzungu* reaction! My entry is more complicated than their exits, it makes sense to postpone me.' Evidently everyone knew everyone else; the Customs officers did nothing, the Passport officers were speedy, quite soon the matatu was on its way. These bureaucrats were brisker and less ebullient than their Ugandan colleagues but equally friendly. The form-filling, however, was more arduous; my ability to support myself had to be proved and passport details recorded thrice, in different offices. Yet within forty minutes I was jolting south, between small shambas of stunted matoke surrounding the minute, distinctive straw huts of newly arrived, timid-looking Rwanda refugees; their dwellings were scattered on both sides of this border, wherever they could find free space to grow food. I assured myself that the surface couldn't possibly be like *this* all the way to Bukoba. And it wasn't; it got very much worse. The war is rightly blamed; nothing less than tanks could have so mangled it, gouging out knee-deep crater-lakes that extended right across the track. Given such a surface, cyclists cannot afford to admire the landscape; one's eyes must be kept fixed on the few yards ahead – or else. So I admired only when I stopped.

The first stop was for elevenses, on a high pine-clad hill. Far below, beyond a matoke slope, lay a boundless savannah plain, golden brown, uninhabited and apparently trackless. Only thirty years ago many elephant herds roamed here. In Bukoba I was told, 'The elephants have moved on.' That's one way of putting it. They were in fact slaughtered, as perks, when politics concentrated the Tanzanian army in their territory.

By noon blue-black clouds were massing to the east, over Lake Victoria. An hour later they delivered as I reached my first Tanzanian village, marred by derelict concrete farm buildings – monuments to Nyerere's ill-conceived collectivisation programme. The place seemed deserted. Under a giant pine Lear and I shared Joy's shower-curtain while thunder shook the world and from the slope beside me large pebbles were swept on to the track by the force of the deluge. This pine marked the entrance to a colonial-looking hospital and medicine-less dispensary. As the rain eased off a nurse in starched white uniform and trim red cap came trotting towards the hospital. Her astonishment on seeing me was comical. There was no doctor nearer than Bukoba, she told me, and all her twenty-four patients had AIDS; no treatment being available for other diseases meant no competition for hospital beds. This epidemic came from God who must have some good reason for punishing people. She didn't believe in 'unnatural' condoms; she thought men should pray more and then they wouldn't need so many women. Tanzania's Kagera district is no less AIDS-stricken than Rakai but has attracted little international attention; it is not so accessible to journalists and TV teams with limited time to spend on their 'AIDS story'.

It was still raining lightly when I continued through an area of flat unpeopled bush, the track now so narrow that elephant grass, bowing from banks on either side, met in the middle and tickled my face as I splashed along. Then came the broad brown Kagera river,

145

its rickety plank bridge guarded (against whom?) by a bored young soldier who mumbled something about this bridge being 'temporary'. Fragments of its more solid predecessor lay in the water. The Ugandan war cost Tanzania some $500 million and no other country contributed to this expensive ousting of Idi Amin. Thus there is nothing left over for bridge-building.

Speke did not exaggerate this region's beauty. I stopped quite often, to give my shaken frame a rest and gaze at miles of burnished savannah, running to the base of long mountains with grotesque rocky outcrops, and compact shambas in deep fertile rifts, and sweeps of ancient woodland – tall evergreen trees that Speke might have looked upon, united by ropes of flowering creeper. On some slopes the coffee, sugar-cane and matoke were ominously weed-strangled. The poverty of the few desolate villages was starker than anything seen in Kenya or Uganda, or anything reported from hereabouts by Speke in 1861. At intervals, all the way from the border, low electricity pylons could be seen away in the distance – not wired up, many lying on their sides, evidently another ambitious project fallen on evil days.

Beyond the Kagera river bigger villages and occasional vehicles appeared, the latter unable to achieve more than walking speed. Here pedal-power gave me the unique experience of overtaking a jeep and two pick-ups. Between Mutukula and Bukoba there is not one yard of smooth surface. Watching cyclists ahead of me, bouncing along comparatively comfortably on their heavy, well-sprung Indian or Chinese saddles, I reflected that for African journeys mountain-bikes should be similarly equipped; the 'lightness' fetish can be taken too far.

Bukoba lies on the shore of Lake Victoria below a high, precipitous mountain which almost defeated me. The gradient was inhuman and underfoot were sheets of raw rock scattered with loose gravel that caused Lear to skid repeatedly as I pushed him up. For several miles the climb continued from ridge to ridge of this mighty barrier, with a few short descents too rough to be cycled. In deep dim ravines below the track frogs were being raucous – the loudest frog chorus I have ever heard. As sunset approached I thought, 'This is ridiculous, you don't have to get to Bukoba, you can stop *here*' – and so I could have, there were many shambas around. But the chemistry of exhaustion was working: at a certain point one is too tired to be rational. The day's goal was 'Bukoba' – only seventy-five miles from Kyotera – and come hell or high water that goal was going to be achieved.

In the brief equatorial dusk I dragged Lear on to the ridge-top. In darkness I descended at reckless speed, uncharacteristic recklessness being another symptom of exhaustion. Within matoke plantations tiny supper-fires glimmered beside hut doors. On the map Bukoba is a city and I looked for urban lights. There weren't any. I had been encouraging myself with thoughts of a long descent but it wasn't like that; the track soon began to switchback through black hilliness – then a half-moon rose, only to be quenched by a wedge of cloud. Here a mysterious convoy of lorries came very slowly towards me: six lorries, seemingly on their way to Uganda. Next day I discovered these were coffee-smugglers doing a regular run. Surely coals to Newcastle? But for some esoteric economic reason their journey – even *that* journey – would be worthwhile. (Speke noted the Bahaya tribe's flourishing trade in coffee, a crop often wrongly assumed to have been introduced by Europeans.)

At 8.15 I arrived in what might loosely be described as suburban Bukoba, a row of still active market stalls on a wide ledge, each lit by oil wicks flickering under straw roofs amidst paltry piles of tomatoes, onions, bananas, limes. The smell was of dust and pombe and kebabs (half fat, half offal) spitting on grills. My mental world had long since narrowed to one consideration: beer. Below the track, behind the stalls, a big shack lit by a kerosene lamp emitted loud argumentative sounds suggesting the availability of alcohol. While pushing Lear down the slope I was noticed and a sudden silence spread over the market – all cheerful chat on my arrival. On an outside bench I collapsed, feeling a puerile glow of triumph – day's goal achieved!

At once Adam, the gentle, elderly bar-owner, took me under his wing. Although shabbily dressed and barefooted he was rich; his twenty acres produced matoke and pineapples, his wife had produced thirteen daughters and three sons – 'All alive!' boasted Adam. Mrs Adam was summoned to meet me; she spoke no English but was shyly welcoming. The level dusty area in front of the shack swarmed with toddler grandchildren to whom Adam seemed devoted though he couldn't remember their names.

That was a weird interlude, my first 'social occasion' in Tanzania, shrouded in darkness with gaunt ragged people edging towards the *mzungu* – tentatively and in silence, not crowding around vociferously like the Ugandans. Quickly I lowered three beers (flat and sour but I wasn't in a discriminatory mood) and then came back to life. When the usual questions had been asked Adam said thoughtfully, 'This is very interesting, to write books about the countries you travel in. It is good for us to know about each other. Big problems happen when people make mistakes about other people, because they know not about them.' Adam then insisted on my sharing with him a glass of throat-flaying banana-spirit.

Two teenage sons were ordered to escort me to the nearest suitable lodging; Adam guaranteed that there I would be 'safe and well-treated'. As we walked up the track by moonlight one boy asked, 'Why do you not stay with your grandchildren, to help them? Why do you run around the world when you are old?'

Cheered by beer and inspired by moonlight I quoted in reply:

> 'You are old, Father William', the young man said,
> 'And your hair has become very white;
> And yet you incessantly stand on your head –
> Do you think, at your age, it is right?'

There was an uneasy silence.

The boys hauled Lear up a steep muddy slope to the Calypso Lodge, standing dark and silent on its hillside. Then they vanished, leaving me in the large square moonlit patio of a standard 'Africa hotel' – so handy for cyclists, allowing machines to be wheeled into rooms. A shout brought an agreeable soft-spoken young man to my side; he made friendly noises in Swahili while showing me into a cell. The door was half off its hinges and unlockable, the window's wire mesh badly torn; the bed sagged like a hammock, neither food nor washing water was available. Then a clinking sound drew my attention to a shadowy corner of the patio where three men sat at a small table drinking, I hoped, beer. A quick nightcap was indicated in lieu of supper; I joined them and it became a multiple nightcap.

Dr Kolimba was elderly, Dr Nyoka not long qualified. Their companion, a Swahili-speaking architect, had come from Mwanza to seek advice on sites for new rural health-centres in the Bukoba area. Both doctors doubted if these buildings would ever get off the drawing-board where they had been congealing for five years, as a direct result of the IMF-imposed Structural Adjustment Programme to which Tanzania reluctantly acquiesced in 1986. The SAP requires debtor nations to cut their spending (never high) on health-care, education and other social services. According to Dr Kolimba, whose English was fluent, the cost of one AIDS test in Tanzania now exceeds the state's annual expenditure on health for one citizen. Dr Nyoka added that by December 1991 even the World Bank and IMF gurus had admitted that the SAP was not working, or likely to work; no country's debt had been reduced. But every country's poorest citizens were suffering extra hardships.

In Kagera district AIDS is now the main cause of deaths in hospitals. The doctors wished more AIDS patients could be hospital-ised because of a frightening rise in the incidence of TB. Throughout Africa, this is among the commonest direct causes of AIDS deaths and in crowded huts the infection spreads fast to HIV-free relatives. Apart from AIDS, said Dr Kolimba, malaria and other water-related diseases were resurgent, even where they had become rare, cut-backs having led to deteriorating sanitation systems. And in the Muhimbili Medical Centre – Tanzania's leading university train-ing hospital, where reliable statistics are kept – shortages of essential drugs and blood had sent the maternal mortality rate soaring. So many women are severely anaemic that post-natal transfusions are frequently needed – another factor putting women at greater risk of HIV infection than men. But in recent years blood supplies have been curtailed, both by lack of transport and the number of HIV + donors. A high percentage of mothers, suffering anyway from over-work, underfeeding and too many pregnancies, develop complica-tions not often heard of nowadays in the West.

Both doctors shared the general scepticism about those African AIDS statistics so confidently announced by the World Health Organisation. All African statistics are suspect and those more than most. Only in certain situations, like the screening of donated blood and the testing of pregnant women in chosen 'sentinel' towns, can the figures be taken seriously. However, the screening of blood (almost always donated by a close relative) was also being hampered by lack of funds. Many healthy people anxiously seeking a test have to be turned away; the limited supply of test-kits must be reserved for screening, or to confirm that patients with significant symptoms are HIV + . The countrywide lack of laboratories prevents most

149

AIDS infections, among HIV+s, from being diagnosed – and even prosperous prostitutes can no longer afford to have their STDs treated. 'From a dozen points of view,' said Dr Kolimba, 'poverty makes it impossible to cope with AIDS in Africa. But we go on trying.'

Dr Nyoka saw a need for many more Western counsellors to help HIV+s adjust to the verdict and live constructively with the threat. His older colleague disagreed; Western counsellors were worse than useless, what Tanzania needed was a TASO. (The AIDS Support Organization, founded in Uganda in 1987 by Noerine Kaleeba, herself an AIDS widow, combines counselling techniques learned in Britain, where her husband died, with the cultural – or spiritual – resources provided by traditional African society. Its emphasis is on Africans learning to cope with the crisis in their own way.)

I applauded Dr Nyoka's next suggestion. 'America looks now for a new enemy, why not have AIDS for that enemy? Why not put all weapons research money into AIDS research? And into helping us with screening and testing and giving soothing medicines to the dying?'

The architect, for whom Dr Kolimba was translating, asserted that could never happen. He was bitterly pessimistic, expecting AIDS research funding to be cut as the West learns how to deal with the virus and comes to see it as a major threat only to expendable others. Drug companies, he was certain, would not continue expensive research if the main market for the end-product lay in the world's poorest countries.

Before this unjolly party broke up, Dr Kolimba invited me to visit his hospital next day. It stood on a hilltop above the Calypso Lodge and had three syringes for 300 patients. A recently built mud-brick annex for AIDS orphans might interest me. Those infants were only being housed pro tem; another solution would somehow have to be found . . . While expressing gratitude for this invitation I knew I would shirk accepting it. My resistance to the sufferings of AIDS patients was decreasing – a curious reversal of the normal emotional pattern.

Trebly painful was my first Tanzanian dawn. That multiple nightcap generated the sort of wish-I-were-dead hangover I thought I'd grown out of; an empty stomach must have exacerbated overindulgence. Then there were my dully aching bones; those fifty malign miles had left me sore all over. Finally, my body was a measled mass of itchy bites – a result of that torn insect-screen. In addition, hunger audibly gnawed at my vitals and I had squandered on beer the small sum changed at the border. Then I felt guilty about feeling self-pity about feeling hungry when thousands of Africans were at that very moment dying of starvation. I was, in short, a mess.

Happily the staff grasped my predicament, though none spoke English, and granted me four cups of weak tea on account: there was still no food in the restaurant. Then I tottered out to find a bank, shrinking from the dazzle of the rising sun.

On the previous evening I had not, after all, reached my goal. Bukoba proper lay two miles away at the foot of the mountain with Lake Victoria beyond, all silver and still. The town is overlooked by colonial remnants on well-wooded ridges separated by cultivated valleys – deep green valleys, in which women do the family washing beside racing muddy streams.

At 7.30 pedestrians were thronging down the battered remains of a tarmac road, past shambas, dukas, closed hotelis and roadside women traders desperate to sell their produce. Cyclists were far fewer than in Uganda and the blatant poverty shocked me. Why such poverty, where hundreds were on their way to work in government offices, banks, schools, markets, factories? Evidently my route was taking me down the scale. Uganda had seemed much poorer than Kenya, Tanzania seemed incomparably poorer than Uganda. But then, entering Tanzania via Bukoba was perhaps like entering a house through the back door and first seeing the neglected scullery. Surely other towns must be less impoverished . . . ? Well, yes – but only marginally so.

Once upon a time things were different. Several large mosques, temples and churches bespoke wealthy worshippers. An enormous filthy covered market, reeking of rotten fish and neglected latrines, offered few goods but proved past prosperity. Two- or three-storeyed colonnaded shops-cum-dwellings, with fine wrought-iron balconies and Asian family names proudly moulded on plaster façades, lined wide streets now almost impassable to wheeled traffic. Many unemployed young men loitered about looking hungry and, like jobless youths everywhere, exuded the musk of latent aggression.

151

Amin's planes bombed Bukoba in 1978 but fourteen years later, in a town so beat-up, it was hard to distinguish between bomb damage and economic collapse. At least half the shops and merchants' residences have been boarded up and abandoned; Asians still run the other half but trading is limited – I couldn't find a pair of shoes. Pale-faced, delicately featured, large-eyed children – dressed as though for a party – gazed down from their balconies or walked decorously beside grown-ups along the dusty streets. I also noticed an unusual number of mixed-race young adults, allegedly the consequence of failing businesses during the Nyerere era. Then the traditional Asian aloofness became impractical and the unthinkable had to happen – marriage into Black families whose political affiliations allowed them to thrive when all around was an economic wasteland. The Asians, too, speak Swahili rather than English, which illogically surprised me; they have, after all, been settled in Tanzania for three or four generations.

While waiting for the bank to open I wandered down to the nearby shore and birdwatched, not very successfully, through shaky binoculars. Then I sat on the edge of the beach, in already hot sun, talking to three amiable characters who saw the Kagera district as 'doomed like with a plague in the Bible – only God can save us!'

This passing of the buck to God had come to irritate me more than a little and being anyway in a filthy temper, for reasons specified above, I said so. 'When people have been educated about AIDS each *individual* can save him or herself from the virus. It's not God's decision.' My companions, all men in the 35–40 age-group, looked awkwardly away. Possibly one or more was, or soon would be, infected, given the scale of the local epidemic. Were this a matter of personal choice – not God's business – they would have to admit to being responsible for their own fate. Afterwards I reprimanded myself for having lapsed yet again into cultural imperialism; but, like the missionaries, I meant well. Scratch any White, I thought gloomily, and you find a cultural imperialist. And to think that this journey had been planned as a therapeutic exercise!

The Forex desk in Bukoba's bank does not attract a queue yet a sullen young clerk took one hour and twenty minutes to change my sterling notes. Tanzania's banking system is surreal. Western banks breed a welter of profiteering bureaucrats whose every devious move costs the customer some hidden charge; but someone (not anyone

I want to know) *gains*. The Tanzanian system has been devised by maniacs to obstruct, confuse, enrage and frustrate without making any profit for anyone. Unlike the Western-owned banks in Kenya and Uganda, they deduct no percentage for charges and 'postage'. (Postage is an infamous con-trick, as though the individual's few sterling notes had to be sent to the City of London in a registered packet for which the customer must, naturally, pay.)

In an excellent Gujerati café I wolfed a three-egg omelette, four chapattis, two liver kebabs, a kilo of chips and five cups of cardamom tea. The sad-looking man sitting opposite me exclaimed, 'You are too hungry! From where you come?' He taught in a primary school eight miles away, on that mountain which almost defeated me. 'In my village you get not many strangers to bring disease. But from our 420 pupils 25 family is orphans. That is 174 children from 420. Can you help us?'

I said I could only help with advice. He should teach his pupils about AIDS in detail. They should know it is not like malaria, cholera, measles, that the virus is easily avoided if they choose to avoid it.

'Not possible!' lamented the teacher. 'For me, *impossible* to tell my pupils all this! You are right, but if I say all this they think I say the dead parents were bad people!'

This Kagera district was a favourite vineyard of the early missionaries. Both the German Protestant Bethel Mission and the Roman Catholic Benedictines arrived in 1910. The Germans were eager to create separate Christian villages, heedless of the grim lesson taught by Uganda's sectarian wars. They built that huge covered market and started a trade mission, hoping to deter Godless Arabs and Asians from moving in – a hope soon dashed. When Tanganyika became a British mandated territory the CMS took over, abandoned the trading strategy and concentrated on (inappropriate) education, enthusiastically supported by the first British District Commissioner, one Mr Baines, who happened to be an evangelical Anglican. Characteristically, the Roman Catholics rejected a Protestant suggestion that Tanganyika should be divided into 'spheres of influence'. Thus the Africans were exposed, for half a century, to the unedifying spectacle of White Christians at each other's theological throats on a daily basis.

Now Bukoba boasts two 1960s cathedrals, Protestant and

Catholic. The former is ugly in a stereotypical '60s way, a see-how-clever-I-am construction, all pretentious angles and curves signifying nothing: it might as easily be a factory, a corporation head office or part of Leeds University. The Catholic effort is something else; I photographed it lest that memory might come to seem, in the future, no more than a hallucination induced by too much bad beer. The photograph lies beside me now, proving that I did see what I thought I saw. Truly there is something diseased about this agglomeration of pigeon-holed concrete walls, decorated by the rains – via leaking gutters – with black, brown and green stripes. The exterior motorway-type pillars are set with plastic tiles, now falling off – and not before time. Little squares and big sheets of pseudo stained glass form a large part of the façade. The whole is surmounted by a metal cross on a metal tripod on a metal globe sprouting four metal objects that might have fallen off a space-craft. Further novelties are available within. The floor slopes steeply down to an altar modelled on a conveyor-belt and the Stations of the Cross appear to have been executed in plasticine by very young untalented children. I sat in a plastic and aluminium pew for half an hour of a Holy Week ceremony conducted by an obese bishop so rotund in his golden robe you felt he would roll away if dropped on his side. He was assisted by twenty priests, in glistening brocade chasubles, and four censer-swinging youths. The congregation was far outnumbered by the pigeons busily flying in and out, shitting on all and sundry. If you will design a cathedral like a grossly magnified dove-cote, what else is to be expected? Later I found that local Catholics are almost deliriously proud of this edifice. But no one could tell me who the architect was, where he came from or went to – I fear the poor fellow may have ended up in a psychiatric ward. How much did the Christian Churches spend on their prestige competition (when one built the other had to) during a decade that saw the local schools and hospitals declining fast?

Bukoba's glory is its lake shore, a golden sandy crescent curving for miles around the wide bay below a vividly green embankment. This sort of place is by now, in most parts of the world, tourist-sodden. I, however, had it to myself as I walked towards the Customs Office. By then the seasonal forenoon wind had risen and white waves frisked on the deep blue water. A few miles off-shore lay a scrubby islet shaped, disconcertingly, like a nuclear submarine –

and inhabited, my binoculars revealed. (Post-breakfast, these no longer shook.) Ahead of me a long wooded promontory sheltered Bukoba's important port. There is no road – not even what Tanzanians call a road – to Mwanza; all traffic must go by water and Tanzanian Railways runs a speedy, efficient ferry service. Now I could see the *Victoria*, spick and span, painted dazzling white. She would sail at 9 p.m. and dock at 6 a.m.; a nine-hour non-stop journey, as compared to the three hours from Britain to Ireland, which helps get Lake Victoria in perspective. At the Customs Office I booked a berth in a six-berth second-class cabin (£4) and bought Lear's ticket (80p). And there I met Mumfi, booking a ticket for the first stage of her return journey to the UK a week hence.

During the hot noon hours I sat with Mumfi on the wide veranda of the Lakeside Hotel, a spacious, solid, very British colonial relic. The bwanas would weep to see that the shore directly below the veranda is now defiled by the sprawl of a rectangular, Marxist-grey café, shop and club – all long since closed.

Mumfi was strikingly beautiful but her disturbed state had been obvious when we met. She talked very fast, never looking directly at me. Her mother had been a Gujerati Muslim, born in Bukoba like her parents before her and brought up in her own wealthy community – in spirit as strictly segregated from the Africans as any Afrikaner. When she eloped, aged 17, with a Bahaya secondary school teacher her family and the entire community rejected her. 'Yet my father was a fine man, kind, honest, intelligent. They had a good marriage, my mother didn't mind becoming a Catholic, they were religious parents who gave me a strict training. Their big problem was only *one* child! When my mother's father died there was a sort of reconciliation with the rest of the family. My mother took me to see them once or twice a year but they were always cold, making me feel inferior, never treating me the same as my nice pale-skinned cousins. I remember being 7 or 8 and walking back from their home in a rage. I was still at school when my mother died – cerebral malaria – I missed her so much! Soon I married Jim, from my father's tribe – he has a good job in the bank. I always wanted to study in England, my mother brought me up to love the English, she said they had no race prejudices. Four years ago I got there, to do computer studies. My father's sister lives next door, she looks after Jim and the kids. Now she's lost one son and another is dying,

155

at home. That's why I came back two months ago, to comfort her. In Croydon I'd decided to stay here, to be with the kids, but this AIDS frightens me too much. I told Jim I wouldn't sleep with him unless he had the test. He refused. He's scared, he sweats at the thought – so he has a reason to be scared, maybe many reasons!'

Mumfi hadn't realised, when she returned, how swiftly AIDS had spread during her absence. I met no other African so openly emotionally upset by the epidemic, and not only because of its impact on her own family. She asked, her eyes wide with horror, 'You know in Kagera district there are more than 3,000 AIDS orphans in institutions?' I did know; Dr Kolimba had told me. I wondered then what the full story was; Mumfi seemed one of those unfortunates tossed by the tide of history on to a rocky shore. Glimpsing factual fragments of other people's lives – when they went where, to do what – can be tantalising if the real 'whys' remain hidden.

Suddenly Mumfi invited me to her home, quite a rare event in Africa. 'I want you to talk to my daughter about AIDS, to back up all I've said. She's 14 but very grown-up – too grown-up! My son should listen, too. He's only 9 but that's when we have to put them on full alert. It's only stupid to pretend they're innocents, at no risk. In Bernadette's school some girls say parents invented this AIDS scare to control kids. They say it's not a virus but witchcraft and how you live has nothing to do with it. Please talk to them in a *scientific* way, explain like I have it's a disease in the West, too, where there's no witchcraft. They may listen to you!'

Mumfi lived down a long, dusty, tree-shaded road not far from the lake shore. The two-roomed concrete hovel – the centre one of three – was entered through a communal yard of extreme squalor bounded by a few matoke plants. Inside all was clean and neat but very cramped. The spectacularly beautiful tortoiseshell cat reclining on a small settee graciously permitted me to stroke him but didn't move to give the visitor more space – a thoroughly spoiled cat, I know the symptoms. In each corner stood stacks of video and hi-fi equipment and thousands of tapes. Tanzania is one of those few blessed lands still without television, or it was then – perhaps by now it has been infected. Family photographs and mass-produced pious pictures (made in Italy: to be found in Catholic homes on every continent) covered the walls. Most conspicuous was an elaborately framed 'Special Papal Blessing' given to Mumfi *personally* by His Holiness John Paul II on the occasion of his visit to Uganda and allegedly signed by the Pope. What sort of racket is this?

Mumfi made coffee while I talked with her stricken aunt. It was of course instant coffee, made in Bukoba and the best such I have ever tasted. Then Bernadette came in, greeted me rather brusquely, said she had to go to a school drama rehearsal and disappeared.

Mumfi was furious. 'I told her I wanted her to listen to you, she is rude!'

Bernadette looked 18 – tall, well-developed, dressed in tight slacks and a low-cut blouse, obviously conscious of being nubile. No wonder her mother was worried. According to Tanzania's Ministry of Health, blood-donor tests had recently revealed a devastating rise in the HIV + rate among 15 to 19-year-olds; and the girls showed an even higher rate of infection than the boys. In Bukoba (population 15,000) the percentage of HIV + women attending ante-natal clinics had risen from 20 per cent to 24 per cent during the previous eighteen months.

Mumfi insisted on both children being involved in the care of their dying cousin in the next-door shack. 'Seeing and smelling and feeling is better than listening to grown-ups' warnings. My kids always loved those older cousins, always admired them because they were champion athletes at school – see those photos of them getting prizes. Last evening I gave Bernadette and another girl cousin one big heavy lecture. My mum used to lecture me about sin and sex but this is different – this is life and death. I was naughty when I was their age and I admit that to them – I don't want to pretend, I'm not preaching like in church. I told them I'm still a young woman of 34 but I don't need sex so much I'd risk sleeping with my husband now he won't have the test. My aunt is upset when I talk so straight but she should know the time for being modest is over.'

The 9-year-old – plump, huge-eyed, copper-skinned – was listening impassively, sitting on the floor leaning against his mother's legs. It baffled me that she should even consider leaving her two children again for the sake of computer studies (if such it was) in England.

I returned to the Calypso Lodge, to collect Lear, by a different route, through old graveyards surrounded by tall pines. The Muslim graveyard was all neatly raked gravel and austere white

157

tombs. Its grassy Christian neighbour was being extended, like many African cemeteries, beyond the original boundary; a man digging out the hedge paused to stare as I counted twenty-seven fresh graves. The dead Christians of past generations were a cosmopolitan lot: mostly Indians and Goans, the rest British, Greek, Lebanese – all in their own segregated plots.

Back on the road, I heard heartrending screams of pain and fear. A tiny boy was being ignored by his mother – tending her stall – as he writhed on the high step of an empty duka, too afraid to get down by himself. He had been bitten by something; his agonised, terrorised shrieks conveyed that as he grabbed frantically at his buttocks. An even tinier girl slowly toddled over and extended a hand of sympathy but was rejected; the boy's eyes were fixed on his mother as he roared with pain – a sound that seemed too large to be coming from such a small body. I timed the incident; after six minutes Mama turned, strode over to her son, picked up a slim switch and repeatedly struck him – hard. Then she pulled him off the step and left him lying shuddering in the dust, shocked into silence, with the tiny girl gazing down at him, solemn and puzzled. Despite the decibels, no other passer-by thought this scene noteworthy.

Back at the port, awaiting embarkation hour, I wrote in my journal:

First impressions: the Tanzanians (the few so far encountered) seem more reserved and tougher, in the best sense, than the Ugandans. On one level it's daft to refer to 'Ugandans' and 'Tanzanians'; on both sides of this border they're culturally the same. Yet they've been set in quite different colonial and post-colonial moulds. My arrival on a scene causes no excitement here, though that catastrophic track from Mutukula is rarely used by non-locals, never mind *mzungu* cyclists. No inquisitive children came streaming from the shambas, no fellow-cyclist pedalled alongside for miles asking friendly questions, no villager beckoned me to stop for a cup of tea or mug of maize gruel. Of course the language barrier is higher here; Swahili, not English, is the non-tribal language. Yet that doesn't sufficiently account for the difference. It's a difference of attitude, a polite detachment from *mzungus*, no doubt bred by Nyerere's gospel of self-reliance. The greetings are courteous but delivered gravely, not with the jolly smiling outgoingness so common in Uganda. I have to admit this Tanzanian reserve is rather a relief at present. Being expected to 'explain oneself', slowly and clearly, umpteen times a day, becomes a bit much.

Nyerere's 'agrarian socialism' was a brave and honest effort to breed Utopia by crossing rural Africa's social traditions with Christian ethics. But then he inclined towards a sort of African Fabianism, a slippery slope leading to much cruel Ceausescu-type social engineering. Even by African standards his well-meant revolution brought about an economic mega-disaster. But maybe it also, paradoxically, to some extent restored Black self-respect, with its emphasis on the value of African social traditions and their relevance for the future. Yet his determination to make *Tanzanians* out of the speakers of eighty separate languages must have done more to kill the local tribal traditions of the remoter areas than either the German or British administrators and missionaries.

Looking back: I feel the British, for better or worse, got a very firm grip on the fertile areas of Uganda that they wished to develop and were genuinely appreciated by the more advanced tribes for bringing 'civilisation'. In Tanganyika, apart from the Southern Highlands and the low-key continuation of Kenya's White Highlands around Kilimanjaro, they didn't get so involved. Throughout most of this vast territory – four times larger than Uganda, waterless, tsetse-fly-infested, sparsely inhabited – there was nothing profitable to involve them. Thus their influence was more political than psychological, which made easier (but not easy enough) poor Nyerere's attempt to defend his country from neo-colonialism.

At sunset I embarked, locked Lear to a strut by my cabin door and for two hours leant on the rail, watching the hectic and strenuous loading of the *Victoria*. This apparently chaotic process was in fact quite well organised; everyone knew when to take what where. Out of pitch darkness into the boat's lights (the only illumination) came a whirlpool of strong colours: shirts and long skirts in reds, blues, yellows and greens, gaudy many-hued bodices and striped headscarves. All passengers over the age of 5 carried prodigious head-loads: sacks of coffee beans, coops of hens and ducks, nylon sacks of charcoal, carrier bags of garments, rolled blankets, baskets of sweet potatoes, crates of beer, airline bags, cartons of Bukoba's justly celebrated instant coffee, bulging smart suitcases – those last the trickiest load, because slippy, yet often with a huge bundle balanced on top. There was even the occasional rucksack, no doubt bought from some destitute backpacker, with long straps hanging over the owner's face; most Africans are baffled by our preference for loading the back.

A crane received countless loads of 'orange' soda, also made in Bukoba, from a badly battered truck. Most of Tanzania's trucks and buses – Mumfi alleged – had been condemned in Uganda as 'unfit for use' and sold off cheap. The Tanzanians naturally enough think these should have been donated, as some meagre reparation for the $500 million spent on Obote's war. It fascinated me to watch the loaded crane platform very slowly swaying up, and up, and up – the orange sodas glinting in the blackness like some fabulous horde of gold. Sodas and matoke – the latter arriving on a succession of tractor-trailers – formed the main cargo. Around Mwanza the lush matoke-growing world ends and sembe (maize flour) becomes the staple food. This was a vivid, noisy, energetic scene, but not a jolly one. There were few smiling faces among these hungry, stressed, exhausted people, men, women and children all struggling with too-heavy loads, a profusion of toddlers getting in the way and being abused, only the babies on backs content as usual.

In my clean and comfortable cabin the other five berths were occupied by a group of friends, luscious teenage girls going to seek their fortunes in, they hoped, Mombasa – 'where is many tourists, Bukoba have none'. For generations Bukoba's main exports have been prostitutes and coffee, in that order. The Bahaya women, I was told all over East and Central Africa, are famous for their beauty and amatory skills and have now become popular scapegoats, castigated for spreading AIDS – as though all African men would live chastely if not lured by Bahaya sirens. In the 1940s, as Elspeth Huxley has recorded, Kagera's chiefs voted money from the 'native treasury' for the founding of a girls' school to provide the region's young ladies with 'other interests'. The scheme failed, as did a chiefs' proposal to compel every woman boarding the steamer at Bukoba to show a travel permit from her own chief. The British

160

Chief Secretary disapproved of this attempt to 'infringe the liberty of the subject'. As Elspeth Huxley dryly noted, 'This answer puzzled and disappointed the chiefs. The liberty of the female subject to go where she pleases is not a concept familiar to African men.'

In Kyotera a White fellow-guest, long involved in AIDS work elsewhere, had questioned the effectiveness of European-devised educational programmes. 'We need to remember', he said, 'that in Africa sex is a *commodity*. Many girls who want what they can't afford – clothes, cosmetics, a hair-do – will earn the money as sex-workers and genuinely not feel ashamed. And rich men like to show their money by buying a variety of girls – again, as a *commodity*. It's another sort of mind-set about sex.' This expatriate opined that if Africans persist in their happy-go-fucky lifestyle the rest of the world will soon lose sympathy and withdraw all AIDS support groups. I commented that this would not displease some of the Africans I'd met on my way. Nor can the West afford to be censorious; we too use sex as a commodity, in more convoluted but no less degrading ways – and without extenuating circumstances.

After a calm voyage, conducive to sound sleep, we docked at 6 a.m. precisely and disembarked in darkness. The area around the ferry-berth had none of the expected stalls selling snacks or tea and coffee, yet hundreds of passengers were milling about, all certainly yearning for sustenance. This seemed significant. Even at 3 a.m., in any Asian or South American country I know (or in Madagascar), these captive customers would be well catered for by scores of entrepreneurs.

As I pushed Lear up Nyerere Road (the surface was too rough to cycle by lamplight) the dissolving darkness exposed numerous crutches pathetically protruding from under sheets of plastic or sacking. Then the cripples beneath the colonnades began to dismantle their 'privacy screens' and prepare to face another day of hunger, humiliation and hopelessness.

Near the bus station other hundreds of passengers were milling but still I could find no sustenance, until I noticed a small bedraggled man squatting in the middle of the road fanning a minute tin of charcoal with a sheet of cardboard to boil a big kettle of coffee. Beside him were incongruously dainty white china coffee-cups, immersed in a large paint-tin of water. The half-dozen men patiently awaiting the magic moment of boiling welcomed me politely but with reserve. That coffee was excellent; feeling uncomfortably greedy, I drank five cups. Each customer's empty cup was rinsed in the paint-tin before re-use; luckily AIDS isn't spread through saliva.

Knowing of no reason to dally in Mwanza – African cities don't grab one – I was on the road to Shinyanga by 6.45. My heart sank when I saw – and felt – that it wasn't a road, *pace* the map, but a deeply and relentlessly corrugated track. Here the wild terrain looked bafflingly familiar; then I remembered that Speke had been inspired to sketch in this area and had accurately depicted these tall, isolated hills of rock, weirdly wind-sculpted, with greenery sprouting at odd angles from cracks in their smooth flanks and coppices of glossy vegetation in the intervening hollows. This was the last of Lake Victoria's surrounding lushness and soon I was in another world, crossing a flat fawn plain, victimised by drought, where withered maize rustled on every side, the few cattle were mere sacks of bones and only *Euphorbia candelabra* and feral sisal plants flourished. I began to feel apprehensive. Had I left the rainy season behind?

That track defeated me. In Old Shinyanga, only eight miles from the day's goal, I gave up. After eighty-five corrugated miles, plus the misery of quite heavy truck and matatu traffic suffocating me with dust, I was broken in body and spirit. As I sat drinking vile beer outside an empty-shelved duka, a barefooted youth and two tattered oldish men advanced from different directions, all looking furtive and clutching cigarette packets. They paused at a little distance, keeping apart from each other and eyeing me speculatively. When I smiled encouragingly and said, 'Jambo!' they advanced, then stopped to confer, then approached me one by one. The cigarette packets contained putative diamonds, going cheap – £5 the starting price. To me these looked like the duller sort of pebble but they may well have been genuine. One of the world's largest diamond mines was discovered nearby in 1940 by a Canadian geologist. As gambles go, a £15 investment would not have been too rash; but Tanzanian jails have an indifferent reputation. All three gazed at me with a terrible despair when I declined to trade, whereupon I broke my rule then and presented them with the money. Tanzania's poverty was getting to me. They uttered no word of thanks, just looked at me incredulously – then rushed away.

I fetched another beer and unfolded my map. In Shinyanga I could get a train to Dodoma from where, if the map were to be believed, a tarmac road led south. At that moment a train seemed a very good – in fact irresistible – idea. Then, miraculously, blond Bruce appeared on his Honda, bouncing down the street in a red penumbra of dust. He had passed me twice during the afternoon and each had wondered about the other. He was an expat with a difference, a Californian who for four years had been setting up windmill pumps in arid regions, always Honda-ing through the bush. Now he sat beside me and said, 'You gotta be mad! In this neck o' the woods you can't cycle on *motor*-roads!'

'That's the conclusion I've just reached. It's the train to Dodoma for me – I'm not in Africa on a penitential pilgrimage.'

Bruce seized the map. 'Look, see all those little paths? You can hardly see them here but on the ground they're as plain as motor-roads – and a lot smoother. And that way to Dodoma is shorter in miles. Just watch out for the big thorns – but they're so big you'll see them the day before! You don't mind camping?'

There are two good reasons why cyclists should be wary of camping in Africa. In inhabited regions a bicycle is quite likely to be stolen; in uninhabited regions there is a remote possibility that the cyclist will be stolen – and consumed. Bruce, however, assured me that neither hazard was to be greatly feared between Shinyanga and Dodoma. He was a young man after my own heart, an unfussy realist. Yes, there were a few leopards and hyenas around, but very few. In his four years of intimacy with the region he'd often had to camp out and never met one. So wouldn't it be very bad luck if I happened to meet one on a four-day trip?

I remember Bruce with gratitude.

8

Trivial Trials

Shinyanga to Iringa

During my Bruce-inspired cross-country cycle I set a personal record by not speaking for four days. (At home I often spend more than four days in solitude, but there I have a dog and three cats with whom to converse.) This unwonted silence was a probably needless precaution; I avoided the sparse population, who in general viewed me with considerable alarm and themselves never tried to communicate – Swahili, never mind English, is not much spoken hereabouts. Although I didn't consciously recall Jill's warning in relation to this area, it may have been fermenting in my unconscious. Each night I camped, though on all but one a compound was within reach, and despite Bruce's assurance I couldn't help feeling slightly neurotic about hyenas. These are notoriously partial to rubber and might eat Lear's tyres – or even chew me around the edges. Hyenas are much more of a threat to campers than any of the big cats. But of course my neuroticism was just that; monkeys constituted the only visible wildlife.

Here I lost track of my mileage, usually marked on the map, but I must have covered about ninety miles each day on these smooth dust-paths across level terrain: through gloriously variegated bush, red-gold savannah and forests ruled by giant baobabs. The occasional settlement of long, low mud huts had flat grass roofs rarely seen elsewhere. Many of the women went bare-breasted while the men wore loincloths, or nothing. Cylindrical hives hung high on many trees, even where there was no other trace of humanity; honey and beeswax are the only local cash crops, as they have been for centuries. The juvenile herdsmen all fled at my approach, treacherously abandoning their lean cattle and plump goats. This is among the least 'developed' areas of East Africa and always has been. From

164

the beginning of the nineteenth century it was controlled by Masai warriors whose reputation discouraged the Arab slavers from moving north of their established route – Bagamoya to Ujiji via Tabora (then known as Kazeh).

Only one problem arose, on the morning of the second day, when my path ended decisively at the edge of a swamp. On either side rose thickly uninviting forest; guidance would have to be sought in the hamlet of Sakamaliwa, a few miles back. I turned – and found myself face to face with an elderly man who might have illustrated Speke's *Journal*. His short tunic was of bark-cloth, he had wild shoulder-length locks decorated with leaves, he wore many copper anklets and carried a sheathed spear longer than himself and a leather shield studded around the edges with coloured beads. His unsurprised expression suggested that he had heard of my presence in the area. And of course the path only *seemed* to end there; below the black mud of the swamp lay a firm causeway of tree-trunks, doubtless visible in the dry season. My companion made no attempt to communicate verbally. Handing me his spear he took charge of Lear, then pointed to my shoes. I removed them and turned up my trousers, wondering if he would remove his anklets. He didn't. The spear was to be used as a walking-stick, an essential aid as the half-mile causeway was calf-deep in slithery mud. Being unable to estimate its width I could not possibly have negotiated it with Lear, even had I noticed its existence. At the far side my guardian angel silently retrieved his spear and, still without any change of expression, returned the way we had come. Plainly he had followed me to the swamp's edge, knowing the *mzungu* would need help. Such gestures are never forgotten.

At Kintinku, thirty-five miles north-west of Dodoma, I rejoined the motor road and found that it had not improved in my absence. A few hours later, approaching the town, another Catholic cathedral caught my eye – red brick and white stone, an interesting mongrel with Romanesque touches, Arab touches, even Georgian Dublin touches. The overall effect, if not exactly appropriate to Africa (or anywhere else), was pleasing enough in its eclectic way. A tall, elderly Tanzanian monsignor, wearing a dog-collar and black cassock, noticed me taking a photograph and with him I broke my silence. He invited me into his little study and took a bottle of Coca-Cola from a crate under the desk. I have to admit it tasted good, after four days of muddy water strongly flavoured with decayed vegetation. The cathedral, Monsignor Mgonda told me, was 'very old', built by Italians (I had guessed that) in 1967. Any building that lasts a quarter of a century is 'very old' in Africa.

The Monsignor was curious about Uganda. He had heard the people were so traumatised by AIDS they no longer reacted normally to bereavement – was this true? I replied that no casual passer-by could presume to judge whether or not reactions were 'normal'. When I added that Uganda's epidemic was not much worse than Tanzania's my host seemed both surprised and annoyed.

As anti-AIDS campaigners, most African clergymen of all denominations are reprehensibly slack but some effort was being made in Dodoma diocese. Recently, said the Monsignor, religious leaders had got together to discuss a united response to the crisis. But alas! the two-day conference ended in shambolic disunity. The Catholics fell out among themselves about whether or not the use of condoms should be promoted. The Catholics and Protestants fell out about whether or not engaged couples, one of whom was infected, should be advised to disengage. The Protestants fell out among themselves about whether or not condom use should be promoted among school-children. The Muslims fell out with the Christians about polygamy; to preach monogamy as the only solution was anti-Islamic – obviously four faithful uninfected wives are as safe as one wife. 'So this was a sad waste of time,' concluded Monsignor Mgonda. 'The Muslims got so angry they withdrew their funding for our leaflet campaign – and that's serious, they're the richest people in Dodoma area.'

Near the cathedral a forgotten campaign is echoed. At one end of a trim military cemetery lie the master-race: Captain P. J. Flytche-Hogg, aged 24; Sister D. A. Fitzhenry, aged 22; many teenagers and one poignant unnamed, 'A Victim of the Great War – Known Unto God'. Across a fifty-yard cordon sanitaire lie the unWhite, below a dignified stone monument inscribed:

God is One. His is the Victory.
In Memory of the Brave Hindus, Sikhs and Muhammadans
Who Sacrificed their lives in the Great War
For their King and their Country.

What an irony! That the purveyors of Pax Britannica should have required Hindus, Sikhs and Muhammadans to die in the wilds of

166

Africa fighting a White man's war! At the turn of the century Euro-peans wallowed in self-righteous condemnations of Black tribal war-fare, an acridly amusing reflex in view of imminent events. The Black-controlled ritualistic warfare involved a far lower percentage of casualties than the Whites' ruthless massacres.

The Chama Cha Mapinduzi party headquarters are in Dodoma and Nyerere once dreamed of moving the capital from the squalid port of Dar es Salaam to this high cool plateau in central Tan-zania – hence those many modern government buildings standing irrelevantly around the periphery. Huge name-plates on already disintegrating façades proclaim the presence within of petrified layers of bureaucracy: National Estates and Designing Corporation (NEDCO) or Small Holder Development Project for Marginal Areas (IFAD). In the town's heart (if it can be said to have one) the Chris-tian Centre of Tanzania faces the recently enlarged Islamic Centre and the very beautiful Shia Ithna-Asheri Mosque – the finest buildings I saw in Tanzania. Full marks to the Muslims for not being seduced by aberrant architectural trends. The combination of evangelical Christian and Islamic influences means that beer is scarce, available only in the archetypically colonial Railway Hotel, where Evelyn Waugh spent a night in 1959. He dismissed Dodoma in one sentence: 'A railway town, scattered, unlovely, noisy.' Thirty-three years later it remained scattered and unlovely – but subdued, not at all noisy: in fact so lacking in character and anima-tion that I looked back on beat-up Bukoba with a certain affection.

For £1.90 the Christian Centre of Tanzania provided a carpeted room with bathroom (and running water!), an untorn mosquito net neatly coiled above the soft bed and a bedside lamp with a *bulb* which shed *light* when the switch was pressed. After three nights in the bush, this extremity of comfort was not unwelcome. The canteen served cheap and nourishing meals and had food for thought above the door:

SMARTNESS IS AN ART.   BEAUTY IS GOD-GIVEN.
MAINTAIN SMARTNESS.

In the grey-blue dawn, scores of small, lean, very black men were moving towards Dodoma at a half-trot. Each carried two grass sacks of charcoal on a wooden yolk and they had been on the move for

167

hours, coming from settlements ten or twelve miles away. These Wagogos migrated to this area only recently, when the drought of the previous two years killed many of their cattle. Observing their gigantic loads and exhausted faces, I remembered the charcoal-merchant cyclists entering Kampala – and Ali's comment that only the rich own bicycles.

That first day out of Dodoma is deeply graven on my memory. The tarmac was smooth but over eighty-five miles of open country a powerful wind opposed me – the sort that necessitates pedalling *down* steep slopes. It kept the tall savannah grass flat on the ground, as though neatly combed, and cyclists with this gale behind them scarcely needed to pedal uphill. There was no moment of respite; I didn't seem to be sweating but I absorbed six litres of water without peeing until the following morning.

At noon I passed the Kongwa junction; it had taken me six non-stop hours to cover fifty miles. A dirt road leads to the scene of the tragi-comic groundnuts scheme, the prototype for the West's count-less inane African projects. This one was a disaster mainly for the British taxpayer, whose £40,000,000 (a considerable sum forty-five years ago) was never heard of again. At the time the ground-nutters – as they were prophetically known from the outset – caused havoc among the primitive cattle-owning Wagogo who had occupied this territory from time immemorial. A small, isolated, aloof tribe, they were demoralised by the importation of 30,000 workers from other tribes. Great environmental damage was also done but is now being undone by time. All aid planners should be made to compare the observations of Elspeth Huxley, who passed this way in 1947, and of Evelyn Waugh who twelve years later followed in – predictably – 'a large, new, fast and extremely comfortable Mercedes-Benz'. Elspeth Huxley saw the very start of the disaster:

> . . . between sixty and seventy men are to push down 3,000,000 acres of vegetation – bush that, I suppose, has grown here since Africa took on its present shape . . . Tanganyika distresses these up-to-date engineers. 'Not a mile of bituminous road in the whole country! Not a single mile! The roads – you can't call them roads, they're enough to make a fellow burst out cry-ing!' We looked down over the mighty rolling plain earmarked for the ground-nut invasion. The terrain was selected from the

air. It is easy to see why this was so . . . It would take a lifetime to clear the bush by hand. No one can really know what emerges from that ocean of thorns: health or sickness, fertility or desert, good soil or bad. And, most important of all, water or no water . . . That is a vital point on which too little is known . . . The ground-nutters are groping in the dark; but from the start they are consulting scientists. A soil chemist and a conservation expert from South Africa are already installed in the camp.

In 1959, Waugh recorded:

A huge clearing in the bush, 90,000 acres of grassland, is all that remains of the Kongwa groundnuts plantation . . . The scheme was conceived in an ideological haze, prematurely advertised as a specifically socialist achievement and unscrupulously defended in London when everyone in Africa knew it was indefensible . . . The aim was benevolent; the provision of margarine for the undernourished people of Great Britain. The fault was pride . . . No considerable quantity of ground-nuts was ever produced; nor was there a need for them – they were piling up in mountains in West Africa, needing only transport to make them available. The site at Kongwa had been selected for its emptiness. It was empty because it was waterless.

Much of the grassland has been maintained, carefully fenced, and is now benefiting rich ranchers; their cattle were improved by the importation into the area, following the groundnutters' failure, of 9,000 head of half-bred European cattle. Meanwhile the Wagogo continue to herd their own tiny animals in the unreconstructed bush. Admiring the baobabs dotted about this pastureland, I recalled Elspeth Huxley's comments on how difficult it was to fell them – even with the aid of bulldozers. In one poverty-stricken roadside settlement I paused to buy heavily sweetened boiling milk from a kettle balanced on a tin of charcoal. These infrequent hamlets were not relaxing places; repeatedly, drunken men shouted aggressively at the passing *mzungu*. One wonders how much long-term damage the groundnutters did by bringing so many outsiders to the area, introducing a cash economy and wrecking the Wagogos' tribal loyalties and social structures.

169

By now I felt seasonally confused; I was moving towards the southern autumn yet recent rains, the most generous since 1989, had given the landscape a springtime brightness. By the roadside, as I climbed to Gairo on its high mountain, the vivid new grass was brilliantly patterned with flowers in a glorious profusion of colours and shapes: tall clumps, orange and purple – tiny individual blossoms, pink or yellow or blue – sometimes sheets of a delicately scented white flower spreading for miles on either side of the road. During the following weeks I discovered that the rain distribution was very uneven, seeming to depend on topography; within one day's cycle I often passed from lushness to aridity and back to lushness.

Gairo is a big village – perhaps officially a town – sprawling attractively for several miles around the flanks of a grassy mountain with a distinctive twin-rock summit visible from afar. The friendly guest-house could provide no washing water because it hadn't rained for twenty-four hours. In a Gujerati restaurant I supped off a compartmented metal platter: rice, beef, greens. Although no alcohol was served in this Muslim establishment the walls were decorated with seductive Page Three girls in glorious technicolor, hanging side by side with texts from the Koran. Watching a group of laughing, gossiping women returning from the well – maybe three or four miles away – I could appreciate the argument against standpipes; these curtail the women's only form of relaxation and leave more time for harder labour. According to WHO statistics (how compiled?), African women do an average of sixteen hours work daily, their menfolk five. One tends to suspect such statistics, yet those accord with my own impressions.

I retired early; that wind had exhausted me, and nobody in Gairo spoke English.

Such dire afflictions as brucellosis (Indian style), hepatitis (Malagasy style), tooth abscesses (Cameroonian style) or broken bones (Rumanian style) put starch into my upper lip. But the common cold unwomans me. Awakening with a throbbing, inflamed throat and a stuffed nose I at once fell into a morass of self-pity and remained there for the day.

After a night of torrential rain the wind had dropped and the air was humid as I crossed the 5,000-foot pass above Gairo – where wandering torn clouds hung so low they seemed touchable. For the next forty-five mainly downhill miles dense forest lay below the road, still and dark, extending from wide valley floors to distant rock-scattered ridges and peaks. Where an earth-track leads off to Kilosa, I stopped for a cup of black tea and three nauseating maize buns, the flour adulterated with something unimaginable. Here I reluctantly started a course of antibiotics. I was beginning to wheeze; since infancy my common colds have always become full-blown bronchitis – a tiresome Achilles' heel. Happily another Concern team is based at Kilosa; Irish hospitality and cherishing were indicated.

This was a lowish, fertile, well-wooded region, the red huts seeming to grow from the red earth amidst maize and manioc shambas. I paused on a rickety wooden bridge spanning the boisterous young Wami which rises in the mountains near Gairo. By the water's edge grew masses of hibiscus: yellow and maroon, or purple-grey, or dark violet. And here too were a few extraordinary trees with round, compact crowns above soaring smooth white trunks – dazzling in the sunlight. Further on, the track was lined with pink jacaranda – its flaky grey bark is popular as an immunisation against witchcraft – and sausage-trees with their dangling sausage-shaped fruits or purple bell-shaped flowers.

Then, about two miles from the junction, Lear's back tyre went flat. I pumped, pedalled on hopefully – he went flat again. I pumped again – again he went flat. I gave up hope and walked. There are certain gifted folk who can mend punctures; I am not among them. Instead, I have a gift for attracting puncture-menders. Within ten minutes a kind fellow-cyclist had offered assistance. He was an odd young man named Saul, one short of the shilling but amiably determined to help. His lack of English didn't matter; sorting out practicalities rarely requires a common language. We agreed that water was needed, walked on for about a mile, then turned into the bush and found a huddle of semi-ruined concrete farm buildings surrounding a selection of long-dead agricultural machinery and – I couldn't believe it – a bicycle mechanic repairing someone's brakes. Two other men, tattered and rather hard-faced, stood under a mango tree queuing with their own diseased bicycles. They ignored the *mzungu*.

Lear's tyres are supposed to be virtually puncture-proof and when

Saul water-tested I saw at once that this was not a puncture but a defective seam in the tube. I hesitated. A new tube, the obvious remedy, would involve removing the back wheel. And could men who had never before seen a bicycle with any gears, never mind Lear's twenty-one-speed system, successfully perform such an operation? I decided on conventional puncture treatment. If that failed I would have to walk to Kilosa; the Concern team must surely be equipped with a talented mechanic. Tensely I watched the patching and replacement of the tyre, like an anxious mum in an operating theatre. Then, as I was reattaching the panniers, one of the silent, sullen men under the mango tree suddenly stepped forward and truculently demanded, 'Give identity papers!'

Smiling sweetly, I handed him my passport. He pretended to read it attentively, before putting it in his trouser pocket and saying, 'Is wrong visa, I keep!'

Discarding my sweet smile, I asked for his identity papers. He had none but claimed, 'In this district, I Big Man!' Maybe his filthy raggedness belied his status and he was some sort of Chama Cha Mapinduzi mini-boss; as a political party the CCM suffered grievously from the poor quality of its minor officials. I didn't like this situation. Lear and the panniers were tempting; we were miles from anywhere; the Big Man was memorably unendearing. Out of the corner of an eye I could see Saul looking frightened; but only out of a corner, this being an occasion to use my tried and trusty weapon of eye-contact. Staring fixedly at the Big Man I moved towards him slowly, with hand outstretched, and said, 'Give me my identity papers – now.' There was a long pause – there always is – while my opponent's eyes showed uncertainty and unease. Then he looked away and a moment later the passport was handed over.

As Saul and I returned to the track I felt slightly limp; the psychic effort required by this eye-contact technique takes its toll. Saul turned to me, before we remounted, and shook hands; I was being congratulated. Here flat bush replaced cultivation, the golden grass tall between acacias and junipers. The track was execrable, grotesquely humpy and very dusty. In the oppressive afternoon heat we made slow progress; it does a cyclist no good to ride fast into deep dust. Since turning south at the junction the Rubeho Mountains had been a long, low, blue wall on my right, not high but steep; now they were nearer and greener. At the next hamlet Saul and I parted; his patch was holding, despite the testing surface.

Now mighty trees lined the track, their canopies disturbed by the capers of unafraid capuchin monkeys. Beyond the big – and rather unwelcoming – village of Msowero came long miles through an elephant-grass tunnel that reduced visibility all round, while the sky darkened. This tunnel led, unexpectedly, to an area being 'developed' (vast sisal and tobacco plantations) by, among other consortia, a Dutch company. I was approaching the village of Rudewa, fifteen miles from Kilosa, when the rainstorm broke at 4.30. As I sheltered, with several plantation workers, in an empty machinery garage, an English-speaking foreman came running through the torrent. He had noticed the *mzungu*, I must spend the night with the project director. It is taken for granted everywhere, by Blacks and Whites alike, that the travelling *mzungu* should be entertained by the resident expatriate.

Will was a fabulously hospitable Dutchman, born in Zimbabwe when his parents moved there from Indonesia. His wife and children were on leave in Harare and my bed had to be moved to the nursery from the guest-room, just then given over to drying long thin red-brown strips of elephant biltong. The meat came from one of a group of five elephants who had been invading the tobacco and sisal. 'On our plantations shooting them's legal,' explained Will. 'If you shoot one the rest push off.'

I thought, 'A bit confusing for the Africans, when it's illegal for them to kill elephants – who presumably damage maize and manioc as much as tobacco and sisal.' And what happens to the ivory handed over, as it must be, to the local police? An obvious solution would be to compel expatriate developers to employ more game-wardens to shoo away the intruders.

Will struck me as a typical White African, not interested in – scarcely aware of – the world outside Africa. As we were talking he noticed one of his servants, a frail elderly man, having difficulty hauling a heavy motor bicycle on to the veranda and at once rushed out to help him. When he said 'we' he meant all Africans, Black and White, yet moments later he could veer to condemning all Blacks as 'bastards'. Or even 'randy swine' which made me wince so perceptibly that he thought it necessary to use AIDS to justify the epithet. The virus was rampant among his work-force, most of whom were migrant seasonal labourers from remote bush villages – the main source of rural infection. Ageing prostitutes whose urban business had declined, because city men reckoned teenagers were less likely to be infected, tended to move to such places as Rudewa. It is almost impossible, Will said, to convince migrant workers that the danger is real because they have not yet seen AIDS killing within their own communities.

A fine drizzle, drifting low over the dullness of tobacco plantations and level ploughland being prepared for sisal, made the dawn seem late. Soon this drizzle turned to a steady chilly downpour which did nothing to improve an already appalling track, adhering – beyond the cultivation – to the base of forested sandstone hills, gashed with wound-like gullies. The gloom of that low-skied morning was relieved only by red bottle-brushes, flaming flamboyantly in the dense bush, and the purple and turquoise sheen of lilac-breasted rollers being aerobatic.

While struggling through liquid mud I fretted about the new 'development' behind me. Sisal and tobacco . . . export crops on all those fertile acres, Africa still providing what the West needs at prices decided in the West – a generation after Independence. It would be absurd to suggest that sub-Saharan Africa could now be flourishing had true independence been granted. Not one of the leaders allowed to take over had a coherent policy about where their country should go, and by what route, once the national flag had been raised. All were sitting ducks for the World Bank and IMF – even Nyerere, behind the scenes, for all his posturing about 'self-reliance'. However, the present shambles would certainly be less shambolic had genuine self-reliance been encouraged by the retreating colonial powers. It is inconceivable that new cash-crop plantations can help to alleviate Tanzania's poverty. Some employment is of course provided, thus slightly alleviating the poverty of a few hundred families at the cost of all the ills traditionally caused by migrant labour – plus, now, the spread of AIDS. But such projects only happen *because* the bulk of the profits flow West. Africans should be employed producing food for Africans; not until enough has been produced (including a stored surplus for drought years, as was the habit in pre-Communist Tibet), should any labour be deflected to cash crops grown by Western consortia. That is a truism. Yet African governments seem too befuddled to see it – befuddled by the miasma rising from the swamp of IMF and World Bank calculations and arguments. (Or can it be that the majority of Black politicians are happy with the opportunities for personal gain inherent in neo-colonialism?) Certainly economists are among the most dangerous animals on earth, skilled at making situations look so complicated that only their own solutions can solve the problems they themselves have created. And by combining insidious bribery, blackmailing bluff and intellectual hypnosis they can pressurise even well-meaning leaders into consistently betraying their own people by collaborating with the West.

Fate has been kind to me over the years, usually (though not always) decreeing that misfortune strikes within reasonable reach of help and comfort. I arrived in Kilosa at 8.30 – soaked through, covered in mud, coughing painfully and much in need of what I received: a *cead mile failte*, a hundred thousand welcomes from the Concern team. Monica – also sniffing and coughing, so I didn't have to worry about spreading my germ – led me to her bungalow on a high hillside amidst the mountainous beauty that heaves around Kilosa. She then left me alone for an hour or so to clean up, service Lear and browse among her hundreds of books. The titles suggested what was later confirmed: I had found another kindred spirit.

Kilosa is a forlorn little town, haunted by German and British ghosts – once important as a colonial administrative centre, now demoted by the new Dar es Salaam–Iringa road. Apart from an impressively well-kept old hospital – revived by Concern – it seems to have decayed beyond retrieval. The project leader drove me up a precipitous, richly wooded green mountain, strewn with the substantial but now slummy residences of the master-races. From a great height we looked down on Kilosa, Michael pointing out various colonial landmarks – like the Gymkhana Club – and suddenly I was overwhelmed by a ridiculous feeling that here only the *past* is real. Evidently the antibiotics were distorting my perceptions. To the Kilosa folk the present is what counts and it made me proud to discover how much Concern is contributing to an improvement of that present – their contribution depending less on the funds available than on the quality of the team members.

175

An item in the Tanzanian *Daily News* explained why the next day was traffic-free:

> The Kilosa–Mikumi road has been closed since April 16 because a bridge across the River Mkondoa, just a kilometre away from Kilosa township, has started collapsing. The bridge is now passable by pedestrians and cyclists only. It was built in 1935. Officials said at least 100/- million is needed to rebuild the bridge.

I mused over that suggestive phrase, 'has started collapsing'. What about the pedestrians and cyclists who happened to be crossing when it decided to complete its collapse? Swiftly I pedalled over, glancing down at the rumbustiously flooded River Mkondoa; to be leaving this ghost town by a collapsing 1935 bridge seemed fitting enough.

A few days previously floods had demolished a local railway bridge and the first few coaches of the Kigoma–Dar es Salaam train (from which Bruce had deflected me) fell into the Mkondoa. No one knew how many died. In the Third World casualty figures are rarely established with precision; only in the West is each citizen of sufficient importance to the authorities for every death to be recorded. The injured, from the derailed coaches that didn't fall in, were brought to Kilosa hospital.

A collapsing bridge wasn't really needed to deter motor vehicles on this road. However, in my view bad surfaces are more than compensated for by that special atmosphere where the worst of the West – an infection carried by motor traffic – is minimal or non-existent.

For five hours the track climbed – sometimes hedged by a fragrant shrub covered in minute yellow blossoms – into the heart of the Rubeho Mountains. This was tranquil country, cloud-swathed and cool, the valleys cultivated, the higher slopes forested.

All day I met only one fellow-traveller, being taken from his village to Kilosa by bicycle-taxi – rare in the bush though common enough in big towns, especially in Uganda. The passenger, riding on a wide soft saddle fixed to the carrier, was an elderly teacher who spoke fluent English. Meeting on the summit of a steep hill we were all happy to rest, leaning on our machines while discussing educa-

176

tion, the SAP and AIDS. It had always been difficult, said the
teacher, to persuade local parents to send their juvenile work-force
to school, even when Nyerere was offering free education. Now it
was hardly worth the effort, so adversely had fee-paying and cut-
backs affected rural attitudes. As for AIDS, that was a city and main-
road problem; there was no need to talk about such dirty things in
bush schools. Yet this teacher's village was only thirty miles from
Mikumi, a popular halt for drivers on the Dar es Salaam–
Malawi–Zambia run. At such moments (and there were many of
them) my heart ached for Africa. Only when it is too late, when the
people of a region are dying in considerable numbers, is the AIDS
menace recognised. Then some villagers, if given advice from an
acceptable (preferably non-Western) source, will be suspicious of
outsiders and abandon customs that could spread the virus – like
tattooing, scarification, circumcision with a communal razor blade
and the ritual cleansing of widows and widowers through copulation
with an in-law. Before we parted the teacher pointed south to a
towering cliff of black cloud obscuring the mountains ahead. 'You
will get very wet!' he said. And he was right.

At noon the rain came, from a sky so low and dark that to shelter
would have been futile; this downpour was certain to continue until
sunset. I pedalled cautiously through russet rushing water, unable
to see the eroded channels beneath the opaque torrent and con-
gratulating Lear on his amphibian skills. I had feared immersion
might wreck his gears but they continued to function while com-
plaining about the intake of grit. Then, as I reached the edge of
Mikumi National Park, the track levelled out and the surface
changed to deep, deep mud – the sludgy sort that makes cycling
impossible.

Here, high in the mountains, the trees are broad-leaved and deci-
duous – known as 'miombo' woodland and a nice change after a
surfeit of acacias. Down on the plain this park protects an abundance
of wildlife but I saw only one troop of yellow baboons, smaller and
lighter in colour than their olive cousins further north. These are
expert hunters, often killing the young (when very young) of reedbuck, impala and other antelope.

Within moments of my reaching the miombo the tsetse flies found
me and for the day's last fourteen miles I had to walk – slither –
while being driven to frenzy by the pain of their bites. As their

177

favourite food is warthog blood they only laughed at Joy's nylon shower-curtain. They come – especially when it is raining – not in ones and twos like our horse-flies, which in appearance they quite resemble, but in a persistent swarm that never for an instant stops feeding. Soon I was covered in sore itchy swellings, each the size of a tenpenny piece. I heard myself whimpering with pain; luckily there was no one around to witness the intrepid traveller's disintegration. Bedbugs used to be my least favourite insects; now these have been supplanted. Why did early travellers not complain more about this entomological torture (then much oftener encountered than now)? I suppose they had real problems on their mind, like dying of thirst, being trampled by an elephant, gored by a buffalo, eaten by a leopard, speared by an unfriendly native. In the bland 1990s, we only have tsetse flies to whinge about. My itch lasted five days and some of the bumps subsequently turned purple; these bites can be so ferocious they actually bruise one. This fly sufficiently explains why much of Tanzania remained unpopulated throughout the centuries. Numerous migrating tribes passed through but none lingered. The tsetse spreads trypanosomiasis, deadly to livestock though Africa's wild animals are immune. Recent eradication programmes to extend grazing areas – inevitable given the population explosion – will if successful destroy the natural habitats of many wild animals.

As I emerged from the miombo, at the start of a long steep descent to the motor road, the clouds began to lift. Below me lay the 2,000 square miles of Mikumi National Park – the third largest in Tanzania – its extent and flatness dramatic yet looking curiously unAfrican in that dim, wet light. My destination for the night was the Mikumi Training College, an Irish-Tanzanian bilateral aid project. In fact I spent three nights there; a five-hour drenching does nothing for one's bronchitis and the antibiotics had to be given a chance to prevail.

Mikumi village, ugly and impoverished, is a typical product of Nyerere's social engineering. Between 1967 and 1977 Tanzania's rural population grew from eleven million to fourteen million and the percentage living in dreary collectivised townships rose from less than 5 per cent to over 90 per cent. These resettlements were intended to improve agricultural efficiency but disastrously lowered food production. Seventy per cent took place within two years in the mid-'70s. The majority were reluctant to move from their scattered homesteads in the bush, for religious and sentimental as well as practical reasons, yet Nyerere, when accused of cruelty, defended himself thus: 'Eleven million people could not have been moved by force in Tanzania, we do not have the physical capacity for such forced movement, any more than we have the desire for it.' Nevertheless, even those most supportive of Nyerere's ends admitted that his means were reprehensible. In *Tanzania: the Struggle for Rural Socialism*, Dean E. McHenry refers to 'a concentrated use of persuasion, inducements, and compulsion by party and state agents – police, militia, and army personnel and equipment – in order to get the job done.'

My hostess took me on a tour of the park, where I saw everything except the big cats, and on our way home we stopped to shop in the market. There people were chattering about an elephant who had been shot during the night on the main street – in theory because he had threatened crops, in reality because there is a lot of meat on an elephant and the Mikumi folk are protein-starved. The game-wardens were furious and rightly so. Yet can one wholeheartedly disapprove of an elephant being shot by hungry people for his meat, as distinct from being shot by greedy people for his ivory?

Mikumi's bilateral aid project seemed to this Irish citizen a deplorable squandering of taxpayers' money. It forms a mini-village on a hillside at the edge of the park – a rather European-looking village, many of the construction materials having been sent out from Ireland. Why pay heavy freight charges on sending such materials to a country that is not short of mud, grass and wood? Who was 'helped' by the dispatching of that cargo? The too-familiar stench of White self-serving hangs about the setting up of the Mikumi Training College. However, Ireland is so comparatively poor that less money has been wasted here than elsewhere. I wondered how my compatriots viewed their project; as a guest it was not for me to ask awkward questions, as government employees it was not for them to make tactless comments. But I doubt if Mikumi gave them much job-satisfaction. They were too remarkable a group to be wasted there – knowledgeable about the area, sensitive to African viewpoints, genuinely caring. On the whole Irish expatriates seem more dedicated than the average to the people amongst whom they work: and this is not mere bias on my part. Between

179

Kenya and Zimbabwe, I heard many Africans making the same observation, often likening Irish aid-workers to 'missionaries' rather than 'experts' – a revealing compliment, on more than one level.

Eleven glorious hours, on a smooth(ish) road with a strong tailwind, took me through the weirdly lovely baobab forest of the Ruaha Gorge, across a hot expanse of level, flower-bright bush, where Masai herders tended emaciated cattle, and up the sort of well-graded escarpment that makes one appreciate the special qualities of a mountain-bike.

Then, near the high but otherwise unbeautiful village of Lutundwi, Saul's patch came undone. This time there could be no postponement of a new tube but Lutundwi looked unlikely to provide expert care. Reluctantly I hitched a fifty-mile lift on a truck bound for Lusaka via Iringa, the next large town. This was a deeply frustrating experience. While toiling up that escarpment, planning to spend the night in Lutundwi, I had been looking forward to fifty level miles on a high cool plateau. As the truck sped towards Iringa, with rock-strewn mountains nearby on the left, I glimpsed on the right tantalising views of jungly plains very far below, empurpled by the evening light. My frustration, I reflected then, was a just punishment for never having come to terms with the mechanical mysteries of life.

The kindly driver was a Muslim merchant from Dar es Salaam, strikingly handsome, with two wives at home and a third beside him in the cab. His 'travelling wife', he called her, and she (aged 23, plump, well-dressed, a Catholic Chagga merchant's daughter from Arusha) smiled at him and said, 'Now only stupid men travel alone, being tempted!' She had not become a Muslim: 'In Dar we don't think about religion. I like to go to church, to meet my friends and sing, and my husband doesn't mind.' While she travelled, the other wives' children looked after her 2-year-old.

At the turn-off for Iringa I asked the driver how much I owed him, as is the custom in Africa, but he firmly refused payment and presented me with a bottle of Pepsi, 'to get you up the hill'. I soon saw what he meant. The climb from a small new industrial zone, on the main road, was formidable. As I pushed Lear up, the broken-tarmac road wound to and fro under towering trees and dusk became darkness. On a broad ridge-top the road deteriorated to a very rough track: Iringa's main street. It seemed the population had already retired; lights were few and dim and without the assistance of an amiable young man ('I good Christian, I want help you') it would have been impossible to find my destination on the far side of the town.

Iringa's Lutheran Centre – a German left-over – is a rambling bungalow in a well-kept garden shaded by mature blue gums. The staff at Reception – three young men doing the work of one, as is usual – spoke no English and were bemused by my arrival, but welcoming. My cell, complete with mosquito net, cost only 75p; the grubby sheets were hastily changed for the *mzungu*'s benefit. At the end of a long corridor two bathrooms supplied running cold water and cleanish Western lavatories. The furnishings and lay-out were institutionally frugal, the atmosphere was restrained but not oppressively pious.

In a nearby would-be tourist hotel the bar was ill-lit and dismal, its décor affectedly 'contemporary', its beer warm and blatantly diluted. My only fellow-drinker was a corpulent gentleman, aged perhaps 40, at whose feet lay a bulging padlocked briefcase. Our conversation opened abrasively when he looked me up and down, then asked, 'You have come to teach us how to run our country? Who pays you? You work for who?'

I explained myself. The corpulent gentleman grunted, thought for a moment, then introduced himself somewhat ambiguously as 'a senior government officer'. Squinting down, I could read the label on the briefcase: Ndugu Godfrey Munisi.

Ndugu Munisi was a man with an industrious insect in his cranial covering. He had the answer – the *only* answer – to AIDS. If every man could have as many wives as he wanted there would be no running around with dirty girls, monogamy was an unnatural restriction. Polygamy had always been part of African culture, African men weren't able to think of having only one woman, AIDS was a direct result of Western interference with African culture.

'But', I protested, 'most men can barely afford one wife! Anyway every population is roughly fifty-fifty, so when many men had more than one wife how did the poor behave? Obviously they shared "dirty girls" – Africa was riddled with STDs long before AIDS came.'

Ndugu Munisi ignored all this boring logic and began to attack

181

the decadent West where men practise a cruel form of polygamy which discriminates against women. Unwanted wives are thrown out, instead of every wife being cared for, throughout her lifetime, as in Africa. His wives were a man's property, yes, but they were also inferior dependent weak beings. Even wives who were barren or mentally defective or crippled should never be thrown out. A first wife might not like a second wife on the scene, or she and the second wife might not like a third wife – and so on – but for any woman polygamy had to be a lesser evil than divorce. The missionaries' worst damage was making men throw out all but one wife. If that sort of brutality was Christ's message he was a bad man and Africans lived better lives before they ever heard of him.

I argued no more. My companion was at that stage of inebriation when one is uninhibited enough to speak one's mind while remaining articulate. His was a not uncommon handicap; he had heard so much about the West that he imagined he understood its weaknesses, yet he had no inkling of what makes it tick. I returned to the Lutheran Centre in a pensive mood. People as angrily confused as Ndugu Munisi always bother me. And in the Africa of 1992 there were a lot of them around.

Unlike most African towns, Iringa is a place you could learn to love. It has a natural advantage, straddling a high, breezy, wooded ridge top, overlooking immense sweeps of countryside – ochre and green, merging into low, vaguely blue mountain ranges in the far distance. Satellite villages straggle away from it on two sides and rural life seeps in from every side, nullifying the urban feel that might otherwise be generated by handsome though decaying colonial offices, ill-kept churches and mosques, an ugly breeze-block bishop's palace, an affluent-looking new bank, a few prefabricated office blocks housing either commercial enterprises (usually stillborn) or Tanzania's superfluity of bureaucrats. I was perhaps becoming used to the incongruity and run-down shoddiness of these remnants of empire where once the District Commissioner and his staff genuinely 'did their best for the natives' and where African administrators now genuinely do their best for themselves and their families. Familiarity was blunting the exasperation provoked by an agglomeration of malfunctioning Western imports – tarmac streets as eroded as cattle-tracks, factories closed or operating at 25 per cent capacity, telephones that don't work, banks that have no currency left, moody

182

electricity, officials who are never in their offices, schools without textbooks, post offices without stamps, hospitals without medicines, courts without justice. Parallel to this world of pretence, the ordinary folk survive – somehow. By setting up a set of bathroom weighing-scales on the pavement outside the bank and charging passers-by a penny a go; by pressing people's clothes, while they wait, with a charcoal-filled iron; by squatting in the wayside dust selling a few combs, mirrors, razor blades, soap bars (probably stolen) spread on a plastic sack; by turning a bicycle upside-down and sharpening knives and axes on a whetstone attached to the whizzing rear wheel – by 101 stratagems bred of desperation. The phrase 'subsistence economy' is cold and hard, an idea in an academic mind unrelated to everyday life. The reality, when one pauses to observe the individuals engaged in it at the lowest level, is harrowing and haunting.

The Lutheran Centre had long since closed its canteen (the reduction of facilities throughout Tanzania is noticeable) and I break-fasted with a fellow-guest in a nearby Muslim-run restaurant – the food good and plentiful. Mr Reweyemamu was expensively dressed, dim-witted and short-legged: he had to trot to keep up with me. He gave me his card – 'Senior Adviser to the Ministry of Education, Dar es Salaam' – and told me he had studied in Britain from 1986 to 1989. This coveted privilege often goes to singularly unsuitable candidates, skilled in manipulating the relevant expatriates; one is left gasping at the ineptitude of the selection system at the benefactor's end (unless of course the cynics are right and such men are chosen to act as lifelong cogs in the exploitation machine). Innocently I asked Mr Reweyemamu what percentage of Tanzanian children attend school. Complacently he replied, '95 per cent', then became quite huffy when I laughed outright. My disbelief being based on personal observations in the bush discomposed him and hastily he sought to cover his tracks – 'I know nothing about bush people, I work on big educational projects for our cities, I live in Dar.' It seemed he really had credited that 95 per cent figure, until challenged. How many Tanzanian bureaucrats live in fantasy-land?

A two-mile walk along a dusty road, between shambas and concrete shacks swarming with children, took me to a startling Palladian edifice surrounded by maize fields. Once these were the playing-fields of Tanganyika's Eton, when Iringa's Teacher Training College was a boys' boarding-school (Whites only). Here I found Jason

Smith, a young English VSO lecturer who removed Lear's back wheel and inserted the new tube as effortlessly as I would break an egg. VSO workers are provided with mountain-bikes, in lieu of Pajeros, and Jason – soon to return home – insisted on giving me one of his spare tubes and an extra set of patches. The College atmosphere was unquiet that morning. A 20-year-old girl student had died during the night while trying to abort with chloroquin, quite an effective and very popular abortifacient but too often taken in excess. It can be bought without a prescription and is also the favourite choice of suicides. Moreover, trouble had erupted a few days previously between the students and a gang of local toughs – town versus gown transposed to Tanzania. The College Director was in Dar, the police refused to intervene, the situation ran out of control and, after several students had been beaten unconscious, the gang leader's ears were cut off.

On my way back from the College I paused to inspect 'The Department for Primary Health Care,' a long line of new one-storey buildings, as yet unequipped. A smartly uniformed askari leaned out from his sentry-hut to tell me the Director was in Dar, where the Directors of things provincial usually are. The Assistant Director, a welcoming young woman named Lily, arrived just then by Land Cruiser, its driver also smartly uniformed. When I asked about AIDS prevention programmes in the schools, presumably a concern of the Department for Primary Health Care, she cheerfully replied, 'We've no schools programme yet, but maybe in September we can start something.' With an effort I concealed the effect of her remark on a *mzungu* aware of the urgency of the problem. 'There's nothing to see here,' she continued, 'we wait for funding from WHO. But come with me to the hospital, meet the area Medical Director and Dr Makwetta – he runs our AIDS Control Programme and gets funding from Ireland.'

We bumped slowly towards the hospital, passing a well-tended pine-shaded British military cemetery. 'Too many dead Whitemen' exclaimed Lily. 'For why did they fight in Africa?' The driver interrupted to ask if I could sell him 'reliable' condoms and then Lily enthused about all the AIDS seminars, conferences and workshops she had enjoyed in the past and hoped to enjoy in the near future. The African penchant for attending such gatherings (as far from home as possible), instead of taking action on the spot, is of course fostered by Western 'experts' for their own reasons.

We were entering the enormous hospital when Lily gave a squeal of dismay – I hadn't signed the Visitors' Book! Even in such institutions as Iringa's virtually non-existent Department for Primary Health Care, Visitors' Books have become a ludicrous – and in this case infuriating – fetish. At once the Land Cruiser was dispatched (an eight-mile trip) to fetch the hard-backed exercise-book, despite my objecting to such a scandalous waste of fuel. Again innocent of her impact on the *mzungu*, Lily explained, 'WHO pays our vehicle expenses.'

The Medical Director was – guess where? Dr Makwetta however raised my spirits; he had never attended a seminar, conference or workshop, being too busy doing his job. Later I heard from several sources that he has a reputation for prudent spending – and for giving back the change, should a project cost less than expected. We established an instant rapport and Lily, who seemed to be in some awe of this Big Man, left us on our own.

Dr Makwetta – a friend of Dr Kolimba's – had previously worked with the National AIDS Control Programme (NACP) in Kagera. He angrily condemned governmental sluggishness; the authorities refused to launch an AIDS awareness campaign until 1990, three years after a Ministry of Health survey found 24 per cent of Bukoba's adults to be HIV + . In 1987, officialdom asserted that this infection came from Uganda and would be confined to remote Kagera. And the locals themselves believed this; initially AIDS was known as 'Juliana', after a popular dress material imported from Uganda. Wearily Dr Makwetta deplored each region's scapegoat-hunting and repeated a Ugandan proverb often quoted by Noerine Kaleeba, 'Finding a snake in the house, you don't argue about where it came from before killing it.'

By June 1990, 16,250 cases of full-blown AIDS had been reported to NACP from Tanzania's twenty regions and Dr Makwetta said it was impossible to estimate how many were dying unregistered in their homes – especially in the south – where shame remains a powerful factor. The NACP 1990 surveys found 81,000 pregnant women to be HIV+ and during that year more than 24,300 Tanzanian babies were born infected. Extreme poverty, in Dr Makwetta's view, was largely responsible for the speed of the virus's spread. For instance, Kagera's economy has been devastated during the past decade by a matoke weevil and the falling price of coffee (falling for the grower, not for the consumer). He therefore supported, with reservations, the latest official idea, 'Intersectoral Co-operation' – a five-year plan based on the collaboration of several government departments and non-governmental organisations whose responsibilities touch on various aspects of the AIDS crisis. He didn't need to explain his reservations. I could visualise 'Intersectoral Co-operation' all too clearly as a menacing new breeding-ground for delay and dissension leading to paralysis.

Dr Makwetta laughed at the notion of any 'behaviour change' campaign being able to avert a catastrophic reduction of the present economically productive age-group. He agreed with Ndugu Munisi that Christianity's demolition of traditional religion had contributed to the epidemic's spread; polygamy allowed men to prove their virility without random matings. Now the most urgent need was for direct action among children, whether school-going or not, from the age of 9 or 10 onwards. But here the cultural barriers were even higher than the financial barriers; both parents and Church leaders continued to oppose blunt speaking about sex.

As I stood up to leave, Dr Makwetta pointed to the poster above his desk. It listed the latest chilling statistics from Tanzania's sentinel towns, below a quote from Camus's *The Plague*: 'Calamity has come on you, my brethren, and, my brethren, you deserved it.'

That evening I met a German White Father – tall, gaunt, malaria-depleted – who had laboured long in southern Tanzania and found AIDS unsurprising; for decades he had been observing sexual activity increasing among schoolchildren. Yet he rejected direct action because of its condom constituent; his AIDS prevention campaign was centred on special church services and more frequent and more fervent praying in the schools 'to deliver these poor young people from temptation'. Such powers of self-deception are doubtless necessary when one has spent a lifetime failing to replace tribal taboos with the imported variety.

AIDS is new, the rest isn't. In 1947, Elspeth Huxley called on an English missionary in Uganda and recorded Miss Hornby's lament:

Immorality is rampant, the sense of obligation to family and tribe has gone . . . Last year three of our (unmarried) women teachers here became pregnant and we had to suspend our senior master, a Makerere man, for seducing a pupil of fourteen.

Miss Hornby was also driven to self-deception:

But we must look to the next generation. We must pin our hopes to them. And I have faith that enough will grow up healthy, self-respecting and God-fearing to leaven the whole . . .

Back in the Lutheran Centre, an excited gentleman informed me that Queen Elizabeth II and the Duke of Edinburgh were about to divorce – yes, it *was* true, it *had* to be true, he'd read it in the *Daily News* (Tanzania's only English-language daily). Months later, when I heard about the genuine royal troubles, I realised how this rumour had started. Its conduit was Dr Musoke, yet another Senior Adviser, this time to the Department of Health. His elderly companion, Mr Lyoto, wore jungle trousers and an anorak – for which he apologised; he had been gathering some rare herbs on a near-inaccessible plateau in the Southern Highlands. He was a botanist, specialising in medicinal plants, and he too worked for the Department of Health which I found cheering. Both men were sitting on a red plastic settee in the foyer, drinking black tea and eating horrible buns. Opposite them sat Joan Mziray, a petite and demure accountant from the Department of Transport in Dodoma, here to do 'an estimate' – of what remained a mystery. I was invited to join the party but excused myself for a moment. After a hard day, I needed something stronger than tea and in my room lurked a bottle of Konyagi, a gut-rotting distillation peculiar to Tanzania. Africa's Christian hostelries were setting me on the slippery slope to secret drinking.

Why were all these government officals not staying in the nearby hotel? My question brought an unexpected and disarming reply: Tanzania was so down on its luck that even Senior Advisers had to look for cheap lodgings. And this was OK. Mwalimu had always preached (and practised) personal austerity, so at the best of times they'd never been used to high living – just a *little* higher than the Lutheran Centre.

Dr Musoke and Mr Lyoto were not soul-mates. The former, who

had qualified in Edinburgh and sounded faintly Scots, remained devoted to Mwalimu – The Teacher, Dr Julius Nyerere, once esteemed as 'the conscience of Black Africa' (even when his collection of imprisoned political dissidents far outnumbered South Africa's). Dr Musoke boasted that resettling the peasants had been 'a big health-care success – we could attend to their needs. Before, they were hidden away in the bush.' Of course many were primitive pagans who made a silly fuss about being separated from their ancestors' graves and since Mwalimu's retirement have been moving back into the bush, leaving 'our excellent free medical care' behind them.

Mr Lyoto beamed at me as I gave a thumbnail sketch of the five rural health-centres I had paused to inspect between Dodoma and Iringa. Airily Dr Musoke dismissed my findings. 'Sometimes we can have temporary problems about the distribution of medicines and so on – we have a fine medical work-force, I think the best in Africa.'

I hadn't been criticising the work-force; those I met struck me as astonishingly dedicated, given their demoralising lack of back-up from Dr Musoke's Ministry. In Dar es Salaam, on my way home, I prised a report out of that Ministry and discovered how much government expenditure on health had declined – from 7 per cent in 1976 to 3.6 per cent in 1987. For 1988 the per capita health budget came to less than one US dollar. No later figures were available. Dr Musoke's evident belief in his own lies mirrored Mr Reweyemamu's illusions about education. When pressed, he admitted that his 'heavy work schedule' allowed him little time to move out from Dar – he was in Iringa to attend a colleague's funeral. As more than 90 per cent of Tanzanians live in rural areas the existence of this segregated urban élite, skilled only at dodging reality, goes a long way to explain the country's present critical condition.

Mr Lyoto made an odd croaking noise when Dr Musoke defined AIDS as a minor problem. The *real* global problem was malaria, now killing at least two million people annually. So why all the fuss about AIDS? Why not concentrate on eliminating malaria as smallpox had been eliminated? Was AIDS so important because it had seemed, when first identified, to threaten the West? Was malaria not important because its victims were rarely Western?

Sharply Mr Lyoto intervened. Smallpox was eradicated, he recalled, by paying chosen people generous sums to report at once on victims, who were then isolated. Malaria eradication requires a whole population to be constantly vigilant in the matter of stagnant water; and in Africa it's not easy to achieve that sort of disciplined communal vigilance. The tsetse fly, he added, presents a similar problem; it cleverly travels underneath trains and vehicles so can't be controlled without cross-border co-operation and equally rigid standards throughout the affected areas.

Joan scarcely spoke while the men were present, then erupted on their retiring. It heartened me that someone in the Department of Transport felt passionate about Tanzania's roads. After her initial outburst, delivered so fast that I got only the gist of it, Joan demanded eagerly, 'You'll write about our roads? *Please*! Make our government feel ashamed! Roads are not like weather – people can *do* something about them!'

I assured Joan that I would indeed write about Tanzania's roads, unsparingly. She calmed down then and spoke more slowly. Her main concern was humanitarian. Tanzania had been spending precious hard currency importing food for the Dar es Salaam market while hundreds of tons of its own maize were going mouldy and being eaten by rats in the south-west, where trucks couldn't cope with the roads. 'So in many areas – you've seen some – villagers go hungry while the rats around Rukwa get fat! Now our government declares it has to give urgent food aid to three million in the north – this last drought was worst there. It's looking for US $3.8 million to transport the surplus from the south. But while it builds new roads the surplus won't wait! In Rukwa there are no good storage places. Not only our government is mad, most Southern Africa governments wouldn't take the drought seriously till last December. The peasants knew how things would be but leaders don't listen to peasants – and they know *they'll* never starve!'

Dr Musoke was Joan's next target. 'That doctor, he's stupid and ignorant! This is why so many of our élite are dying, they think believing in AIDS is a bush superstition and as educated men they know better. For working women like me these men are very dangerous.' Joan repeated what a dozen other women, in Kenya and Uganda, had already told me: many female employees must be prepared to sleep with their bosses to gain promotion – sometimes just to keep their jobs. In Tanzania Nyerere did try to raise the status of women but here too it seems he failed. Joan's sister's husband was then dying of AIDS in Arusha. Her sister told her boss this – adding, truthfully, that she had not been tested. But he was not deterred and to secure the promotion she desperately needed, to support four children after her husband's death, she gave in. Joan said, 'These men are rich, they can afford to keep women in second homes. But they hate independent working women competing with them in their world – or what was their world. Even junior female staff seem a threat. I'm *sure* this is our problem, men want to punish us just for being there. They want us to feel always inferior, dependent, in their power – and controlling our bodies is the way to do it. Everyone notices the women best at their job – the biggest threat to the men – get the worst sex punishment even if they're the ugliest around! When I was in Dar University in the early '80s another sort of control and punishment went on. There was a custom called "Punch" to bully the girl students, to stop them taking any part in university life outside of studies. It upset our studies, too! It was a system of posting up on notice boards very intimate details about a named girl, using very bad insulting words. Any girl who dared to move into the men's world by joining a debating society or something – any normal student activity – was intimidated by "Punch". In '81 – that was my first year – the decent men students tried to have Punch outlawed and found it had the backing of older men, university staff who thought it was a good way of "keeping the women in line"! Those English words were used – can you believe it?'

I said I could easily believe it, sexual harassment also being a problem in the West, though now driven underground by legislation. I wondered how Joan came to speak such fluent English? Her parents, evidently rich, had disapproved of Nyerere's language policy and sent her to a convent school in Kenya – across what was then an officially closed border.

9

Highland Fling

Iringa to Tukuyu

Where I crossed the Little Ruaha River, below Iringa, my path again met Joseph Thomson's, this time on the route of his first expedition (1879), led by the 33-year-old Alexander Johnston who soon died of some undiagnosed tropical disease. The 20-year-old Thomson, continuing alone, walked through the unexplored territory between Dar es Salaam and Lake Nyasa, and from there to the southern end of Lake Tanganyika. This expedition was partly funded by the Royal Geographical Society, with much support from missionary, scientific and commercial interests. Its objective was to advise on the prospects for a road from Dar to the Nyasa region as an alternative to the hazardous Zambezi River route, always threatened by harassment from the Portuguese. The then President of the RGS, Sir Rutherford Alcock, admitted to the subscribers to the expedition fund that many might question the benefit to Africans of such explorations. But, he added, the way to counter such doubts was to show that 'scientific and practical objects could be carried out without necessarily involving great loss of life or conflicts with the natives.' For this purpose, Thomson was the ideal expedition leader; he arrived at Lake Tanganyika having lost not even one porter or quarrelled with even one 'native'.

In this Hehe territory around Iringa Thomson was often delayed; being the first European ever seen in the area, the chiefs were keen both to investigate his motives, which they naturally suspected, and to observe his hilarious habits, like eating with a knife and fork. He found the Hehe 'noblemen of Nature's mould – no one put forth his hand to touch what did not belong to him'. This cattle-keeping tribe, who cultivated little, had become powerful earlier in the century when a strong leader united various clans, incorporated (or

191

eliminated) other weaker tribes and accumulated wealth by export-
ing slaves and ivory to the coast. As fierce but disciplined warriors,
the Hehe were to distinguish themselves in combat with the German
land-grabbers. They annihilated a German 'punitive force' in 1891
and their territory remained 'unpacified' until 1898.

Not far from Iringa I dismounted, the better to see a Hehe witch-
doctor. He came striding towards me down the middle of the road,
robed in a tattered leopard-skin, banging his neck-drum and
screaming – then sobbing, then chanting in a high-pitched voice.
Bright feathers and withered vegetation decorated his long grey
locks; he carried a six-foot spear; bits of animals festooned him –
monkey skulls, a snakeskin, a lion's tail, feline teeth. There was
much early morning pedestrian traffic: women carrying loads of
grain, bananas, onions or sweet potatoes to Iringa's market and
children on their way to school. One sensed unease as this weirdly
powerful figure went on his way – walking faster than any African
normally does, his castrato chant becoming hypnotic. The children
scuttled off the verge into the bush, openly afraid; the adults looked
away, their faces closed – as though to stare at this apparition, as
I was doing, might bring bad luck.

Continuing, I caught myself being again unreasonably irritated
by the African women's cheerful acceptance of their beast-of-burden
role – all those strong young husbands, strolling along carefree and
loadfree, followed by wives carrying weights such as I could not even
lift off the ground, yet chatting amiably with their spouses. Why not
at least divide the load equally? But of course this is literally
unthinkable and She would be as shocked as He if anyone suggested
it. Children are conditioned early. Near here I saw many small
schoolgirls carrying planks on their heads up a steep hill. These were
for a schoolroom extension and on the hilltop stood the male pupils,
complacently watching.

A strong tailwind sped me on my way through a landscape of
round rocky hills, untidily cultivated shambas, stands of feathery
bamboo, swaying pine forests, then mile after mile of newly green
bush from which an extraordinary variety of minute and exquisite
flowers overflowed on to the verges. Yet the local maize was in a
bad way; for it the meagre rains had come too late. So why were
gallons of pombe being sold, outside almost every shamba, to passing motorists and truckers? Because – I learned later – the grain

shortage had so raised the price that families were selling what had been brewed for domestic consumption.

In the bush, remote from any village, I noticed a few of the distinctive Hehe dwellings – very long, low, flat-roofed communal huts, built of poles and red mud fortified with grain stalks. Traditionally cattle and humans shared accommodation. These homes, though in good repair, were unoccupied; the drought had forced herders to take their animals high into the mountains.

Perhaps staring at witch-doctors does bring bad luck. Towards noon I was pedalling slowly up a long, gradual, jungly slope where tall wayside bamboo limited visibility. The collision caught me completely off guard. Out of the bush he cycled fast, a huge jerry-can of pombe lashed to his carrier – and then I was spreadeagled under Lear, being soaked in pombe. For one of those brief but memorable moments we were both lying on the road, staring at each other with astonishment. Simultaneously we scrambled to our feet and my expectation of some sign of apology or concern was not fulfilled. The young man ignored me. Understandably, his main worry was the spillage of all that precious alcohol – as usual corked inadequately with a hunk of cane. Hastily he righted the container, peering anxiously at the contents to estimate his loss. When I offered to hold his bicycle while the jerry-can was being re-lashed, he looked scared; at no stage, during our unfortunate encounter, did he utter a syllable in any language. I walked on then, feeling slightly shaken but thankful that Lear was undamaged and trying to diagnose the damage to myself. My right hip and knee protested as I remounted on the hilltop. Arriving in Mafinga an hour later, I stiffly dismounted; a half-day off was indicated.

Mafinga stands on high ground, its little red mud-brick buildings, with pale grey tin roofs, strewn for miles over wide, lightly wooded slopes. On the main road seedy guest-houses-cum-bars abound, this being a popular truckers' halt. Seediness doesn't usually put me off but these establishments were both super-seedy and unwelcoming to the *mzungu*. Wandering up a dusty track, through acres of failed maize, I came upon a congenial doss-house, its façade half-smothered by a scarlet flowering creeper – a lodging for locals rather than truckers. My room had a disintegrating earth floor, like a well-harrowed field, and the door was unlockable – but that didn't matter, so amiably reassuring were the proprietress and her teenage

193

daughter. Having chained Lear to the bed, I went in search of food.

Mafinga's motel – crudely smart, advertising a nightly disco – was newly built and evidently designed to pull in the best-paid international truckers. The restaurant boasted clean tablecloths and for £1.80 provided an ample meal of soup, bread, butter(!), steak, chips and tomato salad. The dual-purpose waitresses wore tight satin frocks with much cheap jewellery; their lips and nails were dark purple. Mine was a tall slender girl from Bukoba, her darkness accentuated by a sleek shimmering crimson gown, her diamante and gold watch not acquired in the bush. I invited her to have a coffee with me. Three years previously her parents had died of AIDS, aged 42 and 40. She had five younger siblings dependent on her earnings and nothing to sell but her body. AIDS naturally worried her; intelligent and forceful, she claimed to have converted many men to condom use. 'I argue,' she said. 'I tell how my father and mother died slowly and it was like hell. Men are surprised when I tell about my parents but they like me and want me. I show my report, I'm tested and clean. I say I want to stay clean and – OK, they want me, they use condoms! And carefully, not like a joke. Men are not so bad, if women are strong they listen. Many are scared now and like to find a clean girl. I make good money – they come and ask for Margaret because their friends tell them I'm clean. It's not true men won't use condoms but women must be strong – *very* strong!'

Later, in a main-road bar, I watched nineteen trucks from half a dozen African countries coming to rest on a vast dusty area by primitive repair depots. At dusk teenage girls swarmed out like mosquitoes to forage among the truckers. For them to reckon 'It can't happen to me', when it has already happened to at least 26 per cent of this town's married women, seems suicidal. But then of course they know nothing about these statistics. This aspect of the epidemic was troubling me increasingly. In Iringa Dr Makwetta had assured me that Tanzania 'keeps to the UN rules about AIDS and human rights'. This means that no one knows which individuals in sentinel towns such as Mafinga test positive. But is it ethically admissible to test people – even anonymously – without their consent? Arguably such testing is necessary to determine the rate at which the virus is spreading. Yet what practical purpose does that serve? How does it help infected communities? Statistics are of absorbing interest to the countless academics now so profitably riding on the AIDS industry gravy-train, but how does their collection help Africans? Is there not something intolerably paternalistic about this refusal to treat the infected as responsible human beings, entitled to know the worst and make appropriate decisions? The husbands of those infected Mafinga mothers may well develop AIDS first, causing some of their wives to sleep around to earn money to buy alleviating medicines – or witch-doctors' 'cures'. What right do experts have to reduce individuals to statistics, using their tragedies as 'research material'? Does this happen in the West? Were it discovered that 26 per cent of pregnant women in some English town were HIV + would all agree that they should have been tested without their knowledge and should not be given the opportunity to respond to their condition as they judge best? Is this choice not a human right?

From a cycling point of view Tanzania's Southern Highlands were even more enjoyable – because more varied – than my bush short-cut from Shinyanga to Dodoma. Beyond Mafinga, a seventy-mile detour through the Mufindi Tea Estates allowed me to glimpse another world – high, cold, wet, windy, very beautiful. This was a magical world of noble forests, steep terraced slopes neatly clothed in tea-bushes, sudden heart-stopping views over many lower mountain ranges and criss-crossing valleys all wooded and secret-looking. On the Kilima Estate I was lavishly entertained – by pampering servants and affectionate dogs – in Kibwele House, the home of Mary and Jonny Niblett, who unfortunately were on leave.

Then down and down to Makumbako, a larger than usual township where I rejoined the main road and next morning continued to descend along a narrow ridge, many miles in length, with tremendous expanses of low, golden-brown bush and jungle stretching away on either side – only limited, on far horizons, by the faint irregular blueness of other mountain ranges. Where this ridge merged into savannah I was surrounded by a red-gold ocean, restless in the strong wind – and then I saw, in the distance, what seemed to be quite a large though short-legged animal moving slowly by the roadside. Moments later it became apparent that this creature was a grotesquely crippled young man, dragging himself through the dust, using only his stick-like arms. His destination, I assumed, was an isolated compound five hundred yards away, just

195

visible through its pathetic crop of failed maize. I braked. Should I stop and try to help him, or would he mistake my concern for vulgar curiosity and feel angry and humiliated? Then I realised that he was unaware of my presence, being totally absorbed in the pain of his effort to move. I dismounted and suddenly felt overwhelmed. All the strong but futile emotions generated by Africa's manifold problems and tragedies, and normally half-suppressed, took over and shattered me. The young man's breath was coming in short wheezy gasps, saliva dribbled from the corners of his wide-open mouth, his small thin face was twisted with agony and despair, his filthy rags revealed an emaciated torso and dreadfully distorted legs. Leaving Lear in the middle of the road, I approached him; possibly he would accept a piggy-back home. Then he noticed me. Terror filled his eyes and he whimpered and writhed like a wounded trapped animal. Hastily I turned away and remounted, abandoning him to his lonely misery and confusedly wishing that someone would put him down, as though he were indeed a disabled animal. Obviously he was uncared for and unloved – a piece of human trash in his community – otherwise he would not have had to move thus, nor would he have given off such a powerful aura of every sort of suffering.

Soon after came a grim drought area: mile after mile of stunted maize and withered sunflowers. The trees too were burned up, the few inhabitants looked wretched. Their square or oblong huts, unusually neatly built, were thatched to match the dead maize and blended almost invisibly into the shambas. Amidst thorny scrub wandered flocks of brown and white fat-tailed sheep and herds of small skinny cattle tended by small skinny boys.

I spent that night in the rather unfriendly township of Igawa – low-lying, dusty, hot – where begins the long climb to the Mbeya escarpment. Tanzania's main-road townships keep the *mzungu* at a distance, though one always meets a few welcoming individuals. Unlike homogeneous bush villages, these are mongrel communities of uprooted people from disparate regions – a bit of this tribe and that, everyone hoping somehow to scratch a living by selling something (food, charcoal, pombe, poultry, handicrafts, bodies) to the comparatively rich who pass that way. Even bus or matatu passengers are comparatively rich, otherwise they couldn't afford a ticket. International truckers are very rich; their smuggling opportunities, if not their wages, see to that. Passing expatriates – rich beyond imagining – like to get a wayside handicraft bargain and boast to their neighbours who paid three times as much for the same thing in an urban market. And so on . . . Yet in my experience most Tanzanians, however poor, do not beg or seek sponsorship from the *mzungu*; their activities are proudly commercial.

The next day's long climb to the Mbeya plateau involved only a few miles of non-gruelling walking and many miles of slow cycling. On one long steep hill, during the hottest part of the afternoon, I walked behind a middle-aged man pushing an old man – who looked at death's door – to the nearest hospital, ten miles away. I marvelled at the skeletal patient, his eyes glazed with suffering, being able to balance on the carrier. Then an FAO Land Cruiser overtook us, empty but for the expatriate driver who sped past, unseeing, vividly illustrating the reality of Western 'aid' to Africa. Hundreds of such vehicles, normally carrying only one or two expatriates, zoom around rural areas; but the locals, to whom transport would be a boon, know better than to expect a lift. Ten minutes later, near the top of the hill, a Toyota pick-up stopped and a well-dressed Tanzanian got out to rescue the old man. A front-seat passenger moved to the back and the patient – too weak to walk – was lifted into the vehicle. His son cycled on, there being no room for a bicycle in the crowded back. Following him, I mused on the manifold uses of bicycles in Africa – as carts, ambulances, bath-chairs, hearses (the rigid corpse, wrapped in sacking or bark-cloth, is laid across the carrier), as mobile dairies and dispensaries and of course as vehicles for a family outing. Later that same day I saw a father transporting two small sons on his cross-bar while his pregnant wife rode side-saddle behind him, with baby on back and toddler in lap.

I arrived at Uyole, a trading centre marking an important international junction, just too late to cover the final ten miles to Mbeya. In these dreary little places one tends to concentrate on *bia*; food is too hard to find and too repulsive when found. It surprised me to be greeted by three English-speakers, sitting outside a crowded noisy bar; since leaving Mafinga the language-barrier had been insurmountable.

Mr Luhala, from Arusha, had recently moved to Mbeya as sales manager for a tyre company, leaving his wife and four children behind. 'Education must be a parent's first priority and here the schooling is bad.'

Mr Maskini, a retired lawyer, told me, 'The mission schools, with strict discipline, used to produce the best pupils. It's good our Prime Minister Malecela now says religious communities can again run secondary schools – but not primary, which might too much influence the formation of the child. President Nyerere allowed only secular education, he thought all those different Christian sects would be divisive – as in Kenya and Uganda – against the unified nation he wanted to create.'

'And *did* create,' said Mr Luhala. 'At least we can be proud of our unity. We've hundreds of tribes but could never have tribal troubles like Kenya and Uganda.'

Mr Mpondele, a hotelier and 'international merchant' from Mbeya, rather smugly agreed: 'We have become politically mature, a grown-up nation – thanks to Mwalimu!'

Mr Maskini frowned at his *bia* bottle and wondered, 'Politically mature? That remains to be seen, when we have our multi-party elections in 1995. Anyhow you can't compare us with Kenya or Uganda. We don't have the same history of conflict. Our tribes were mostly small and scattered over a huge territory, not competing. But it's true Mwalimu cleverly stopped trouble-makers from stirring up tribalism. He encouraged nationalism instead, using Swahili to give us a sense of superiority – we haven't remained tied in our thinking by the colonial language.'

'But that was a two-edged weapon,' said Mr Mpondele. 'It also cut us off from the advancing Western world. And people laugh at us for keeping English as the medium of university education while refusing to have it taught in primary schools, and having it taught only very badly at secondary level. Now our academic standards are shameful – most students learning by rote, without understanding!'

'Soon this may change,' said Mr Luhala. 'Lately the expat teachers at our training colleges decided all future exams should be in Swahili.'

Angrily Mr Maskini asked, 'Why should expats make such decisions for us?' His question was ignored. This conversation helped me to understand the common Tanzanian assumption that all *mzungus* should speak Swahili; among the unsophisticated, failure to do so can provoke mild antagonism, as though their collective self-esteem had been wounded.

Despite the disasters wrought by Nyerere's head-in-the-clouds socialism, my companions still saw it as a better way of life than unrestrained capitalism. Mr Luhala asked, 'Why do Western politicians talk so much now about "socialism" being dead? Only Communism is dead and these are different ideas – our Mwalimu is a humanist, not a Communist!'

I explained that at present the West is led by manic capitalists who find it expedient to blur this distinction.

'You are correct!' exclaimed Mr Maskini. 'Not only African politicians are dishonest!'

It was getting late. As the truckers who had been drinking nearby began to move off with their bar-girls Mr Luhala suddenly admitted to being in a panic, as a grass-widower. 'For me now celibacy is the only safeguard, but even at 48 that's not easy. I ask myself if castration would be better than the risk of AIDS? I'm only half-joking! Maybe that's the answer for all men who have completed their families!'

When I too made a move it transpired that Mr Mpondele had already paid for my *bia*. He then invited me to spend the following night as his guest in Mbeya's Grand Motel – 'My wife Janet would like to talk to you about many things. She very much enjoys foreign conversation.' He had offered a lift – Lear would fit in the back of his pick-up – and had been puzzled by my declining it. The concept of cycling for fun is hard to get across in Africa.

My doss-house cell was decorated with by-now-familiar AIDS prevention posters and on the bedside table lay a six-pack – 'Made in Alabama: Electronically Tested'. (The notion of electronically tested condoms inspires some interesting but unprintable thoughts.) A graphically illustrated booklet, produced by the Benedictine Ndanda Mission Press, represented a loftier approach to the problem; it emphasised the behaviour change angle, the weakening of self-control when drink has been taken, the miserable lives led by widows and fatherless children. This was an excellent publication, but once a couple have closed the bedroom door are they likely to pause for a read?

Mbeya on its high plateau seems protected by semi-surrounding mountains, their majesty cloud-veiled when I arrived soon after dawn. This provincial capital is thinly spread over the valleys, slopes and ledges of a fertile ridge gradually rising to a blunt, perpendicular central peak. Steep, wide, rough streets alternate with even rougher narrow laneways, winding between huts or dukas or bungalows in shaggy gardens. As in most such cities, the atmosphere is more rural than urban, the bush lifestyle much in evidence. To me the people seemed jollier, and more relaxed and friendlier, than elsewhere in Tanzania. 'We are like the Malawians,' said Janet; and I found that she was right.

Mr Percy Mpondele's Grand Motel is a new one-storey building in a valley opposite the bus station – a hyper-active place at 7 a.m. Recently a law forbidding nocturnal bus journeys had come into force, provoking much indignation. Its laudable purpose was to prevent all those fatal crashes inevitable in the dark on Tanzania's average road, but its only perceived effect was to add alarmingly to travellers' expenses. Instead of bussing from A to B by night, doing what had to be done in B during the day and returning to A in a bus departing at sunset, *two* nights had to be spent in B – and no one considered the extra safety worth the extra cost.

From the road the Grand Motel is invisible behind its high mud wall, fortified with broken glass and softened by overhanging acacia and frangipani. Having pushed Lear up the eroded slope – almost steep enough to be called a cliff-face – I found a locked gate and a sleeping askari. Within, below the veranda, three thatched, bamboo-walled drinking booths were conspicuously labelled 'Lourdes France', 'St Francisco of assis' and 'St Bernadett'. These set the tone of the establishment. The Grand Motel was devoid of sex-workers and more genuinely 'respectable' than some of the Christian Centres I had stayed in. (Later I discovered why.) By Western standards it seemed ungrand, though clean and comfortable; in contrast to my usual lodgings it seemed Hiltonian.

I spent much of the day exploring Mbeya and its environs. The large shops are still owned by Asians (or Levantines) and stocked a few 'luxury' goods – edible biscuits, coloured candles, tinned butter, powdered milk – imported from nearby capitalist Malawi. But, as one Asian merchant explained dolefully, it was hard to sell those exotic items; inflation was galloping so fast you couldn't see it, yet no wage increase would be allowed until July. In the bank I discovered that all Forex controls had recently been lifted; it was now possible to exchange hard currency in any freelance bureau de change, at negotiable rates.

200

Far up in the mountains a coolish breeze blew, even at noon; I was moving into the southern winter. All Mbeya lay below me, hundreds of flat tin roofs glimmering amidst thriving crops: maize, bananas, coffee, cocoa. Here on the heights grew woods of mighty blue gums where women foraged for fuel, then gracefully carried their long heavy loads, tied with vines, in and out of narrow gullies on precipitous paths. This region, enjoying every natural advantage, should be prosperous. Its extreme poverty, being man-made, arouses as much rage as pity. And now it walks, with the rest of Africa, in the shadow of death.

The Mpondeles belonged to the local élite; they owned another hotel in 'new' Mbeya, the slightly industrialised zone on the main road to Zambia, and Percy's international trading was almost too obviously profitable. As Janet and I settled down to a sunset *bia* session on the veranda she described herself as 'a pious Catholic' – then added, 'But I'm not a spoil-sport or narrow-minded. I'm a liberated woman, if I want a drink I have it in public.'

Soon Janet was confiding that Percy disapproved of her 'purity policy'. 'He says it's impossible to run a successful hotel without bar-girls but I say he's wrong. This hotel is my personal AIDS prevention programme. Men away from home should have such places to stay, now more and more they want to avoid temptation. If they can have nice surroundings, good food, happy talk in the bar and no women hunting them – then they can safely travel. A year ago I told my husband we must have this sort of hotel, in time it will become popular – and already this is coming true, my hotel is getting a reputation for safety. I had to nag and nag at Percy, he didn't want to know about the figures that put me in this mood. Sixteen AIDS deaths were reported in Mbeya in '86. Four years later we had 1,776 *reported* deaths – and how many more? Now we are the third worst town in the country. That's what made me *do* something, it's crazy to say nothing can be done! If everyone does nothing, it gets like a sort of mass-suicide. If we don't change, who will be left in twenty years? All my darling children could be dead, there are families who have lost *all* children . . . I don't know how those parents go on living! Everyone has to *do* something, not only talk about how bad it is – or pretend it *isn't*!'

Janet also fretted about her children – should they escape AIDS – becoming drug-addicts. There is, she said, an increasing cocaine problem in Tanzania and her blaming some of the backpacking Whitemen seemed not unreasonable. We were into our fourth beer when she confessed to her major worry – Percy's behaviour in the other hotel (stocked with up-market bar-girls), where he often spent the night on the pretext of 'needing to supervise things'. 'We have a good manager there,' said Janet. 'I don't believe him. I've stopped sleeping with him, it's too risky and my children must come first. Orphan children are the worst nightmare for every African woman educated about AIDS. We are not fools, we know what men are, we must act independently – a complete change of attitude and behaviour is our duty. If husbands lose the wife's trust, that's their own fault.' She spoke briskly, stoically; but there was sadness and hurt in her eyes. I remember her now as another 'source of hope', my generic name for those exceptional African women whose response to AIDS is imaginative and courageous, who know their feminist hour has come.

After supper, as I wrote in my room, Max appeared in the doorway – a cheerful, good-looking young man who worked with his wife in the hotel kitchen. Without preamble he asked, 'What medicine do you have for this *ukimwi* disease?' The following dialogue then took place.

Me: There is no medicine for *ukimwi*. The only solution is to avoid the virus – one man, one woman, no bar-girls!

Max: That is impossible! *Very* impossible for my age – I am twenty-eight, young and fit, one woman cannot satisfy me. Always I must test myself with others.

Me: Then in five years you will probably be dead – certainly in ten years. Is it OK for your wife also to test herself with others?

Max: (looking bemused, then angry) What do you say? You say my wife should be like a prostitute? This is not a nice thing to say to me, I am an educated man, I want no prostitute for my wife!

Me: Do you test yourself with prostitutes or friends?

Max: Of course with both, I have many friends who admire my body. Our bar-girls in this town need money and enjoy very much different men. They learn many things truckers know from different countries – I like this, it is good for me. But

I love only my wife because she is the mother of my children.

Me: How many children?

Max: (proudly) Five and soon another!

Me: How old is your wife?

Max: Twenty-five or twenty-six – I am not sure, maybe twenty-four, she was from school when we married. My father paid very much because she is educated like me, to secondary.

Me: So now you have enough children?

Max: (giggling) No, no! We must take all God sends, it is a sin to stop children coming – the Pope, our Holy Father, says this.

Me: What does our Holy Father say about men testing themselves with many women?

Max evaded my stern gaze and asked how much Lear had cost in sterling. Would I sell him at the end of my holiday? If so, please would I bring him back to Mbeya and sell him to Max? At this point Max's wife summoned him to the kitchen where there were chickens to be plucked for four government officials who had just arrived from Dar es Salaam and sought the temptation-free Grand Motel.

Max's phrase 'I must test myself' reminded me of Dr Makwetta's comments on polygamy. To have fathered a baby once a year for six years is not enough to prove virility; fidelity to one woman indicates weakness and poverty, even meanness. It must be evident to one's peers that one can cope, physically, emotionally and economically, with a variety of females. I fell asleep pondering: Could an epidemic like AIDS have inspired – where it was inspired – the religious requirement to be monogamous?

On 6 May Lear had his finest hour – actually eight hours, up to and down from the 7,300-foot Mbogo Pass on a track my map described as 'non-motorable'. When I noticed it, while considering how to avoid returning to the Uyole junction, my pulse quickened. A Tanzanian route designated 'non-motorable' (which is how most people would describe most Tanzanian roads) is guaranteed to be just that. From Makumbako we had been on the main road and, though traffic is light on even the 'mainest' Tanzanian road, I craved the solitude of a mere track. This one – the old, history-haunted German road from Mbeya to Karonga – joined the main road near the Malawian border. Decades of disuse render even a German road

203

indecipherable and it took some time to find its starting point in the large village of Mlowa, twelve miles from Mbeya along the road to Zambia. Once I went astray on wide, bright pastureland, silvery green in the rising sun and rippling under a cool breeze. This very beautiful mistake led to a shoddy collectivised dairy-farm where a small boy became hysterical with terror on seeing me. His father spoke no English and seemed almost equally scared, though in a more restrained way. Even the cows took fright and tried to break out of their filthy milking-shed.

From Mlowa 'the German road', as it is still known locally, ran level for several miles through lavishly fertile country between blossom-laden hedges. Then cultivation was left behind and gradually the climb began, in a treeful valley where a mountain stream raced and sparkled beside the track – now a sandy path. Amidst the variegated greens of the wayside vegetation wild flowers rioted, their colours matched by darting birds and dancing butterflies. Little can have changed here since August 1914, when Captain von Langenn Steinkeller set out from Mbeya to invade British-held Nyasaland, leading 21 White officers and 800 spearmen and askari.

When the serious climb began Mbeya soon reappeared, away to the north-west and far below. Directly behind me Mount Mbeya dramatically dominated the whole region – an 8,500-foot cone, the only break in a smooth-crested range that stretched north and south as far as the eye could see. On both sides of the track, beyond profound ravines, occasional isolated homesteads overlooked precipitous slopes from their narrow ledges. Each slope was cultivated in long thin contrasting strips: the old gold of ripe maize, the sombre green of potatoes, the rich red-brown of ploughland, the strident yellow of something unfamiliar. Lear should now have been fulfilling his destiny as a mountain-bike but it wasn't quite like that; perhaps the inventor had another sort of mountain in mind. Sometimes instead of Lear carrying me I had to lift him over rocky protuberances – is it time to invent a jumping-bike?

About halfway up I saw something unexpected, an elaborate complex of ruined red-brick colonial buildings on a distant hilltop. These, I later discovered, were a long-abandoned German Mission. Why missionaries ever settled here I cannot imagine, unless the region was then much more heavily populated. From such remotenesses thousands were drawn to the German cotton and sisal plantations – where workers were regularly flogged and treated as slaves – and, in British days, to the tea estates of Mufindi and Tukuyu.

The Mbogo Pass is not straight up-and-down; having attained an exhilarating 7,000 feet, the grassy path undulates across a series of wide saddles linking mountain to mountain – some slopes bare, short-grassed, boulder-studded, others darkly forested. Here the vast panorama of the Mbeya plateau is no longer visible; this is a world withdrawn and touched by mystery, silent but for the echoing shouts of shepherd boys in deep green valleys and the singing of the wind in isolated pines.

The summit happens amidst a magical forest of indigenous trees, wild bananas, towering ferns, convoluted vines, multicoloured fungi. Rarely does one come upon an unviolated forest – not secondary growth, recovered from past depredations, but the original woodlands of Africa. I paused to nut-munch and commune with those trees, as one feels free to do once well away from the negative vibes of motorised territories.

For some time the path had been dwindling and I saw now that it vanished below the pass, where forest was abruptly replaced by a naked slope of scree and tufted grass. I hesitated. Should I remain on the heights and turn south towards Malawi, plunging into the forest and trusting to luck? No – the undergrowth was too thick for Lear to be forced through without extraordinary effort. The alternative was to descend, traversing the scree and hoping the track would eventually reappear and turn south. Cycling was not of course an option on so fearsome a gradient; the exertion required to restrain Lear was scarcely less than that required to push him up.

On that three-hour descent I completely lost my always feeble sense of direction. Eventually the path reappeared, following the course of a swift sparkling stream, and led me round and round a bewilderment of very steep mountains wearing a seamless garment of dark dense forest. This path might or might not be going to Malawi; given such a topographical frenzy anything seemed possible. Then the landscape widened; expanses of rough grassland separated the mountains, groves of trees replaced the forest and the path again acquired road status. Where it had been hacked out of sheer red cliffs it overhung, on my right, a wooded gorge in which the stream was growing to riverhood. When this gorge broadened to a

205

valley, chequered with plots of maize, bananas and coffee, I knew I was on the wrong road.

In a tiny village I was stared at with wide-eyed disbelief or fear – or a mixture of both. A mile further on I sat astride an old but still sturdy stone bridge, eating bananas bought by the wayside from a brother and sister, aged perhaps 6 and 7, who were too alarmed to indicate the price of their goods. Below me brown flood-water foamed and roared over and between giant boulders, seeming more a waterfall than a river. Not long after I found myself on the main road – ten miles north of Tukuyu and forty miles north of Malawi.

Tukuyu is a biggish town draped over a high mountain; post-Mbogo, that long ascent from river-level used up the last of my energy. Since mid-afternoon clouds had been lurking along the horizon; at 6.15 a cold gale sent them swarming blackly across the sky. Mercifully I arrived at the first bar-cum-guest-house just as the rain came – a torrent that within moments had made a river of the street.

Two English-speakers, an elderly government official and a young doctor, sat morosely drinking in a corner of the grubby lamp-lit bar. (Tukuyu is only erratically electrified.) The official deplored Tanzania's kow-towing to the IMF and slow drift towards multi-party democracy. 'This new fashion in Africa, this pretending to want democracy – *who* wants it? Who understands it in the bush? This is Western racism, forcing Western ways of politics down our throats. Is it right to threaten "No more funding!" if we don't have "human rights"? Human rights! What do they know about human rights in the bush? All they want is food!'

'And medicine,' said the doctor.

His companion snorted angrily. 'Medicine! What good is medicine now? There is no medicine for *ukimwi*!' He glared at me. 'You see Africa as a nice place for WHO to study this interesting new virus – and for drug companies to make experiments. You think we're dirty immoral ignorant people who deserve to die! Well, we *are* dying – around here many, very many.'

The doctor added, 'We'll never know how many. Here people are still ashamed, not willing to report the true cause of all these deaths out in the bush. But we see the funerals, more and more every month. You know what's the problem? Women will do anything for money – *that's* the problem!'

206

I was too cold, tired and hungry to pick up even this gauntlet. Instead I moved to the cramped restaurant behind the bar, where one could see the cook dismembering a bull's hindquarters in a leaking lean-to while his juvenile assistant fanned a bucket of charcoal.

My last Tanzanian supper was memorable: a pile of pale, limp, grease-sodden chips and three slabs of dauntingly tough fried bull – I spent forty minutes chewing through it and was left exhausted, with aching jaws. My table was half-obstructing the door of a chronically neglected latrine, much used by drinkers from the bar, and each time the door opened ammonia (plus) threatened asphyxiation. Meanwhile two teenage prostitutes were drawing blood while competing over a truck-driver. He had brought one of them from Dar es Salaam as his semi-permanent travelling concubine, thus provoking a despairing local lass to physical violence. She knew the driver, he had always slept with her before, now she would have no supper. For that youngster, no man meant no food. In such places as Tukuyu bodies are sold not to acquire luxuries but to survive.

10

One-Man-Banda

The Two Faces of Malawi

When travelling alone one can behave childishly without fear of derision. It was dotty to leave Tukuyu at 5.50 a.m. in rainy darkness – 'But so what?' I said to myself, pushing Lear up a steep main street pitted with craterous pot-holes. I was too impatient for my first glimpse of Lake Nyasa to be detained by the sort of steady cold rain not unknown in Ireland. Then the first light glimmered over the Kipengere Range – sulphurous streaks amidst heavy clouds lying along the summits. Free-wheeling down from the ridgetop, I thought of the runner who left Tukuyu (then Neu Langenburg) on 15 August 1914, bearing an urgent message from Herr Stier, the German Imperial Administrator of the district, to his friend Mr Webb, the British Resident at Karonga, sixty miles away. Poor Herr Stier had heard rumours of war but his anxious pleas for information from Mbeya had been ignored, or not received. So he wrote to Mr Webb: 'I am not clear whether England is at war with Germany or not.' Courteously Mr Webb replied, clarifying the situation; and that, one supposes, put an end to a beautiful friendship.

During the Scramble for Africa this region was much coveted, despite its being so inaccessible. Germany and Britain – with Portugal protesting in the wings – laid claim to here or there and one morning in 1885 several tribes around Lake Nyasa woke up to find that the cartographers in Berlin had given them new identities by drawing international frontiers through their territories. Henceforth there would be Portuguese and British Angonis, British and German Wakondes, and so on.

In 1875, Europeans ruled less than a tenth of Africa; by the end of the century they had appropriated almost the entire continent.

(There wasn't enough widespread organised armed resistance to talk of its being 'conquered'.) Yet the speed of the political take-over was deceptive; not everyone knew precisely what it was they were taking over.

As a British Protectorate, Nyasaland was treated as a reservoir for labour in the South African and Rhodesian mines and plantations. There were some misgivings about this policy at official levels; in the British colonial administration those who didn't like what they found themselves doing quite often said so, but were rarely heeded. In 1935 a Nyasaland government inquiry reported:

> The whole fabric of the old order of society is undermined when 30% to 60% of the able-bodied men are absent at one time. It is easy to criticise that old order, but it worked: the community was stable; and there was give and take within the community. Emigration destroys the old order, but offers nothing to take its place. The family-community is threatened with complete dissolution.

This alarm bell rang in deaf ears and a decade later there were 200,000 migrant workers in Southern Rhodesia (now Zimbabwe), 62 per cent from Northern Rhodesia (now Zambia) and Nyasaland (now Malawi). Their families remained at home in moribund villages, a pattern already seen in Uganda. However, the British – despite their mixed motives – unquestionably did more good than harm in Nyasaland. Without outside intervention the whole region might have been depopulated by the turn of the century, so efficiently were the Arab slavers raiding when Dr Livingstone arrived in 1861, and so ruthlessly were the Angoni slaughtering those who escaped the Arabs. (The Angoni, a sickeningly bloodthirsty tribe originally from Zululand, spent much of the nineteenth century killing every African who had the misfortune to get in their way as they rampaged from southern Africa to the shores of Lake Victoria.) Thus Pax Britannica really was urgently needed around Lake Nyasa; and it was initially imposed not by detachments of the British or Indian army but by a scattering of resourceful, fearless missionaries and a handful (sometimes no more than two or three) of extraordinarily courageous traders, armed with obsolete weapons that as often as not didn't work.

209

Livingstone's ambition to bring 'Commerce, Christianity and Civilisation' to Africa is often unfairly quoted as summing up Victorian racism-cum-profiteering. Although Livingstone the man was unlikeable in many ways, greed was not among his personality flaws – his whole career proves him to have been singularly unmercenary, he only wanted to stop the Africans exploiting each other for the benefit of the Arabs. Any humane European, arriving on the southern shore of Lake Nyasa on 17 September 1859, would have seen a need to import 'civilisation' – and fast, before the local tribes became extinct. Livingstone naturally thought Christianising the 'natives' was the best way to go about civilising them. And a profit-making exchange of non-human goods seemed the quickest way to wean them off their enthusiastic collaboration with Arab slavers – by whom they were paid only the pittance needed to secure their collaboration.

Our road of ravaged tarmac ran level for a few miles through Tukuyu Tea Estates, not far from the town, where pickers were already at work – the women's bright garments like confetti strewn over distant green slopes. Then abruptly everything disappeared; a cloud had sat on the mountain, reducing visibility to thirty yards and imposing the strange silence of fogginess. But soon the long, gradual descent began and the meridian cleared, though on either side immense grassy valleys retained in their depths small separate cloudlets, drifting like misshapen ships on an ocean of space. At every shoulder I looked for the lake but saw yet another mountain – wooded or sparsely cultivated. A delightful lack of traffic puzzled me; soon that mystery was to be unpleasantly solved. Then the mountains opened out and to the east, beyond a wide, shallow, tree-packed valley, rose four free-standing, oblong forested hills crowned with lines of pale grey rock obelisks. Eagerly I scrutinised the southern horizon and there, fringing a vast flat hazy plain, lay Lake Nyasa – a remote blueness, a mere line of light that might have been mistaken for sky. The plain still lay a thousand feet below me but from here the descent was steep and soon I had joined – disconcertingly – an EC-type highway complete with harshly coloured obtrusive signs. One of these informed me that it was five miles to Malawi. This new road and the open border celebrate a reconciliation between neighbours; because of Banda's cosy rela-

210

tionship with South Africa, Tanzania and Malawi were non-speakers for many years.

It pained me to cross the flooded Songwe River on one of those starkly functional concrete bridges to be found everywhere from Norway to Calabria. I paused to gaze at this famous frontier between Tanganyika and Nyasaland, hurrying brownly between low shrub-lined banks with a long smooth mountain ridge in the background. In anticipation, the next four or five weeks filled me with excitement. I had a detailed map, showing me how to avoid areas now tourist-infested, and Malawi was to be the centrepiece of my journey. For some reason lost in the mists of time, Nyasaland – as it was when first I read about it – had always enthralled me even more than Masailand, Kilimanjaro, the source of the Nile, the Mountains of the Moon. And in 1992 there was the added interest of a complex political evolution – too complex, as events soon proved.

The new Tanzanian border-post comprised a few beat-up por-tacabins at the foot of a cliff in the middle of nowhere. A sudden brief heavy shower coincided with my arrival. The only other border-crossers were local peasants; they had moved freely before the reconciliation but now were required to produce documents. As we huddled together in the shelter of the cliff there was a vague unease in the air. Then I hauled Lear into Passport Control where my health documents were checked, for the first and last time, and my cholera certificate found to be out of date; in London I had forgotten to replace the old with the new. From the Tanzanian point of view it couldn't have mattered less; I was now leaving the country. However, I had broken the law and provided another bribe-seeking opportunity not availed of; the officer registered shock! horror! – then lectured me at length before accepting my grovelling apology and waving me on. While crossing no man's land I paused to forge an up-to-date vaccination on my old certificate.

A customs officer and a policeman – both polite but distant – awaited me outside a solitary, freshly painted little bungalow. The former glanced cursorily into one pannier, the latter told me the 'formalities' happened twelve miles farther on, at the village of Kapora. This seemed odd, until I studied the landscape and realised how difficult an illegal entry would be with Lake Nyasa on the left and high, bulky, pathless mountains quite close on the right.

At 9.45 the ominously hot sun was tempered by a headwind against which I couldn't pedal much above walking speed. It came tearing across the plain of Nkonde – flat, fertile, bright green – and here I remembered with grief the fate of the Wankonde, a tribe who lived next door to Paradise before the slavers arrived. (One can and does mourn uselessly in certain places.) This plain was once a haven of tranquillity and abundance, protected to the north by the mountains I had just crossed, to the west by the mountains I was about to cross, to the east by Lake Nyasa – and never encroached on from the south because no one bothered to find out what went on at that extremity of the inland sea. (Livingstone imagined Lake Nyasa to be a hundred miles shorter than it is and none of the Africans he met on its shore was in a position to put him right.) 'Nkonde' means 'banana'; this tribe took its name from the plant that supplied not only its main food but fuel, roofing material, plates, umbrellas, soap from the sap and fibre for weaving into blankets. (The Wankonde went naked during the day, apart from the women's token apron of bark-cloth, some nine inches square.) Plump cattle grazed the pasturelands between the banana groves, and the stands of cotton trees and sycamore, and Thomson wrote ecstatically, 'I felt as if I had fallen upon some enchanted place'. But a decade later came the Arabs from Tanzania, who had heard talk of these happy people, lacking a warrior tradition and there for the taking. Monteith Fotheringham, an African Lakes Company employee then managing the Company's new store at Karonga, described the slavers 'burning village after village, slaughtering without stint, and those women they did not kill they put in irons and reserved for a fate still more severe'. All this was the standard prelude to the enslavement of the most saleable members of a tribe. Fotheringham – the only European in the region – at once took it upon himself to organise an ultimately successful campaign against the Arabs and their local half-breed ally, the infamous Mlozi. But by then the tribe's 'perfect Arcadia' – Thomson's phrase – had been destroyed forever.

Malawi's Department of Tourism proclaims to the world: 'You'll fall in love the moment you discover the spectacular beauty, the charming friendliness, the mysterious moods of Malawi – THE WARM HEART OF AFRICA!' It wasn't quite like that at Kapora, apart from the mysterious mood which led to my being given only a ten-day visa and told that I must go no further south than

Kasungu. I almost wept, so grievous was this blow.

Kapora's atmosphere differed grimly from all the other border-posts on my route. It is true that to qualify for admission to Malawi men must be 'short back and sides' and women skirted to below the knee; I had half-suspected these off-the-wall regulations to be a travellers' tale. Men with hair likely soon to touch the collar are turned back unless they consent to be shorn on the spot. Those for whom long hair is a 'significant statement', and who therefore try to hide their flowing locks within capacious headgear, are dealt with extra-severely. I was curtly ordered to put on a skirt; when I pro-tested that no one could ride a bicycle with a cross-bar wearing a long skirt the hard-faced immigration officer snapped 'No excep-tions can be made!' and handed me a thick book of rules. Luckily I read on, out of curiosity, thus discovering that writers and jour-nalists require written permission from Lilongwe to enter the coun-try and are not allowed to travel without a 'guide'. That was a narrow squeak; instantly I became a 'retired teacher' and during the next ten days was surprised by the strength of my own reaction to this deception. Enforced concealment of one's identity is oddly disorientating, especially among a people as endearing and affably curious as the Malawians. On being told 'retired teacher' they always sought details about my long and presumably honourable career.

Donning my wrap-around skirt, bought in Mbeya for this pur-pose, I cycled on in a miserable and puzzled fury. Beyond sight of officialdom I stopped to adjust the skirt, rolling it up into a thick pad around my waist and incidentally discovering that those silly old colonialists were right after all and a cummerbund greatly ameliorates the savagery of the midday sun. I knew nothing of recent events in Malawi, which is a measure of how little interest most Africans take in each others' problems – understandably, their own being all-absorbing. In fact to be Irish in a Malawian Immigration Office on 7 May 1992 was singularly unfortunate; Bishop John Roche, a brave fellow-countryman, had recently set a much-needed cat among Malawi's over-fed pigeons – of which more anon.

Approaching Karonga, I saw that tall bango reeds still mark the Kombwe lagoon. Here, on 27 October 1887, the Arabs' African mercenaries (the dreaded ruga-ruga) attacked the Wankonde. Fotheringham described how:

213

The war whoops of the ruga-ruga smote the Wankonde hearts with terror. Armed only with spears they were no match for the Arabs who, keeping at a safe distance, poured volley upon volley into the reeds, soon red with the blood of the dying. Every black who jumped out of the lagoon was shot in the open . . . Maddened by their success, the ruga-ruga rushed upon the natives and drove them farther back, spearing those who stuck fast in the mud. They then fired the reeds and, as the flames rose, the yells of the poor creatures behind might be heard far and near above the steady discharge of the guns. Now another enemy, more dreaded than the Arabs, rose against the natives in their dire extremity. This was the crocodile, who swung his hideous jaws out of the pool and made an easy prey of the bewildered blacks . . . Few succeeded in struggling through to the other side. While the attack was in progress the three Arab leaders, in order to gratify their morbid curiosity, climbed into trees, and with diabolical interest watched and regulated the work of extermination. Darkness only put an end to the slaughter. The native chiefs with the remnant of their people fled to the Songwe river, while the Arabs who had captured a great many women and children, encamped at the lagoon. Surely was never such a cruel massacre as this day had witnessed! It was the butchery of a simple people who had done wrong to no one.

Post-massacre, Mlozi, the slavers' leader, arrogantly informed Fotheringham that he was now Mlozi I, Sultan of Nkondeland, and expected regular tribute from the African Lakes Company. So began a small but momentous war that continued until 1895 and afforded Frederick Lugard his African initiation. Oddly, it was scarcely noticed in Britain though the Siege of Karonga out-Hentied Henty.

It felt strange to arrive in Karonga with my mind full of the town's century-old drama and to be at once confronted by the current drama. All the shops were shut; the town centre was near-deserted; jeep-loads of heavily armed paramilitary types were patrolling the streets, their expressions suggesting direct descent from the ruga-ruga. In an unobtrusive one-storey tourist hotel by the lake I sought beer and information. For all I knew, it was normal in Malawi to have armed men cruising around a town but surely it was abnormal for shops to be shut on a weekday. In the hotel bar a grey-haired, elegantly dressed man was trying to get the World Service on his transistor. That seemed healthy; it is illegal to listen to foreign broadcasts that might occasionally criticise Banda or encourage the populace to think for themselves, but at least this gentleman was not being cowed by the cruising paramilitary.

Having cycled through the noon heat – fierce at lake-level – I finished my first beer before asking, 'What's going on?' Gladly Sylvester explained, though I had feared my question might discomfit him. On the previous day, in Blantyre, a few hundred workers at Lonhro's David Whitehead textile factory had turned off their machines, picketed the factory gates and urged others to go on strike. As they marched into the city hundreds more joined them. The police tried to break up the demo, violence inevitably ensued and twenty-two strikers (the official figure: the true figure was not expected to emerge) were shot dead. Whereupon the unrest rapidly spread.

'We get all our credible information from the BBC,' remarked Sylvester, resuming his twiddling of the knobs. 'And in this hotel we can safely break the law. Malawi's image as "the warm heart of Africa" is very important – no police will intrude here, frightening you and all those out there.' He nodded towards the veranda, where a score of overlanders – English, Australian, New Zealander – sat gazing across the clear sparkling blue of Lake Nyasa towards the hazy blue mightiness of the Livingstone Mountains, rising sheer from the water on the far Tanzanian shore.

A small slim sandy-haired man hurried in, very agitated. He had just been on the telephone to Lilongwe, where lived his wife and little daughter. Things were much worse today, with thousands rioting and looting. He had also rung the boss of his Johannesburg road-haulage firm and been told to get his family out immediately. They would be leaving in an hour, on the next flight to Nairobi, from where they'd fly to Jo'burg – an eccentric route but the only quick exit.

Malcolm, a regular in Karonga's tourist hotel, was a friend of Sylvester, who now accused the Jo'burg boss of over-reacting. 'This is a beginning,' he said, 'but it isn't a revolution. Things won't be the same again – *never!* – but Whites are safe if they keep off the streets.' I thought then of the 1915 Chilembwe Rising, when one visitor to Nyasaland commented, 'The White population of the Protectorate were thrown into a very great fright over a very little thing.' Given a whiff of crowd violence, the Black/White relationship quickly collapses into mistrust and fear – witness my fleeing downhill from those angry Ugandan Muslims.

Having heard about my visa disappointment Sylvester sighed. 'Those immigration officers were also over-reacting, fearing a big uprising putting foreigners at risk. But nothing is organised, this is only the signal it's time to organise. And of course those officers wouldn't like your passport – maybe you're a colleague or ally of Bishop Roche! We're very sad about him, deported recently for demanding human rights for us – he'd lived in Malawi for twenty years and he loves us.'

Bishop John Roche was indeed central to the disturbances. Having led a chorus of clerical protests against Banda's intolerable ill-treatment of 'dissidents', he was arrested in his cathedral during the Easter ceremonies and deported at twenty-four hours' notice. Then, largely as a result of the religious leaders' bold public stand, seventy-five dissidents met in Lusaka and formed the Interim Committee for a Democratic Alliance in Malawi (immediately acronymed into ICDAM) to oppose the Malawi Congress Party, otherwise known as the One-Man-Banda. On 16 April the 52-year-old trade unionist and apostle of democracy, Chakufwa Chihana, returned from exile in Zambia to lead this opposition, despite his having previously spent seven years in one of Banda's notorious jails. A small crowd of Malawians and senior Western diplomats went to Lilongwe airport to meet him and witnessed his arrest as he left the plane. (The Malawians were few only because a rigorously censored press had been forbidden to announce Chihana's return.) In times past that would have been that: but 1992 was different. Several Western governments promptly issued formal statements denouncing Chihana's arrest and in a personal letter to the Life President the US government demanded his immediate release. All this 'interference' was ignored by Banda & Co. but widespread public awareness of outside support undoubtedly encouraged the strikers.

Malcolm went to the telephone again and came back white-faced – now expatriate vehicles were being stoned in Blantyre and Lilongwe. Sylvester asked dryly, 'Are you surprised?'

As the afternoon and evening passed more detailed news came through, either on the telephone via Malcolm or on the World Service. In the overcrowded and destitute townships around Blantyre and Limbe violence was increasing, the looters concentrating on PTC supermarkets owned by the Press Trust, which controls most of the Malawian economy and has Banda as its principal trustee. In Ndirne township women wearing Banda-decorated skirts were being stripped and beaten and the Malawi Congress Party offices had been destroyed. Meanwhile, in Lilongwe, some 3,000 of Chihana's supporters had gathered outside the High Court to glimpse their hero, chanting, 'We want to see the one who is brave!' When the police failed to bring Chihana to court, as ordered by a judge, the crowd ran riot through Lilongwe old town where the PTC supermarket was the first shop to be looted.

In the intervals of learning about Malawian politics I used this opportunity to study a phenomenon even odder than backpacking – overlanding. Overlanders are youngish (usually) people who pay large amounts of money to travel by truck from, for example, Nairobi to Cape Town, bringing most of their own food with them and camping each night at predetermined places like Karonga. This way of seeing Africa is apparently gaining popularity among those with more money than sense. At least backpackers retain autonomy, even if they exercise it with timidity. Overlanding I found utterly incomprehensible. Consider the sheer physical misery of travelling the length of Africa – or even half the length – by truck: the jolting, the dust, the diesel fumes, the frustration of being confined all day to a motor vehicle with companions not necessarily congenial . . . Who wouldn't gladly pay thousands of pounds to avoid such a fate? It relieved me to find much discontent among this truckload; reality was falling far short of the 'adventure and discovery' promised by advertisements. A young New Zealand woman complained, 'I thought we'd learn lots about Africa but our expedition leader is an ignorant lout. And we never seem to get to meet with Africans – we're all stuck together, or with other travellers, like now.' As we spoke the 'lout' was sauntering in and out of the bar; I would have described him as a wide-boy – tall, handsome, cocky, smooth-talking and knowing as much about Africa as a dog about a holiday.

Returning yet again from the telephone, Malcolm reported all borders closed, presumably to prevent the import of arms should that be under consideration. Sylvester smiled at me. 'So you're lucky you got in, even for ten days!' Malcolm hurried out to tell his four truckers they could not continue into Tanzania with their loads of grain for the drought areas. Then Sylvester advised me to spend another day in Karonga, awaiting developments; should events prove him right, a visa extension might still be possible. I followed the truckers to a large nearby guest-house set in a spacious, well-tended garden; my hot windowless cell, halfway down a long prison-like corridor, cost only £1.20.

The clock changes in Malawi, a change for the worse from my point of view as darkness falls at 5.45 p.m. After a dawn swim the hotel restaurant served an excellent breakfast at 6.10. People get going earlier in Malawi, perhaps because of the changed hour – or the Banda work ethic?

By 7 a.m. it was unpleasantly hot as I walked to the town centre – awkwardly, in my long skirt. The World Service had reported that unrest was spreading to various plantations in the south but Karonga seemed back to normal, apart from jeep-loads of the para-military Young Pioneers ostentatiously wielding their weapons as they patrolled the town and environs. I looked for the David White-head showrooms, as advised by the Tourist Board – 'Remember: No trip to Malawi is complete without a visit to David Whitehead and Sons (Malawi) Limited. Brilliant colours, bold patterns and high-quality 100% cotton are turned into works of art by our design team.' Alas! my trip to Malawi had to be incomplete; the Karonga showroom was closed – naturally enough, this firm's workers hav-ing sparked off the unrest. No one knew (or would say) whether the local workers were on strike or had been ordered to close the premises for security reasons.

Karonga's small PTC supermarket displayed an astounding range of products unseen for months: familiar brands of chocolate, tinned soups, breakfast cereals, preserves, fruit drinks, biscuits, washing-powders, toiletries, wines and spirits. I went for the powdered milk at 16 kwatchas (£2.60) per kilo; had I realised then how two-faced is Malawi – what Spartan fare lay ahead – I would have bought very much more. All these goodies are of course beyond the reach of the average Malawian. Yet an Australian overlander, queueing with me at a state-of-the-art till, exclaimed, 'So really Banda *is* a good guy! I wondered, but look what he's done for his country – there's no store like this in Tanzania, even in Dar!'

I remained discreetly silent. Sylvester had mentioned that PTC staff are reputed to be reliable Banda stooges.

After Tanzania's drab and uniform poverty Karonga seems almost First World. Its freshly painted public buildings stand in grounds trim and flowerful; all its shops, including a bookshop, are well-stocked; its sleek middle class is conspicuous; its Carlsberg Special beer is superb. (In Malawi, Carlsberg hold the brewing monopoly.) Tourists inured to the deprivations of neighbouring countries naturally ask, 'If this is the result of a benevolent dictatorship, who wants democracy?' Karonga does not suggest a country with the fifth-highest infant mortality rate in the world (320 per thousand in the first five years) and one of the lowest (4 per cent) female literacy rates.

His Excellency the Life President Ngwazi Dr H. Kamuzu Banda, Malawi's leader since 1963, fancies himself as successor to the region's old Maravi kings and claims 'divine right' and absolute authority. Ngwazi means 'Champion, Conqueror' and the President's megalomaniac title must be used in full whenever he is publicly mentioned. He exercises his absolute authority mainly through a 99 per cent share of Press Holdings, used to control not only agriculture, and retailing and distribution, but also Malawi's finance – including the two major banks. During the 1960s he gave some half-hearted support to smallholders but his long-term economic strategy was based on the development of estate agriculture. Between 1969 and 1973 Press Holdings took over the tobacco estates and Banda began to endow his courtiers and their families with carefully chosen assets in industry and agriculture, assets that would keep them loyal. The cunning and skill with which he turned Malawi into his incalculably profitable personal property is deserving of a book in itself. One is tempted actually to admire his adroit manipulating of the World Bank, which at first was properly suspicious of his machinations, then gave in and allowed them to flourish.

Because Banda abhorred the Soviet bloc and fitted neatly into the capitalist scheme of things he was for long, in Western eyes, 'a good guy'. Anyone who dared to defy him came to an unpleasant end – in exile, in prison or in an early grave – but that little weakness was overlooked. Before Portugal's African empire collapsed he was on friendly terms with Lisbon. In 1967 he established diplomatic ties with South Africa; three years later he received Prime Minister Vorster, paying a return visit to Pretoria in 1971. Ever since, he has carefully cultivated diplomatic and commercial (including tourist) links with South Africa. No Western tongue praised him aloud for this but in powerful circles his 'pragmatism' was quietly applauded. And it has to be said that it was less morally – if not politically – repugnant than the furtive collusion with Pretoria practised by some ostensibly anti-apartheid Black leaders.

Seen from afar (and 'afar' could be a luxury hotel in Lilongwe) Banda looked like the glorious exception to African leaders, the man who knew how to ensure political stability, sustain a sound economy, pay national debts. It seemed sensible to make agriculture the backbone of the economy; only when agribusiness became profitable was industrialisation – concentrating on light industries – to be considered. It seemed even more sensible to disdain 'Africanisation', retaining expatriates in key positions in both the private and state sectors. However, Banda's fondness for expatriates did not extend to the automatic acceptance of the rulings of an English judge. As Robert Jackson and Carl Rosberg have recorded in *Personal Rule in Black Africa*:

In one High Court trial, Banda not only refused to accept the ruling of its English judge – who, for reasons of insufficient evidence, had dismissed charges of murder brought against five men – but also blocked the release of the men and proceeded to give the traditional African courts the right to retry the cases and pass sentences of death upon conviction. Banda warned: 'Those five men are not going to be let loose, I can tell you that . . . Never, never, never. No matter what anyone says or does . . . I am in charge and I am not from England, either'. In addition, Banda secured from Parliament a Forfeiture Act, which empowered him to withhold the personal property of all persons whom he judged to be 'subversive'. An amendment permitted the law to be used against allegedly corrupt or negligent officials, and no prior conviction had to be obtained in the courts.

Well might Banda claim, in an argument with the directors of a British multinational giant, 'Anything I say is law. Literally law. It is a fact in this country.' Malawi's official motto is 'Unity, Loyalty, Obedience and Discipline', a list of virtues with considerable appeal for the multinational heirs of the bwanas.

While Nyerere's adherence to a chimera was depleting Tanzania's wealth, despite varied natural resources, Banda's 'state feudalism' was increasing Malawi's wealth, despite limited natural resources. Those neighbours had only one thing in common: both reduced the peasants to abject poverty. Malawi's 'economic miracle' is largely based on overpopulation, on an agricultural and industrial work-force which must accept slave-wages. Much is made of Malawi's capacity to feed its people and have enough over for export; in truth food is normally available for export only because most Malawians can't afford to eat enough. The drought has of course left them as dependent on imported grain as the rest of Southern Africa and on 15 November 1992 the Reverend Canon Peter Price reported in the *Guardian Weekly*:

Two weeks ago I visited the drought-stricken regions of Malawi. The hunger of many in the villages was painfully evident. Equally apparent was the fact that in rural communities the price of food was loyalty to the government. Parish clergy spoke of the inequitable distribution of maize in government hand-outs, revealing that many of the most needy are 'simply not entitled' . . . During the worst drought in history, any restoration of aid would need to be accompanied by the closest monitoring to ensure that the most at risk receive its benefit . . . Recent news reaching church agencies in the United Kingdom suggests that church leaders are in immediate and considerable danger, and various threats and coercions have been applied.

After a not very thorough exploration of Karonga – the lake-level heat is peculiarly enervating – I sweat-replaced in a small down-market café (comparatively down-market: anywhere else along my route it would have been up-market). A slogan plastered diagonally across the window said: 'KAMUZU KNOWS BEST' and two of my female fellow-customers wore wrap-around skirts displaying the Life President's portrait – on their bottoms, which struck me as a

221

comical case of *lèse-majesté*. A handsome young man stood by the counter, looking rather pensive and sipping a coke as though he wanted to make it last. He watched me drinking six cups of very sweet, milky tea, then followed me on to the street. 'I feared to talk in there,' he said, 'but I like talking to visitors. What is your opinion of my country? You've come when we make history! This is the beginning of the end – maybe the beginning of something horrible and violent but we *must* have change! Can you understand what it means for us to see this crack? It's only a crack, of course. And big buildings last long after they've shown a crack. But now people know there's a crack and if they push, and keep on pushing, more and more cracks will appear, faster and faster!'

Throughout the day this view was expressed, in different ways, by eight casual acquaintances. I found the Malawians' openness surprising, heartening – and touching. But their underlying message frightened me. I seemed to sense a people preparing for bloody conflict; dreading it, yet containing within themselves so strong an awareness of injustice that when the moment came they would contribute to it. I hope I was mistaken.

Near my guest-house stood Karonga's public library, reasonably well-stocked (the educational and fiction sections especially strong) and very well-organised. It is open all day, five and a half days a week, and much used – including by ragged little urchins unable to afford school but pathetically absorbed in the Ladybird series and excited by the excellent range of illustrated children's books. They spoke only a smattering of English and longed to be fluent. My engaging them in conversation displeased the librarian who chased them out of the building; I had trouble controlling my reaction.

The noon hours were spent sitting in breezy shade by the sapphire lake where white wavelets whispered and hissed on fine golden sand. In the intervals of bird-watching (mainly three species of heron) I talked with the passers-by or those laundering in the shallows. Karonga that day was invaded by a swarm of censorship-bred rumours: all borders and airports were closed – H.E. had fled to South Africa – the army and police were fighting each other in Lilongwe – Chihana had been strangled in jail by the Young Pioneers – the Presidential Palace had been burned down/blown up/looted – the Tanzanian army was coming to capture H.E. No rumour was too wild to be debated at length.

A few girls passed wearing big brightly coloured buttons on their bosoms, buttons inscribed around the periphery: SAVE OUR GIRLS FROM AIDS. NATIONAL AIDS CONTROL PROGRAMME. The central lettering preached the behaviour change message: SMART GIRLS SAY NO TO SEX! Banda's neurotic puritanism has done nothing to protect his country from AIDS; Malawi has the second highest total of reported cases in Southern Africa. It was unnecessary to visit any clinic or office to get the depressingly familiar figures; a large notice-board in the library displayed them prominently, together with numerous newspaper cuttings, urgent pleas for 'behaviour change' and extracts from WHO reports. In 1985, 17 cases were reported in Malawi, by 1988 there had been 2,586 reported deaths and by March 1991 that figure had risen to 15,715. As elsewhere, health officials believed the true figure to be higher, probably much higher. One newspaper cutting praised Chief Mponda of Mangechi District for having ordered every initiate to bring his own razor blade to his circumcision rite. Dr George Liomba, Manager of the National AIDS Control Programme, was quoted:

In the mid-1990s, AIDS will be the major cause of death in the age-group 20 to 49 years. This group has suffered 77% of our AIDS cases. Already we have more than 20,000 children who have lost one or both parents to AIDS. In urban centres about 20% of the women attending antenatal clinics are HIV +, as are 20% of our blood donors and 80% of prostitutes. Out of a population of about eight million, more than 300,000 are HIV + – 20% of urban adults and 8% of rural adults.

Malawi must be given credit – I said to Sylvester – for not sweep-ing the virus under the carpet in the interests of tourism. Swiftly he replied that the agricultural industry – as the mainspring of Malawi's economy, employing 85 per cent of the work-force – is much more important. 'This country will fall apart if we can't stop the epidemic. Most of its export earnings come from tobacco, tea, sugar – all needing a big work-force. Other countries have the same problem but we're more conscious of economic well-being, for the élite, so the government tried from the start to alert people. They haven't had much success, AIDS education is hard when you've such a high illiteracy rate and most families are too poor to own even a cheap transistor.'

Sylvester's brother worked for an insurance company in Lilongwe; it had recently doubled its premium and shortened its life-policy duration to ten years for untested clients. Only a minority had so far refused the test though no insurance is available for the infected. Time may reveal a statistically improbable number of false negatives on insurance company files.

Malcolm had joined us at the bar looking more cheerful, his family (including the dog) having landed safely in Johannesburg. He questioned the value of AIDS education. His employers, a South African haulage company, provided a hundred free condoms monthly to each driver of its fleet of seventy trans-Africa trucks and it was Malcolm's responsibility to issue them and get a receipt. 'Then the trucks come back to base and I find the rubbers stashed away in the back of the cab, spoiled by the heat, or the boys admit they've sold them. They'd rather get hell for selling them than have me thinking they'd used them – that's not macho!'

Hitchhiking White girls, Malcolm asserted, were still sleeping with his drivers in considerable numbers. 'It's all part of their "African Experience" – and they don't even insist on condoms. We go on about Blacks being suicidally fatalistic but those White bitches are no better.' Malcolm himself was the reverse of fatalistic. In Blantyre the family's Indian doctor had convinced him that mosquitoes could spread AIDS so he and his wife and 5-year-old daughter were tested every six months.

At sunset the World Service reported that thirty-eight were known to have been killed, by police and Young Pioneers, in Blantyre rioting. Later Malcolm heard that in Lilongwe and Blantyre the army (at present an insignificant force, though it may prove crucial in the years ahead) was passively siding with the rioters by refusing back up to the police and Pioneers. At which point I stopped hoping for a visa extension and settled down to some serious planning – as is not my wont.

By dusk on 17 May I must be over the border, in Zambia. Memories of that immigration officer deterred me from trying any tricks, like overstaying and pretending I'd got lost. Therefore impulsive detours, loitering in beautiful places, dismounting often to bird-watch, accepting delaying invitations – all those indulgences of the happy wanderer must be eschewed (more or less) for eight days. Carefully I worked out my route and mileage, allowing for the fact that most of those 420 miles would be on execrable tracks. At Karonga one has to choose between extremes: there is no middle way. The flawless lakeside road takes tourists where they want to go (and where Banda wants them to go), while the Stevenson Road – closely resembling that track from the Ugandan border to Bukoba – climbs into the Misuku Hills. I didn't really have a choice. Apart from other considerations – like avoiding tourists – the lakeside temperature rivalled Kenya before the rains and I longed for mountain coolness. The Stevenson Road would take me north-west into an atypical – because infertile and sparsely populated – area of Malawi. This 'highway' was designed to link the northern extremity of Lake Nyasa with the southern extremity of Lake Tanganyika. When the Royal Geographical Society sponsored Thomson's first expedition someone dreamed an impractical dream – as lunatic as the worst of modern 'aid' projects. To overcome the difficulties of land transport in Africa, the Mediterranean should be linked to Central and Southern Africa via the Nile, Lake Victoria, Lake Tanganyika and Lake Nyasa. An ill-advised Glasgow merchant named James Stevenson donated what were wrongly calculated to be the necessary funds for one of the link roads. This money ran out when the road reached Chitipa, on the present Zambia-Malawi border, but James Stevenson's reward is immortality of a sort. Not everyone has a road called after them in the remotest corner of Malawi.

225

11

Over the Hills and Far Away

Karonga to Lundazi

Unexpectedly, the first half-mile of the Stevenson Road was lined with parked trucks, their drivers and passengers having been tempted by the closed border to sample the flesh-pots of Karonga. The dawn light revealed a reassuring number of discarded condoms in the vicinity.

Soon the climb began: up and up, around mountain after forested mountain, the trees ancient and grand, sharing matted vines, the red-rock cliffs swathed in flowering creepers. Each jutting shoulder overlooked the wide brown Rukuru River, curling through a deep gorge and occasionally spanned by swaying footbridges cleverly constructed from tree-trunks and grass ropes. Then both river and forests were left behind and long, level saddles linked one smooth-topped scrubby mountain to the next. Sometimes the track plunged down, seeking a way through these tight-packed obstacles, then steeply rose until I was high enough to see again Lake Nyasa's farthest shore – a silver streak at the base of the powder-blue Livingstone range.

Mr Stevenson's road provided the toughest stage of my whole journey. This track suffers from every ill to which a road is heir: hideously rutted gradients, skiddy loose gravel, erosion channels deep as a grave, jagged slabs of rock twenty feet long, corrugations demanding clenched teeth and a camber more appropriate to a circus-ring than a public highway. On downward slopes this camber – unique in my experience – forced me to dismount at every bend; even pushing a bicycle at such an angle was difficult enough. One needs no specialist knowledge to diagnose that here the African Lakes Company employed unskilled labour; and their in-charge was either an amateur or an engineer sacked from all previous jobs.

The sixty miles to Kapoka took twelve and a half hours with only three brief stops and this challenge was mightily therapeutic, an escape from everything but the testing of one's body. AIDS and drought and Malawi's political crisis faded away as I relished the space, the silence and the lonely splendour of these mountains. My joy was shadowed only by the lack of animals in a region swarming with wildlife less than a century ago – a dark enough shadow.

By mid-afternoon I was on an undulating plateau – cool, green, higher than the surrounding ridge-tops. Near a few isolated shacks, malnourished children herded bony cattle. At 5.30 the track descended slightly towards wide fields of maize and sugar-cane, promising Kapoka's nearness. Here the Stevenson Road had been attended to, after a fashion, and at last it was possible to cycle above 5 m.p.h. A strange rosy light suffused the plateau as a huge red sun perceptibly slid towards a wall of mauve mountains on the near horizon. Then the cloudless western sky became a sheet of gold – and suddenly the sun was gone. Moments later a bronze-tinged twilight gave way to darkness.

How much further to Kapoka and food? I had little hope of an evening fix; Banda disapproves of alcohol, though even he has never tried to impose teetotalism. But one can buy beer only in bottle-stores, shops licensed to sell it and not numerous.

Fifteen minutes later I dismounted at a crossroads under towering trees. Even by daylight Kapoka – small and scattered – seems less a village than a trivial mark made by man on the wilderness. A lamp glowed faintly through the open doorway of a solitary square hut, the only visible building. This was a duka and on the counter stood a transistor radio surrounded by four men struggling to hear the World Service through an aural blizzard of static. More importantly, behind the counter stood four crates of Carlsberg Special. Next morning I saw that this mud duka had 'Bottle Store' crudely painted on one gable-end.

The men were incredulous, they had never heard of *anyone* travelling with a bicycle from Karonga to Kapoka – and to do it in a *day* . . . ! I shared their incredulity. Undoubtedly this was a minor feat and I allowed myself to enjoy being admired, while relaxing on a narrow wooden bench drinking beers at a rate that would have appalled Banda and eating six hard-boiled eggs from a dish on the

227

counter. These, I was to discover, are Malawi's 'fast food', on offer in many bottle-stores.

For an hour we talked of this and that: mostly domestic politics. Then the young store-keeper's 16-year-old wife brought me a plate piled with chips, scrambled eggs and fried onions. Payment was reproachfully rejected – was I not *Irish*? During the next week, official hostility was more than compensated for by the gratitude and praise so illogically lavished on me by ordinary Malawians. Being a compatriot of Bishop John Roche meant travelling in reflected glory; I lost count of the beers stood to me by impoverished men in desolate dukas because I came from the same country as the hero of the year. I wondered if public opinion would have been so unanimous further south, in Chewa territory. Banda is a Chewa – Malawi's largest tribe, comprising 45 per cent of the population.

Anxiously the men debated where Kapoka's guest should sleep. I suggested the floor of the bottle-store but that wouldn't do; they thought it more fitting to introduce me to the Chief's compound. The youngest man led me through several fields, on twisting pathlets, by the light of a half-moon. A high fence of wooden stakes enclosed this large compound where a dozen tin-roofed huts accommodated a bewilderingly extended family. In the newest hut – six feet by eight and so new the mud still felt and smelt damp – a grass mat was unrolled on the floor. On that I spread my flea-bag and slept for ten hours.

From Kapoka the Stevenson Road continues for another fifteen miles to Chitipa; but at dawn I left it, without tears, and turned south towards the Nyika Plateau. Here the switchbacking track's main defect was very deep powdery dust, often masking treacherous craters or hunks of smooth stone embedded in the surface. At noon I reached Chisenga, having advanced only forty miles through uninhabited hilliness.

Chisenga was once a minuscule outpost of empire; now this district is administered from Chitipa and Chisenga feels at the end of the world – a widespread settlement of shambas, impoverished, welcoming and very beautiful. A mile or so to the west rise the Mafinga Mountains, the Zambian border – a massive blue fortress, sheer, flat-topped, radiating the mystery of the inaccessible. There are no paths across, I was told; this is a natural boundary, not a cartographer's decision. To the south-east stretch lower mountains –

cinnamon brown, arid, uninhabited, apparently endless – and there my track was visible at intervals, crossing the heights.

In mid-village it startled me to come upon a red-and-white striped pole blocking the track. Nearby stood a well-maintained police-cum-customs-post in a neat garden where the Malawian flag fluttered high. A customs officer, Mr Mayinga, sat on a bench in the hot sun wearing an air of dejection and an overcoat. Only two days before he had been transferred from Marka, on the sweltering Mozambican border. 'You see me *dying* of cold! But I'm happy to be away from those refugees, 980,000 Mozambican refugees are in our country – nearly one million and we are only eight million! The aid agencies give them food – but not enough so they become thieves, making big problems. In February our government told Mozambique they must go home, by July all food reserves will be gone – but still more come!' Mr Mayinga paused to light a cigarette, then wondered plaintively, 'Why am I here? No one crosses this border, the road is too bad.'

When the policeman arrived I stood up to shake hands, hoping he would not arrest me for skirtlessness. He was markedly less cordial than Mr Mayinga but called me 'Sir', an error based on tact, I felt. He advised me to stay overnight in Chisenga; a mega-rainstorm was due during the afternoon in the mountains on my route and where could I shelter? Nowhere! This advice was not unwelcome; the previous day's minor feat had left me with a slight muscular hangover. And besides, I had fallen in love with Chisenga.

Neither of the two dukas sold food (their shelves were seven-eighths bare) and a small boarded-up colonial rest-house has been 'in a state of constant disuse' – the policeman said – for twenty-five years. But there was a hoteli, a white-washed two-roomed shack, its dishevelled thatch hanging so low over the door one had to duck to enter. Inside, Mary welcomed me warmly and offered tea, though the making of it at midday was troublesome. Food could be provided at sunset: chicken and *nsima* (mealie-meal dumpling). Mary was a tallish, slender, good-looking 30-year-old wearing a wrap-around skirt depicting the map of Africa, a torn but clean white blouse and a white headscarf. Her 10-year-old first-born – the first of seven – had stick-like limbs, jungle sores on his ankles and a grossly worm-swollen belly. Behind the counter two shelves held half a dozen dusty bottles of soda. A shaky table and four chairs furnished this outer 'restaurant' room; I could sleep on the earth floor after closing time which was 6.30 p.m. The family lived in the equally small back room.

When I went exploring Lear was left unlocked in the hoteli. To fuss about his safety would have seemed impolite and in certain places – usually the remotest and poorest – one can sense honesty in the air. A narrow path sloped up from the track through dense green vegetation, lively with birds. I dawdled along it, bird-watching, then suddenly came out amidst a glory of giant magnolia trees in full flower. These semi-encircled the District Officer's residence, one of those magnificent colonial bungalows that have a palatial air despite being single-storeyed. Now it is sadly battered and weather-worn, the windows broken, sacks of maize and salt stored in the high-ceilinged drawing-room, chickens roosting on the deep pillared veranda – facing the Mafinga Mountains – and countless underfed children everywhere.

I was thinking the obvious thoughts when two youths, Patrick and Declan, emerged from the old servants' quarter – yes, both their fathers had been educated by Irish missionaries. Excitedly they took charge of me. I must visit their school, they were boarders, their families paid 70 kwatchas a term. I wondered why, on seeing three long sheds which Amnesty would condemn as a prison. Here the boys provide and cook their own food and five teachers (none very bright) instruct 320 pupils. Such bush schools are proliferating in Africa, encouraged by the pathetic ambitions of parents who naïvely imagine them to be an improvement on the calamitous state schools.

The rest of the day was spent with Patrick, Declan and various of their friends. When the rain came we crowded into the hoteli to continue our discussions of multi-party democracy, marriage and AIDS. Everyone was outspokenly anti-Banda and fearful of his heir presumptive, an unsavoury and by now extremely powerful character called John Tembo. All but one were devoted to the notion of multi-party democracy without even slightly comprehending it. For many young Africans it has become a fetish; given that reform, all problems can be solved overnight. No one thought women should be given the vote – 'In our country they are not educated and can't understand politics.' It shocked them to learn that in the West young people choose their own marriage partners and brides come free.

'That is *very* bad!' exclaimed Patrick. 'Then the husband does not *own* his wife – she may run away!'

Chisenga lacks a bottle-store. 'Here are no kwatchas for luxuries,' Mr Mayinga had observed gloomily. 'They don't even have much pombe – and none left at this season. People drink tea.' So I too drank tea, a novel experience at sunset. None of the boys would accept my offer of a soda, nor would Mary accept payment for my lodging and supper. The tourist trail was far away.

The policeman's advice was fortunate; I needed a rest-day before crossing those mountains between Chisenga and Nthalire on a track too closely related to the Stevenson Road. So steep were the gradients and so lamentable was the surface that a mere forty-two miles took nine hours. Yet this was among my Top Ten days; every summit, every shoulder, revealed another desolate expanse of many-hued beauty. On one high ridge I got very wet and very cold but by then I was too exhilarated to care. This unpeopled corner of Malawi (it really is a corner: see map) has a special quality of remoteness, of anonymity; one is not conscious of being in any particular 'nation-state', only of being in Africa.

Nthalire is a town – in miniature – and on arrival I was pursued by a policeman of the bullying sort who confiscated Lear until I had tucked my skirt into the waistband of my trousers. Here too the colonial rest-house had long since fallen into disuse but there was an 'Africa hotel' and there I slept extra-soundly after more mealie-meal and chicken. In all these cases, 'chicken' is a courtesy term.

The Nyika Plateau was the place above all I had longed to see in Malawi. Although a national park, vigorously advertised to tourists, I had been assured that only a trickle visit it – and I was that trickle on 12–14 May.

All morning the plateau was visible, filling the southern sky. The country between was a wilderness of russet bush; as usual my track could be seen at intervals, redly snaking over distant hills and gradually descending towards a green plain below the plateau. At 8 a.m. I stopped to nut-munch and rashly scrutinised that apparently sheer escarpment. My binoculars revealed a discouraging pale grey squiggle on a massive wall, a track evidently engineered with monkeys or antelope in mind. From a distance it seemed quite unsuited to human traffic, an impression in due course confirmed.

At the base of the escarpment a road-block is manned by two amiable, smartly uniformed National Park officials whose abundant offspring, spilling excitedly out of their mud huts, were riveted by Lear. I should have been charged a 3-kwatcha entry fee but the officials had run out of receipt dockets so please would I pay instead at my destination, the Chelinda Lodge?

That climb was mind over matter all the way, partly because the matter had been seriously underfed for days. Towards the end I had to stop every twenty yards or so to summon the strength for the next twenty yards. Feelings of humiliating inadequacy afflicted me. Most Africans are underfed not for a few days but all the time. How do they keep going? What feeble creatures we Whites are! Then I remembered Thomson's description of his ascent to the Mbeya Plateau: 'The hard work of an entire day seemed concentrated in each step I took. Every few feet I had to stop, gasping for breath and blowing like a broken-winded horse, while my heart palpitated in a most alarming manner. My mind became dazed and stupid, while my poor limbs seemed made of jelly . . .' This is a clear case of the knocks, aggravated in Thomson's case by repeated attacks of malaria. He had a dangerous obsession about 'keeping going' and but for his youthful vigour might well have succumbed during that expedition, as Johnston did at the outset. Perhaps he wouldn't have died at the age of 37 had he punished himself less.

That grey squiggle, seen from afar, was only stage one. It led into a green and secret place – the rest of the world invisible, all around precipitous slopes, anciently forested, with the depths of the ravine on my left hidden by dense vegetation. There was no sound: when I rested I could hear my heart thudding. Then, beyond a jutting shoulder, there was a sound: the faint magical music of a waterfall across the ravine, a whiteness streaking down through the forest from the edge of the plateau, singing sibilantly on its way – not breaking the silence but accentuating it.

An hour later I arrived, after a final brutal gradient on which I had to stop every ten yards. That was a dramatic arrival, emerging from the confinement of those dark precipices on to the immense brightness of Nyika – an apparent infinity of golden-grassed space, broken by low rocky hills. On an improved track, no longer erosion-torn, I pedalled joyously towards Chelinda Lodge, fifteen miles ahead. And then I froze. I had arrived sweat-sodden, I was at 7,000 feet or more, the sky was overcast, the wind icy and winter coming to Malawi. Dismounting, I noticed how unpleasantly diseased one looks when a dark tan is combined with purple gooseflesh. As Nyika is an uninhabited game reserve there was no one to observe me stripping by the wayside and donning *all* my garments – one vest, three underpants, one nightgown, two skirts, spare slacks.

A few miles from Chelinda I too got the knocks, for the first time in years. The only effective treatment is to lie flat and eat, while the palpitations slow down and protein unjellies the limbs. Reclining on grassland by the track, using my skirt as a blanket, I ate the last of my nut-supply and considered camping. But my equipment didn't match the rapidly dropping temperature; foolishly one thinks of Central Africa as a uniformly hot place. Dying of hypothermia on the Nyika Plateau seemed a silly idea. A little later I stood up and continued, on my reserve tank, confident that a Malawian *tourist* lodge would provide a good meal.

Then came a thin icy rain, very wetting and – given my condition – rather dispiriting. It turned the track to skiddy mud as I slowly pedalled towards a forested ridge-top where Chelinda at last appeared, far below, most of its buildings still hidden by towering Mexican pines. Here the track deteriorated and I continued on foot through the fading light, my mouth already watering, and arrived, with numbed hands, at Reception – an architect's enlarged imitation of a 'native' hut.

The place was empty. Long minutes later Ben – a lounge-suited young man, trained to be nice to tourists – strolled in and welcomed me effusively. Accepting my K3 National Park entry fee, he requested a daily vehicle charge of K7.50. Remembering that escarpment, the sheer injustice of having to pay a *vehicle* fee outraged me – as did the demotion of my noble Lear to mere motor status. A bicycle, I argued forcefully, is not a 'vehicle' but an aid to self-propulsion. Ben indicated a long list of regulations hanging on the wall; one clause deemed bicycles to be 'vehicles' for the purpose of fee-collecting. As I was sulkily counting out K22.50, Ben stopped being professionally nice and became genuinely so. Of course the charge was unfair; he must charge for one day, the other two he would overlook.

Chelinda offers two grades of accommodation: several expensive self-catering bungalows on the lake-shore below Reception and four less expensive (£5 a night) self-catering tents a mile away high in the forest.

'*Self-catering?*' I queried, with a sinking heart and rumbling stomach. 'Is there no restaurant?'

'It's closed, but in our shop you can buy food. And beside the tents lives Francis, who for a small fee will cook it.' Ben then guided me through the pines, in Stygian darkness, to the duka. Its stocks had run low; I could buy only one small tin of repulsive corned beef and half a kilo of rice. Happily it was also a bottle-store and I drowned my hunger before setting off to find the tents – hidden in dense jungle and not easy to find. Each was hut-sized (ex-army) and erected permanently on a raised wooden base under a thatched roof. The 20-year-old Francis and his 16-year-old bride and her 9-year-old sister shared a miserable nearby shack of brushwood and grass. Their kitchen was a three-stone fireplace under a rough thatch upheld by six stakes. My arrival disconcerted Francis; he had no saucepan in which to cook my rice, I must wait until the morrow when he could borrow one. I shone my torch into the kitchen and said firmly that he could use his own saucepan. He objected that it was dirty and there was no water left to clean it. I retorted that I didn't care how dirty it was; I needed my rice cooked *now*. When the fire had been lit the 9-year-old squatted beside it, attempting to do her homework by that faint erratic light and screwing up her eyes as the smoke gusted. Her English reader was filthy and tattered. Boys can get their homework done by daylight while the girls are about their various chores: mainly fetching wood and water. When I visited the little school next day (it caters for the children of the National Park labour-force, who all live in Chelinda) I realised that that girl was lucky to have a book; it had been given her, Francis said, by a kind tourist.

The howling of hyenas often woke me, perhaps because the cold was so extreme; next morning the little water left in my container on Lear's carrier was frozen solid.

Few places in the world can rival the beauty of the Nyika Plateau and I would have liked to spend a week on those heights. But after a day's wandering around Chelinda, on foot, I had to hasten away. Leaving the tent site just before dawn I met a leopard; he crossed the path scarcely ten yards ahead – my one and only sighting of a big cat. However, several sets of leopard pad-marks (among many others) appeared in the deep dust of the track during the day. When I had desperately sought a chicken, or some eggs, in Chelinda, the duka-keeper explained that poultry would attract leopards to the settlement and are therefore forbidden.

Eleven hours and seventy miles later I was back in the populated world, approaching Bolero, where this journey's most bizarre lodging awaited me. Rumphi had been my goal: the first town since Karonga, where there was sure to be a supermarket and restaurant. But after an exceptionally gruelling descent, on a Stevenson-type surface, I shirked the final ten deeply corrugated miles. Of the wide range of surface defects available in Africa, corrugations are, for the cyclist, the most uncomfortable though not the most tiring.

Bolero, a big village, has attracted lavish German aid – according to an enormous sign, in German and English, on the outskirts. All the dukas were closed because this was Kamazu Day, Banda's birthday and a national holiday. The bottle-store was also closed but a garrulous old man, full of yarns about his days in the British army, led me through a German-inspired housing estate to a hidden source of Carlsberg. In an incongruously vast pre-fab secondary school, built of imported German materials, what the donors had designed as a small kitchen is now a bar (or was on 14 May 1992). Three middle-aged men, sitting on plastic beer crates, welcomed me wonderingly. Two spoke fluent English and all had their quota of the Malawians' distinctive charm – in the best sense of that ambiguous word. One was a local Chief, therefore a Banda protégé. Another introduced himself simply as 'a government inspector'. The third and least fluent was, significantly, a teacher. The teaching profession lacks prestige in most African countries – strangely, it might seem, given the universal craving for education. But teachers are so badly paid that talented youngsters usually choose a more lucrative career.

Outside, schoolboys came crowding around the window above the sink, the smallest being lifted up to observe me sitting on the draining-board – the only space available.

'They are amazed', said the Chief, 'because we talk together socially. Our tradition condemns this mixed-sex talking, we say it leads only to misbehaviour. Men and women have nothing in common to discuss, they live in different worlds. But we know you have another tradition.'

Predictably, all three opposed the notion of multi-party democracy and praised Banda who has given Malawi 'peace, stability and a respectable place in the world'. An interesting ambivalence tinged everyone's reaction when I asked, innocently, about John Tembo's role. No one denigrated him, nor did they praise him.

The Chief recalled his youth, when the people of this area only had to go hunting to secure an adequate meat supply for their families. He was not enough of a Banda-man to eschew the World Service and had recently heard a WHO spokesman mentioning the victory of medical science over many African diseases. He mused, 'Was it good to check those diseases that kept the population down, when the West couldn't give good health to the extra millions? Isn't there more happiness in the world if an area has five million well-fed people, with enough wildlife to give them protein, instead of ten million always hungry, never rightly developing their minds or bodies?'

When the teacher deplored there being only 4 teachers to this school's 575 pupils I asked him to repeat those numbers, fancying I must have misheard. Everyone agreed that a bigger staff in a less grand building would make more sense. But of course donor countries decide what to donate and who in Bolero was going to say 'No' to such an imposing edifice?

After dark I tentatively enquired about a restaurant. My companions looked faintly embarrassed, then said I could eat well in Rumphi's restaurant on the morrow. Remembering Francis's equally unimaginative reference to the morrow, I began to suspect that Africans see no need to eat regularly, even if one has just cycled a long distance over testing terrain. But it wouldn't have done to complain about acute hunger pangs; someone might then have felt bound to feed me.

As the trio were leaving they decided I should sleep in the schoolroom. 'It is eighty metres by forty,' smiled the inspector. 'You'll have space enough!' True, but there was a snag. Next day the senior pupils faced their important final examination and thirty of them sat revising in my bedroom, sharing books by the dim light of three Aladdin lamps suspended from the ceiling's metal struts. The luxurious German desks were so jam-packed that I had to walk across them to mount the high teachers' 'stage', extending the width of the room. Yet this was also the examination hall. 'So little space!' lamented the teacher. 'It makes cribbing too easy!'

My entry did revision no good. Feeling like a solo act, I performed on the empty stage, emptying my pockets and removing my boots before wriggling into my flea-bag – the cynosure of thirty pairs of incredulous eyes. Everyone stood up to watch me arranging my boots as a pillow, then they settled down again and studied diligently though noisily until past midnight. I wondered how far this diligence would get them, given their academy's limitations. Education has long since acquired the status of magic in Africa, the only magic that can lead to an improved (that is, urban) lifestyle. All the secondary-school pupils I met, without exception, were aiming for university and puzzled to hear that only a minority of secondary-school pupils in the West do likewise. Without a degree, they argued, nobody can find a job worth taking.

From three-ish, as though to make up for Chelinda's lack of poultry, I was kept awake by the loudest cacophony of non-stop cock-crowing I have ever heard – all happening within a hundred yards or so. I was up before dawn, mixing the last of my dried milk by candlelight to get me to Rumphi's restaurant.

From Rumphi a tarred road, only mildly hilly and mildly traffic-busy, accompanies the – usually invisible – Kasitu River through a long cultivated valley (its drought-stricken fields were grey-brown) between two ranges of the Viphya Mountains. While lodging that night in the dull little town of Ekwendeni, I heard Malawi State Radio announcing the Minister of Finance's return from Paris 'where donor countries had sympathetically considered Malawi's future needs and remarkable economic progress', a good example of misreporting. In fact Malawi's funding had been cut at that Paris meeting, in an attempt to curb the regime's ill-treatment of dissidents. Luckily, in almost every village someone listens to the World Service and spreads the truth.

Early next morning, as I sped through the outskirts of Mzuzu, hundreds of workers were converging on handsome red-brick factories set in landscaped flower-filled grounds. Bright little gardens surrounded the attractive workers' bungalows, their tin roofs painted green. Mzuzu, only thirty miles from the lakeside tourist centre of Nkhata Bay, is one of Banda's showpieces.

My brief traverse of northern Malawi contributed a dispropor-tionate number of my Top Ten days and this was to be another, though I didn't yet realise it. The levelish Mzuzu–Mzimba highway seemed brand-new and was furnished, every few miles, with speed-limit signs and giant Pepsodent and Surf advertisements, the first hoardings seen since leaving Nairobi. Gloom was looming when a foresters' track appeared on my left, a legacy of the British develop-ment of a vast forest reserve. The map told me that this track is spatially though not temporally a short-cut; it climbs high to cross the 6,000-foot Viphya Plateau, then rejoins the road which curves around the plateau's base.

During the next nine hours my solitude was undisturbed, though the Viphya Reserve employs 8,000 men and I passed two of their isolated settlements. At first the track rose and fell through a planta-tion of 55,000 blue gums. This sounds boring, but in such mature reserves Nature has had time to adopt intruders and one is hardly conscious of human meddling. Higher up, many inaccessible moun-tains support only indigenous forest, moss- and creeper-festooned and full of interesting little noises. Twice an unidentifiable animal, about the size of a badger, crossed the track. The climb was tough but enjoyably so. I was now well-fed, with ample supplies in my pan-niers, and on a track engineered to accommodate heavy vehicles the gradient was rarely extreme.

Truly the Viphya Plateau is a Paradise, a dazzlingly lovely world containing a multitude of brilliant birds, butterflies, shrubs, flowers – the delicate scent of wayside blossoms mingling with the heavy pungency of forest decay. Even in drought years these mountains attract heavy rain and many sparkling streamlets raced down the slopes or beside the track. Ecstatically I pedalled or pushed (mainly pushed) Lear around mountain after mountain, never able to guess at the configuration of the terrain around the next shoulder. This was a gloriously unpredictable range, in contrast to some African landscapes where it can seem as if the Creator ran out of ideas on whichever day they were created. Finally came miles of green wind-swept grasslands directly below sheer, rounded rock-peaks – and here it was very cold, as the afternoon clouds gathered.

Eventually we rejoined the main road and two more miles revealed Chikangawa in its deep hollow between wooded ridges – a

238

small town where hope of a visa extension was to be revived.

Chikangawa is the headquarters of the Viphya Forest Reserve where foresters live in many rows of identical dwellings – more than shacks but less than bungalows, with one 'sentry-box' earth-closet for each four families. In the cramped bottle-store taped reggae, amplified to the point of aural crucifixion, made conversation impossible. On the counter sat Lovegod, a short muscular young man wearing ragged jeans and a 'MAKE MALAWI GREENER' Carlsberg T-shirt. He insisted on standing me a beer, then beckoned me outside to talk. He was called Lovegod because his parents loved God and he worked as a forestry transport officer. At school he heard a call to the Catholic priesthood and then spent three years in a seminary, his fees paid by an Irish sponsor, before 'the devil got into me and I left. Now I regret that but with a wife and son I can't change again.' He invited me to stay for a few days and made light of my visa trap; his father was a senior police officer with the Immigration Department in Lilongwe and could surely 'fix it'.

Two hours were spent getting through to Lilongwe on the telephone. The off-duty operator had to be found and then bribed, with beer, by Lovegod. We walked to the telephone exchange by moonlight, between groves of magnificent Mexican pines, and when various technological complications had been overcome I was appalled to hear Lovegod describing me as the Irish sponsor who had paid his seminary fees and was now in Malawi seeking help. He spoke with pathos but Daddy said 'No!' Crestfallen, Lovegod reproached himself – 'I am a crazy man! I made a big mistake, I should have said you were British. Here we love the British and not the Irish any more. Daddy said those priests and nuns make too much trouble about human rights and maybe you're helping them . . . This is sad but come to my home and sleep well after meeting my family and we will talk about politics because I have views not like my father's . . .'

I did sleep well, on a camp-bed in a tiny living-room lavishly decorated with pious pictures. Lovegod rose at 5 a.m. to cook me a mega-omelette on the wood-range and make a quart jug of tea. 'Forgive my wife doesn't come, our boy is getting teeth and disturbed her, now she must rest. She works *too* hard, teaching 160 children!'

On the tough pre-dawn climb out of Chikangawa's hollow a gale was blowing and the full moon seemed to race between low speeding clouds. Then sheets of cold rain drenched me but were soon left behind. During that long fast descent through the Viphya foothills – twenty miles on velvet tarmac – the road crossed many high narrow saddles affording limitless views of an apparently uninhabited land-scape, all golden and blue in the early sunshine. On the most exposed saddles the powerful crosswind made it advisable to walk.

Soon after 8.30 a small battered signpost, pointing west, faintly said, 'Lundazi: 45 miles' and now I had the wind behind me. Moocha is not a popular crossing; between junction and border-post the traffic consisted of one cyclist, coming from Zambia. He was so amazed to meet me that he fell off his bicycle. The track across the final low jungly foothills – innocuous-looking from a distance but very steep – was strewn with pretty, pale pink stones, sharp-edged and hell to walk on. Then, down on a sparsely populated, level plain extending far beyond Moocha, the gale took charge and pedalling was hardly necessary. Here the track consisted of two deep smooth sandy ruts separated by tall vegetation. In this region the Malawian-Zambian border is an abstraction, in no way reflecting those years of Banda-Kaunda hostility. Approaching Moocha, and again over stretches of the Great East Road from Lundazi to Lusaka, the highway itself forms the frontier and one can picnic freely in either country. The same tribe (its name forgotten: I neglected to make a note) lives on both sides – cheerful friendly folk, very black and very poor, who view the border as a ridiculous politicians' irrelevance.

The tailgale relieved me of any anxiety about getting to Lundazi before dark – until Lear's back tyre slowly softened, on the only day of our journey when destination-reaching was important. Over the last ten uninhabited miles I had to stop repeatedly to pump, then pumping worked no more – another defective seam, or a real punc-ture? Walking on, I felt pessimistic about Moocha as a repair depot.

In the attractive Malawian Customs and Immigration hut, set in a neat garden, both officers were relaxed and chummy, unlike their main-road colleagues; Moocha provides little to be unrelaxed about. My trousers were commented on between themselves, in whispers, but there was no hassle. That came at the nearby Zambian post, a concrete shed manned by a tall lean immigration officer and a short plump customs officer. Both greeted me with some

240

astonishment and at once it was plain that the former saw this mad-woman as An Opportunity. When I had patiently filled in the ludicrously long visa application form, requesting a thirty-day visa and leaving the 'Address in Zambia' space blank, we disputed as follows:

IO : This is not good, please give your Zambia address.

DM : I've no Zambia address, I'm touring.

IO : Then I can give only a seven-day transit visa, for longer we need an address to get in touch with you.

DM : About what?

IO : It is necessary, it is the rule.

DM : OK, please give me the address of a Lusaka hotel and I'll write that in.

IO : There are very many hotels in Lusaka, we have no addresses. Who do you know in Zambia, who are your friends?

DM : I know nobody.

IO : Then why do you come here? You have a map? Show it, show me why you need thirty days.

DM : I've already explained, I'm on a cycle tour and I've had no problems like this on other borders.

IO : (frowning at map) Zambia is different, we have our own rules. You cannot cycle from here to Zimbabwe in seven days, it is impossible!

DM : That's why I've asked for a thirty-day visa.

IO : Without an address you cannot have.

DM : (picking up pen) Then I'll give the Irish Embassy as my address.

IO : (rolling his eyes) This is very bad, you have lied! You know people in this place!

DM : I don't, but I'm an Irish citizen entitled to use this address.

IO : No! When you know nobody you cannot use it, that is false information and not good. There is no solution for your problem.

A long silence followed. The two officers stared at me while I stared at a large AIDS poster above the counter – 'Your next part-ner could be that SPECIAL PERSON who gives you AIDS. The *only* safe sex is with one partner *only*.' This anserine bribe-hunt had so infuriated me that I needed time to simmer down before seeing the obvious solution.

Folding the map I said, 'Fine, that transit visa will do. I'll get a bus to Lusaka and tell the Irish Embassy I was refused a tourist visa at this border-post.'

My problem evaporated. The customs officer gave a comical yelp of alarm and his friend exclaimed, 'No, no! To get to Lusaka you must have twenty-one day visa, then you get extensions for one month, two months – in Zambia we like Irish people very much! My teachers were Irish priests, holy clever men!'

Then it was the customs officer's turn to assert himself, legitimately but maddeningly. Ignoring my luggage he asked, 'You have enough money to live in Zambia?' I assured him that I had and showed my Visa card. Its details were carefully inscribed on a docket, I was given a carbon copy (why?) and then my cash had to be shown – a demand never made elsewhere, and one which induced slight unease. Public entertainments are scarce in Moocha and fascinated locals – the majority young men – had long since gathered around the doorways to enjoy my pilgrimage through this bureaucratic Lough Derg. They watched, awe-struck, as £820, in ten- and five-pound notes, were carefully checked through on the countertop, then replaced in their sweat-proof bags and stowed away in my money-belt. The sun was near setting, Lundazi lay thirteen miles further on through unpeopled country and Lear was punctured. I would however have felt much more uneasy at a busy main-road border-post; Moocha's atmosphere was reassuringly innocent.

This tiresome episode had a happy and typically African ending. My seeking someone to mend the puncture stimulated the officers' milk of human kindness and they magnanimously offered to do the job themselves; again it was a leaking seam. I then considered staying the night in Moocha but was advised, 'Here is little food and no lodging, better continue to Lundazi.'

At 5.35 I rode into the sunset, towards a glory of rose and lemon cloudlets imposed on paling blue. Half an hour later I dismounted; this vile track took corrugations to such an extreme that cycling by lamplight was unsafe. But I hadn't walked far when a pick-up – it had been parked near the border-post – overtook me, stopped, backed, offered a lift to Lundazi. The two young men – Newstead and Chibeza – were Barclays Bank agricultural credit advisers and one question from me triggered an avalanche of information.

Zambia has some 350,000 subsistence farms, 170,000 small to medium-sized commercial farms and fewer than 1,000 large farms using modern technology. Little more than half the land is cultivable, everywhere the soil is poor, in many areas tsetse-control has been abandoned and rainfall is variable at the best of times. Maize has proved an unsuitable successor to the traditional crops – bulrush and finger millet, sorghum, cassava, beans and groundnuts. The encouragement of hybrid maize, with its need for imported artificial fertiliser, has been a disaster. Yet the tsetse-free areas support nearly three million cattle, 80 per cent in bush herds, and since the territory fed its population in pre-colonial times it could surely do so again, 'with modern assistance like we give', were enough emphasis put on farming. Newstead quoted ex-President Kaunda who once rightly described rural development as 'a matter of life and death'. Chibeza pointed out that in practice Kaunda's regime had neglected to invest in agriculture, the obvious (and only) realistic alternative to copper mining. Instead of investment there was too much state interference by corrupt and incompetent bureaucrats ignorant of the nature of the problems they were supposed to solve.

'Governments only make problems,' said Newstead, 'they can't ever solve them. Now our quarrelsome politicians are making worse the effects of this drought. They say our '92 maize harvest will be 60 per cent down on '91 and last month our stocks ran out and we need to import a million tons of maize and 100,000 tons of other grains. This isn't only because of drought. Last year our maize-farmers were promised higher prices but never delivered the expected yields – they couldn't get the essential inputs, Zambia couldn't afford to import enough. And where they did deliver, the government had no money to buy the maize or no transport to collect it. The politicians of all these drought countries are partly to blame. Now in our southern province people are eating roots and wild pods, not just because of drought – there's bad distribution of what's available. South Africa is sending 86,000 tons of maize – will it ever get to the hungry?'

Newstead drove very slowly – 'otherwise this road will injure us' – and we arrived in Lundazi at 7.30. Without consultation my rescuers delivered me to the British-built tourist hotel. 'Here you must stay,' said Chibeza firmly. 'Zambia is a dangerous country, you will be robbed if you walk in the dark. And Lundazi's lodgings are dirty.'

So was the Castle Hotel; a gang of bedbugs lurked under my pillow, awaiting their prey, and several colleagues – upset by the light – stampeded across the bedside table. The sheets were damp, the towel was blood-stained, the wash-basin had neither water nor soap. The communal lavatories stank, there was no shower and the British bath was coated with scum and pubic hairs. The bar had closed at seven, there was no food left in the restaurant and when the electricity failed at 7.50 no one thought of providing the guests with alternative lighting. In Zambia the tourist trade is not big – and won't be, at this rate.

My unsavoury room had a quasi-medieval fireplace and was circular because in a turret. As an outpost of Scottish Baronial, in a Central African trading centre, the Castle Hotel's idiosyncracy makes up for a lot. It was built in 1953, perhaps to celebrate the birth of the short-lived Federation of Rhodesia and Nyasaland, and is a corny red-brick joke complete with battlements, turrets, parapets, Gothic windows and arches, spiral stone stairways, purposeless vaulted embrasures here and there along dark passageways, and low nail-studded doors leading into enormous circular rooms furnished only with a bed in the centre of the floor and a worm- (or ant-)eaten colonial wardrobe.

From the open central courtyard a steep flight of steps leads down to a small pseudo-dungeon dining-room where at breakfast-time the only sign of life was cockroaches – hopping, crawling and flying. Eventually three waiters appeared to serve five guests; overmanning is one of Zambia's many problems. There was no menu to study; we were each served with a bowl of mealie-meal dumpling and a plate of fried fish. This tasted as though bred in a sewer and was most curiously constructed: tough skin contained 10 per cent meat and 90 per cent long, hard, sharp bones. Each had been cooked whole – innards and all – yet the three men at the next table left not a scale on their plates, folding the fish in wads of dumpling, then gulping them down not daring to chew. I watched apprehensively, wondering about perforated guts . . . Although not a pernickety eater, I drew the line here.

It was time to go shopping. Lundazi might most aptly be

described as a rural slum, scattered in an unplanned way over a square mile of ominously dry hillocky country. The trading centre recalled Bukoba; it had the same abandoned or half-empty large shops and forlorn-looking Asian traders, the same air of past prosperity and present hardship. Zambia has the highest per capita foreign debt in the world and 42 per cent of the urban population are said to live below the poverty line – a credible figure, when one looks at them. I could find only a half-kilo tin of dried milk (made in Mallow, Ireland) and two tins of nauseating fish which I ate in my room for elevenses.

At lunch-time the Castle Hotel's soiled tablecloths remained *in situ* but there were fewer cockroaches. A waiter offered us (there were two other would-be lunchers) rice with beef or chicken. Some time later we were told that there was after all neither beef nor chicken, only fish. I shuddered and opted for rice unadorned. More time elapsed and we were told that there was no rice left, only *sembe* (that dumpling again). Meanwhile teetotalism prevailed; the bar-girl had absent-mindedly gone home with the key and wouldn't be back until 3 p.m. My companions, two health inspectors from Chipata, took this shambolic scene for granted, including (despite their profession) the tablecloths and cockroaches. One was suffering from AIDS; by then I knew, too well, the significance of the rash on his face and hands. They told me about Lundazi's Irish colony: four nuns, to be found in a compound near the Catholic church.

I spent most of the afternoon with that remarkable quartet – and not only because they fed me, non-stop, with homemade shortbread tasting like the food of the gods. These Sisters of Mercy taught at a local school and were the sort of adaptable modern missionaries who do a lot to make up for the sins of their foremothers. Their affection – and *respect* – for the Zambians, and the extent to which they had been accepted by Lundazi, gave them some unusual insights into Zambia's difficulties. They saw AIDS as having overtaken all other problems since the first case was diagnosed in 1985. Out of a population of approximately eight million, some 250,000 were HIV + by March 1992. The reduction of the professional class was already having serious social consequences. Within the previous six months Lundazi had lost two doctors ('highly trained and dedicated') who had been achieving much-needed reforms in the local hospital. These were a married couple, aged 28 and 30; the husband's widowed mother was left with their two orphans and her other sons, long settled in Lusaka, gave her no support. Both emotionally and financially, the lost son had been her mainstay. 'But at least those two tinies will get regular meals,' said Sister Brigid. 'According to UNICEF, Lusaka has about 12,000 AIDS orphans more or less destitute – many homeless, wandering the streets. Watch your possessions there!'

'Since '89,' said Sister Catherine, 'one of our commercial banks has lost fifty-five of its top staff – it's had to close some branches, it couldn't find enough skilled replacements. Now people are dying faster than replacements can be trained.'

'Compared to other epidemics,' said Sister Teresa, 'the economic threat comes from the age-group affected. Epidemics used to wipe out whole familes and villages but AIDS leaves the most dependent, the young and the old. And this in countries that couldn't begin to cope, *before* AIDS, with their health care and social welfare needs!'

We switched then to education, a subject not much less depressing. As compared to other British possessions, Zambia was under-privileged during the colonial era. In the late 1930s, when its copper mines were yielding a profit of over £4 million annually, not one secondary school was available for Black children; the authorities claimed the country couldn't afford such a luxury. After Independence English became the language of education from primary school upwards and school enrolment rose by more than 200 per cent between 1964 and 1979. Since then there has been a grievous deterioration, especially since the mid-1980s. Primary education is not now compulsory, there being inadequate facilities; 200,000 children failed to find a school place in 1991 and less than one-third of the new generation can hope to receive seven years' education. Although ex-President Kaunda was genuinely keen to harness women's talents, his ideal of 'equal educational opportunities' couldn't be realised even before Zambia's economic collapse. At second and third levels fewer girls enrol (respectively one-third and one-quarter) and their examination results consistently fall far short of the boys'. Having left school, they find it correspondingly harder to get jobs – and inevitably that brought us back to AIDS.

Standing to take my leave, I asked, 'So what's the good news?'

The quartet beamed and exclaimed in unison, 'The Zambian people – you won't meet better!'

246

12

The Last Frontier

Lundazi to Karoi

Kaunda was an optimist. (I doubt if he still is.) As the national motto
he chose 'ONE ZAMBIA: ONE NATION', a legend first seen on the
border and subsequently in many public places. Again one wonders
why tribes who had never even heard of each other in 1890, and who
have not coalesced voluntarily, or by any gradual natural process,
should have been expected to behave like a nation seventy-four years
later. In 1890, half the area of what is now Zambia (a territory three
times the size of Britain) was tsetse-infested, which restricted the
keeping of cattle. Hunters and gatherers occupied the north-west;
in the west and east, the raiding of richer neighbouring tribes sup-
plemented cultivation. Then, during the 1890s, the European
appropriation began with the signing of treaties between local chiefs
and the mineral-questing British South Africa Company.

Until 1924, when the British government took over, the BSA
administered the territory under a Crown charter and White rule
gave a spurious unity to a disparate collection of tribes technologi-
cally at the level of early Iron Age cultures – here was no equivalent
of the Baganda. Around Fort Jameson (now Chipata) the BSA
allocated the best land to White settlers, of whom there were over
700 by 1921, in farms varying from several thousand to a few hundred hectares. During the late 1920s the British government set up
'Native Reserves' which soon became alarmingly overcrowded,
especially in the Eastern Province, and therefore eroded. Black farming was positively discouraged, in reaction to some Blacks showing
signs of being able to compete successfully with the settlers, thereby
threatening to bring down the price of maize. A Northern Rhodesia
government *Agricultural Survey Commission Report* (published in Livingstone in 1933) bluntly advised:

Any land with poor soils, inadequate water supplies, low nutrition grasses unsuitable for European cattle or overgrown with impenetrable bush, is not suitable for Europeans and instead should be allocated to Africans.

By the late 1920s copper mining dominated the economy and the hut-tax dirty trick had been used to uproot the village men. Ever since, a rural labour shortage has limited agricultural development. Because Northern Rhodesia (which became Zambia in 1964) was developed solely as a mining area, seven of Zambia's ten towns – even Lusaka hardly qualifies as a 'city' – are mining settlements where more than half the population now live. Since the irreversible decline of copper mining, many would be better occupied back in the bush (where it's cultivable) instead of drifting into urban criminality. But such a move could only be brought about through the use of force.

In 1964, President Kenneth Kaunda hoped to be able to run Zambia as a one-party democracy – which to us sounds like a contradiction in terms, though it need not be. He fervently believed in 'Africanisation' and increased state intervention in the economy, to counteract the unequal opportunities of the colonial era. In theory this was fine and Kaunda's philosophy (Humanistic Socialism: 'Production by the masses, not mass production') seemed more flexible and practical than Nyerere's African Socialism. But alas! it led to over-simplification of the problems, over-centralisation of the institutions coping with them, corruption on a grand scale, fierce tribal rivalries within the grossly over-manned bureaucracy and a series of cock-ups that would be laughable were not their main victims the poorest of the poor. For instance, in 1970 the Credit Organisation of Zambia, established to support co-operative farming, died a sudden death owing more than 22 million kwatchas to small farmers all over the country. Two years later Kaunda tacitly admitted that his initial experiment had failed and set up the non-democratic Second Republic – to be replaced by the Third Republic on 31 October 1991, when a democratically elected multi-party government took over from Kaunda.

Copper had boomed soon after Independence, providing 94 per cent of Zambia's foreign exchange and 47 per cent of government revenue in mineral taxes. A decade later its price was halved and continued to fall during the next eight years, devastating Zambia. As a result of irresponsible borrowing on the international financial market the country's per capita indebtedness is now more than double its per capita income. However, copper continues to be Zambia's most important hard-currency earner; in 1989 it made up 87 per cent of total exports. By now most mines are nearly worked out and social unrest looms ever more menacingly, with some 175,000 16-year-olds annually joining the would-be work-force. Inevitably, many Zambians complain that the mining companies robbed them of their natural wealth, which of course is simplistic. The Zambians could not possibly have extracted that wealth for themselves; even now they cannot efficiently maintain industrial plant.

Several expatriates familiar with my proposed route from Lundazi to Lusaka through the Eastern Province, where the population density is less than one to the square mile, had commiserated with me. 'Poor you, it's so *boring*! Hundreds of miles of nothing, you'll hate it!' Those motorists' judgements didn't cast me down; cyclists and motorists see landscapes with different eyes. The map showed few villages, no town beyond Chipata and many, many mountains; whatever other snags might arise (food and water shortages?) boredom would not be a hazard.

Those 500 miles were covered in six days. I was by then in top condition, despite intervals of malnourishment, and between Lundazi and Chipata I set my personal record for the journey: 115 miles in eight hours on a smooth, level, almost traffic-free road – much of it with Kasungu National Park, which is in Malawi, on my left.

My lodgings were varied: in Chipata – by mistake – a tough brothel (that was quite a tense night); in Katete a convent of young Zambian nuns; in Nyimba village a stable-like doss-house; in Rafunsa hamlet a one-roomed police station; in Chungwe trading centre the home of a teacher met in a bar. Food was scarce throughout this drought area and in both Nyimba and Rafunsa, where I arrived just after sunset (after supper-time), none was available though I waved a K500 note – to the locals a vast amount of money.

Although my population-sample was small, during these days, it seemed to confirm the Lundazi nuns' analysis. The good news, in

Zambia, is the Zambians – warm-hearted, open-minded, high-spirited against all the odds.

Lusaka is tiny and charmingly fails to project an urban image. Of course it tries; there are a few high-rise (but not very high) status symbols, several pretentious banks, the usual airline offices, embassies, shopping arcades and pseudo-supermarkets (their stock reminding me of Rumania), an international airport, a few of Zambia's seventeen cinemas, an elegant residential area (mainly occupied by expatriates) and the offices of the usual plethora of UN free-loaders. But none of this, somehow, adds up to a *city*. One is much more aware of the desperately impoverished shanty towns around the edges – known, for some obscure reason, as 'compounds'. These seem to be (and are, numerically) the real Lusaka, where tens of thousands endure poverty with fortitude. But of course that poverty breeds crime and in the city-centre pickpocketing has been brought to a fine art. On Day One my spectacles were stolen from the buttoned-down side-pocket of my jungle-trousers. That didn't matter; I had a spare pair. On Day Two the tragedy happened – I know not how, Day One having put me on Red Alert. Yet again the deft fingers got there and this time it was my (African) address book. The implications were, and remain, harrowing. This theft cut me off from all the people who had been kind to me, to whom I owed letters of thanks. Now, looking at the map, I see it littered with places where generous people have written me off as yet another White exploiter of Blacks. However, when one compares the lifestyles of the expatriate colony and the compounds it is hard not to see White pockets as 'legitimate economic targets'. This reaction shocked my Zambian friends; they accused me – probably rightly – of being sentimental.

Miles of flat open wasteland surround the compounds and I wondered why these have to be so squalidly overcrowded, often with two large families sharing a small oblong shack. Then I was told that just before Zambia's economic collapse a speculator bought this land, planning some grandiose urban development, and he is still hoping his dream may come true. But as the drought drove more and more starving villagers into Lusaka, significant piles of mud bricks were accumulating on the wasteland – for illegal building, it was rumoured.

Lusaka has a large, lively and long-established colony of Irish expatriates who at once took me to their collective bosom. In a

secluded, shrub-surrounded bungalow, complete with swimming-
pool, Maire and Seamus O'Grady – assisted by four endearing
small daughters – undertook my resuscitation. For two days I
devoted most of my time to eating five-course meals, with snacks
in between, while trying not to think of those villages where the next
one-course meal would happen only when the next truck-load of
relief maize arrived. Then I was invited to stay in a city-centre
counselling clinic for HIV + and AIDS victims, which was also a
hostel for those victims who had been rejected by their families.
There I felt more at ease; in Africa it is not easy to adjust to luxurious
living, however congenial and welcoming one's host and hostess. In
a storeroom with sacks of mealie-meal piled in one corner I had a
comfortable divan bed and a table and chair – the latter items more
important to a writer than the former.

For bedtime reading I was given the May/June 1992 issue of *AIDS
& Health News*, published in Lusaka by the Kara Counselling and
Training Trust. None of it promoted sweet dreams; one item,
illustrating the extremity of African women's victimisation, promoted nightmares. I quote:

> From childhood the Zambian woman has been taught various
> ways of coping with and sustaining marriage relationships, car-
> ing for husbands and children and various other aspects of
> adult life. The teaching is prolonged and thrives on the princi-
> ple of repetition which inculcates in the women a strong attach-
> ment to traditional beliefs. The feminists of today, therefore,
> not only have to deal with men's subjugative attitudes towards
> women but has [sic] to deal with the women's continued practis-
> ing of these strongly held beliefs . . . Women themselves do at
> times perpetuate their own subjugation by accepting that men
> are free to have several other partners. This puts them in
> danger of being infected. In accepting this, the women then
> begin to take measures to hold on to their husbands – to be bet-
> ter in sexual ways than women their husbands may go to.
> Methods of doing this vary but an interesting one is Dry Sex.
> In a study – 'The Behavioural Aspects of Dry Sex practice in
> Lusaka Urban' – Meya Jenny Nyirenda, RN, DNE, BSC Nurs-
> ing, describes dry sex as a sexual practice in which the vagina
> is dried of its natural secretions before or during intercourse.

This is done in the belief that it enhances sexual pleasure for the man. Scientists and researchers have established that genital lacerations, bruises or cuts make infection much more possible. During the sex act and because of the dryness achieved, there is extreme friction which causes these lacerations and the woman would be much more vulnerable not only to being infected but also to infect her partner. The practice of dry sex in Lusaka Urban is widely spread and cuts across all social and ethnic boundaries. It is practised not only among the illiterate but even among the educated women. In the high-cost areas of Rhodes Park, Northmead, Olympia Park and others wives admitted to Mrs Nyirenda that they practise dry sex.

Having pedalled almost 3,000 miles along 'the *ukimwi* road', I was by now sharing fully in the Africans' anger at the shameless development of the AIDS industry. At Entebbe there is a White-run Virus Research Institute, one of three in the world, where all enquiries about the ethical standards applied to its work in Uganda are side-stepped. Other Western academics briefly visit Africa to pick up information painstakingly gathered and collated by African colleagues. They then fly off to present these findings – apparently the result of their own research – at one of the AIDS industry's numerous and extravagantly run international conferences. These jamborees encourage AIDS 'experts' to mouth earnest platitudes and relay dramatic statistics for the benefit of the media, and to read papers written in impenetrable jargon for the benefit of each other, all by way of competing for funding for the next unconstructive project. Unconstructive, that is, for AIDS victims in Africa or anywhere else but lucrative for the experts. Meanwhile, out in the bush, the genuinely caring and knowledgeable Whites – always too busy to attend conferences – cannot afford basic medicines to relieve the agonies of the dying.

Another variant of the AIDS industry – I encountered this in its most extreme form in Lusaka – requires the insertion of 'an AIDS component' into a larger donor project, AIDS in Africa having become a 'good fund-raiser back home'. When I bought a copy of the April/May *Southern Africa Economist* from a street vendor on the Chacha Road it didn't surprise me to read:

According to the World Health Organisation, AIDS has given rise to the 'helicopter scientist' – the Western researcher who flies into hard-hit Third World countries to collect blood samples to take back to laboratories at home. The results of the research are never relayed back to the country. Some privately-funded researchers, WHO says, have taken advantage of lax regulations in some countries to carry out tests on people. Investigators for WHO's Global Programme on AIDS found that of the AIDS research done in sub-Saharan Africa in 1988–89, nearly 95% of the 559 projects identified were of no immediate relevance to the local populations.

That reminded me of an English doctor's outburst in Tanzania – 'For seven years now we've been tormented by sociologists, anthropologists, psychologists and otherologists, all studying the 'African Response to AIDS'. Then they write papers about "guilt patterns" and "denial syndromes" and whatnot. They never mention that many Africans can enjoy even a life they know is doomed. Western academics have their metaphysical knickers in such a twist they can't recognise, when they see it, the courage needed for *that* response to AIDS. Maybe it's too simple and they need something more complex to bump up their wordage.'

That simple courage (if it is simple) made my stay in the Lusaka hostel an extraordinary experience: moving, inspiring and – strangely – comforting. For months, as a casual passer-by on the African scene, I had been encountering almost daily the effects of AIDS in one form or another. I needed this opportunity to meet the tragedy on, as it were, a more intimate level, to share – if only for ten days – in the inner life of some of its victims, to be able to discuss AIDS, within the framework of friendship, on a philosophical rather than medical/sexual plane. One might imagine such a hostel to be depressing; in reality those young people lifted my heart. While their condition permitted, many worked as AIDS prevention educators, visiting schools, factories, government departments, commercial offices, army and police barracks to speak honestly and eloquently of their personal experiences, seeing this as the most effective way to spread the urgent 'behaviour change' message. They proved what heights of imagination and compassion can be scaled by those who look upon AIDS as a challenge and have taught themselves to cope with the imminence of death. One 24-year-old said to me, 'If I'd lived to be 80, I might never have learned how to enjoy life as much as I'm enjoying these few years. Maybe God plans best for us.'

The eighty mountainous miles from Lusaka to the Zambezi River (the border between Zambia and Zimbabwe) are mainly downhill, through parched deforested country, and were easily covered by 3.30. Beyond the Otto Beit bridge I booked into the only available lodging on the edge of the Zambezi Game Reserve. This big well-run tourist motel was at the other end of the scale from the Castle Hotel, luxuriously geared to White Zimbabweans and Western tourists yet comparatively inexpensive at £11 a night. A conspicuous notice over the bar reminded me that Zimbabwe was, until quite recently, Rhodesia. It warned:

STRICTLY SMART CASUAL. No Vests, Overalls, cut-off sleeves or track-suits. No Hats, No Bare-feet! THANK YOU.

It seems jungle-trousers and a bush-shirt are not Strictly Smart Casual; I was viewed with disfavour by the tall, slender, bow-tied young barman. This bar is modelled on an old-fashioned English pub and was being decorated by two well-equipped painters using steady aluminium ladders. Even on Zimbabwe's fringe there were hints of a prosperity and orderliness not met elsewhere along my route. The few other drinkers sat outside on the wide veranda, overlooking a green – because sprinkled – lawn where juvenile baboons gambolled.

As I stood at the counter, questioning the barman about the local wildlife, a youngish White man entered – very Strictly Smart Casual but not very civil. He grunted in reply to my greeting, then ordered two beers. Soon his friend arrived: fair-haired with a crew-cut, broad-shouldered and beer-bellied, his stubby fingers clutching a bulky gold cigarette-case. He was in a rage, his vehicle had broken down twice on the way from Harare, he was 'vomit-sick of this coun-try – it's no place to live any more, not since those bloody mindless kaffirs took over'.

I felt a sick tightening in my stomach; there were three English-speaking Africans within earshot. I looked closely at the speaker. Was this an act being put on for my benefit? No, clearly not; the two men were launched on a letting-off-steam exercise that disregarded the presence of the tourist as well as the 'natives'. They ranted on about 'bloody stinking savages' and 'flat-nosed swine' and the impossibility of continuing to live in a country going down as fast now as Zambia did a decade ago – 'and those thick brutes can't learn from Zambia's mistakes!' It all seemed unreal, as though I were in a time-warp. The barman had disappeared; I glanced at the painters, no more than six yards away, expressionlessly concentrating on their work. When the talk turned to poaching it was agreed that all poachers should be shot on sight and buried in the bush with no questions asked – as is, I gathered from this conversation, the custom in Zimbabwe. (They were of course referring to Black poachers; White poachers are 'wildlife merchants'.) As I left the bar I glanced again at the painters and this time one of them caught my eye and grinned: but it was a camouflage grin, hiding pain.

The Zambezi Game Reserve is well-stocked; mounds of elephant dung lay around and when I hung my briefs out to dry they were stolen by an adolescent baboon who sat on the roof above my room derisively waving them at me. His tribe were all over the place and into everything – fiddling with parked trucks, grabbing glasses of beer left unguarded, invading any room incautiously left open.

Settling down to write my journal, I found I couldn't; my mind felt numbed – and not only by that overheard dialogue. At 5 p.m., inexplicably, I wanted to sleep. For two hours I did so, then went to the restaurant and failed to enjoy an excellent dinner. Something was wrong; a tummy-bug, evidently, which surprised me – my guts have long been immune to the slings and arrows of outrageous hygiene.

For nine hours I slept deeply, then failed to enjoy an excellent breakfast, served at 6 a.m. sharp as promised. I still felt weirdly drowsy and slightly queasy yet this indisposition seemed minor; the important thing was to cross the low-lying game reserve in the cool of the morning. So off I went, irritated by my lack of energy but confident of reaching the Zambezi escarpment before noon.

A few hours later, near the base of the escarpment, the fever flared. Dismounting, I put a hand to my forehead and belatedly diagnosed 'malaria'. Dizzy, trembling and wanting to vomit, I dragged Lear into the bush and collapsed, laying my pulsating head on a convenient pile of dry elephant dung – the size and shape

255

of one of those round fat sofa-cushions beloved by our great-grandmothers. But the ground beneath felt unlike a sofa; flinty stones, swarming ants and long thorns, shed by the leafless tree above, suggested a move. But to where? For forty miles in every direction stones and thorns prevailed. Anyway I felt incapable of moving. This was my first experience of malaria: why had no one ever told me that when the collapse comes an irrational lethargy takes over?

I thought, 'Thomson didn't react like this, he just bashed on regardless up the next escarpment.' I remembered Ali in Kyenjojo asking, 'You get a fever alone in the bush, who helps?' I recalled Mary Livingstone, lying dying of fever on a mattress spread on three tea-chests – that was at Shupanga, not far from here, during the ill-fated Zambezi Expedition. Then I thought, 'Must move, must take Halfan.' Halfan is the very latest malaria cure; not a prophylactic, only for the stricken. I looked at Lear, leaning against a baobab tree eight yards away. He seemed virtually inaccessible. Four baboons loped past, then paused to survey me. In game reserves they don't feel threatened by humans. Feverishly I resented their insolent staring. The big male sat scratching his private parts – a misnomer in the case of baboons. The curious baby laid both hands on a pedal and when it revolved took fright. Her family followed; she was too small to be left unprotected.

I thought, 'This is crazy, lying here getting worse.' I stood and swayed, lurched towards the pannier-bags, groped for the medicine box, extracted the Halfan, returned to my pillow. The instructions emphasised, in capital letters, that Halfan must be taken only after consultation with a doctor. Hysterical rage swept through me. *A doctor*! Who were the cretins responsible for this leaflet? Malaria is now a tropical disease. Doctors are scarce in the tropics. I heard myself give a manic laugh which alarmed a herd of Thomson's gazelle grazing on nothing visible beyond the baobab. It struck me as comic, in a skewed kind of way, that the nearest doctors were in a Zambian town thirty-five miles north and a Zimbabwean town forty miles south – while for me walking eight yards required heroic effort. I then swallowed two Halfan and soon my head had stopped pulsating. The other symptoms remained unaffected: leg-pains, shivering, nausea, lethargy. I felt absurdly complacent; I had done the responsible thing and taken my medicine and it was working.

Maybe the next two capsules, six hours hence, would cure me.

As the sun climbed I wriggled around the tree, desperate to escape those deadly rays. Then came the noon silence of the bush – which verges on the eerie, where no human noises intrude. The sun takes charge, immobilising even the ants. One knows that nearby are many living creatures: insects, reptiles, birds, monkeys, antelope, elephants, hyenas, leopards, lions – all now utterly still, under a sky pallid with heat. Not the slightest current of air stirs the parched vegetation. All sound, colour and movement seem to have been wrung out of the earth. Freed of the ants' tickling torment, I slept.

Awakening at 3.40 I felt both better (the fever) and worse (all the other symptoms). My mild delirium had abated and with it my optimism about Dose Two; the full course was six Halfan, not four. It then occurred to me that it is imprudent to leave oneself lying around all night in a well-stocked game reserve. Alarm took over, until I remembered the tsetse-control posts: there must be one at the foot of the escarpment to protect the plateau cattle. But it was still much too hot for action. I slept again.

Soon after five I got going; having Lear to lean on helped as I crawled hopefully along the road towards the massive brown fortification ahead – defending the cool fertile heights from the hot arid depths of the Zambezi valley.

Instead of a tsetse officer I found a game-warden. Initially his little thatched hut, twenty yards off the road, persuaded me that I was hallucinating – perhaps a side-effect of Halfan? In the porch sat Simon, peeling potatoes for his supper. He came forward to greet me, wearing a neat khaki uniform and a wide kind smile. Then anxiously he asked, 'You have a fever?' I nodded. 'No problem!' beamed Simon. 'You rest here, there is room. When you recover, you continue.' It was as simple as that.

The hut boasted two solar panels (inoperative) on its thatch but lacked any furniture apart from pink nylon curtains. In the outer room Simon slept on the floor in an army flea-bag beside his complicated radio equipment. In the inner room I slept on my own flea-bag beside several large guns propped against the wall. For the next thirty-six hours I drifted in and out of feverishness and lost all sense of time. At intervals Simon brought enormous enamel jugs of very sweet, very hot black tea. 'You must drink much,' he said firmly, helping me to sit up and supervising my intake. He also provided an eclectic range of medicines – Andrew's Liver Salts, Panadol, Lemsip, Anapolon, Lomotil, Burrough's Tonic, Fulford's Gripe Water – only some of which I contrived to evade. 'All these are *very* good for you, *please* take! When tourists go, they leave me their medicines.'

As radio officer, Simon received and transmitted coded messages from four countries. Cunning must be employed, where armed and ruthless poachers abound, and he spent most of the day and part of the night holding conversations like this:

Half-litre says storm hits lake. Lake denies. Two bananas fell into whiskey. Over.

Coca Cola looks for three long boats. Boats avoiding because of smallpox. Over.

Peru five hours late. Beer goes to sun. Happiness fights tree. Over.

Four teas spilled. Half-litre requests Berlin. Storm and sun dancing. Over.

On first hearing these arcane messages I resigned myself to being in a terminal delirium. Later, Simon explained.

I had collapsed on a Friday. By Sunday morning I felt ready to take the bus to Karoi, the nearest town on the plateau. This uncrowded vehicle (where would a crowd be coming from?) passed at about eight every morning but Simon was touchingly reluctant to discharge his patient – 'Here I live without people, it is nice for me to have a Mamma in my house.' As he pushed Lear to the road I confronted a dilemma: to tip or not to tip? The former, I decided, though no amount of mere money could express the gratitude I felt. But when Simon saw my wallet a hurt look appeared. He thrust Lear towards me saying, 'The radio calls! I go!' And away he sped, without even shaking hands.

A lugubrious elderly clergyman shared my bus seat. 'This Zambezi Valley malaria has become very bad,' he said grimly. 'You think you are better, in two weeks you relapse, this time it is cerebral malaria – quickly you die. Even in a Jo'burg hospital, you die. For cerebral malaria there is no cure.' He looked at me with protruding, bloodshot, melancholy eyes. 'You are foolish to think you are better. Every year malaria kills *millions*! People now fuss too much about AIDS. AIDS is nothing, it kills only people living dirty lives. Malaria kills *everyone* – people like you, like me.' He stopped and sighed. I felt he was visualising my funeral within a fortnight. I rested my head on the seat in front and slept.

In Karoi's bus-station hotel the staff didn't conceal their distaste for Whites who are dirty, dishevelled and able to afford only a bicycle. Grudgingly a small room with smelly bedding and no bathroom was allocated: expensive at £5 a night. Even more grudgingly payment was deferred to the morrow; outside Zambia its kwatcha are waste-paper. The sour woman receptionist commanded, 'By 9 a.m. you must pay, our banks open at 8.30.' I was again feverish and dizzy and couldn't imagine myself getting to a bank, or anywhere else, within twenty-four hours – except perhaps to the grave hinted at by my lugubrious companion. But tomorrow was another day. I explained that I had malaria and asked for drinking-water. The receptionist sneered. 'At this season we all have malaria, it is not important, we work on.' True enough; many malarial Blacks do keep going until they either recover or drop dead.

Having locked Lear to the bed, lest I fall into a coma, I subsided on to the malodorous quilt. Perhaps Simon had been right and my moving was premature. All day I tossed and turned, aching and muzzy-headed. From 4 p.m. until 1 a.m. the hotel's heavy metal disco inflicted a peculiarly diabolical form of decibelical torture. Then I fell into a strangely deep sleep and awoke at dawn in a cold sodden bed. At last I had sweated it out; all the bedding and the thin mattress were soaked through. A raging thirst tormented me but the lethargy was gone. I dressed and wobbled weakly to the door; it was piercingly cold, my breath visible. A grumpy young man rejected my order for two pots of tea and some dry toast; breakfast was served *only* in the restaurant. I shocked myself by repeating the order in a memsahibish tone. The young man looked startled, then sulkily meandered towards the kitchen and returned in thirty-five minutes with a tray. In fact I couldn't face the toast and had to lie down to rest between each cup of tea. I looked at my watch; it was 7.15, bank time loomed. I considered appealing at Reception to Sour-puss's better nature – but probably she didn't have one. Also, according to an advertisement in the loo, that heavy metal band would be performing nightly during the coming week. So another refuge must be found, preferably in the local hospital; the prospect of being *nursed* was appealing. When I left the hotel the ground seemed to be moving like the deck of a ship in a slight swell; but extreme weakness, unlike malarial lethargy, does give way to the mind-over-matter approach. I sought the nearby taxi-rank and a sympathetic driver readily agreed to await his fare outside the bank.

Although Karoi's Barclays looks like anywhere else's Barclays, the Forex clerk's time of arrival could not be specified. If I tried to stand in the long queue I would certainly faint; dragging a chair from a corner, I sat in the queue. And there Shayne found me.

Shayne was tall, fair and slender, an angel of mercy disguised as a young White Zimbabwean woman. I first noticed her as she looked sideways at me with some concern. Concern became alarm when I asked the whereabouts of the hospital.

'You can't go there!' exclaimed Shayne. 'It's only for Blacks!'

This information did not deter me. I was feeling increasingly end-of-tetherish and it seemed more fitting, and somehow *tidier*, to die in a hospital than in a squalid hotel. Anyway, as I explained to Shayne, I've always enjoyed being ill in hospital. One is no longer responsible for oneself – a relaxing reversion to infancy.

Shayne didn't think I'd find Karoi hospital at all relaxing: and she may well have been right. Firmly she decided, 'You'd better come home with me, we'll look after you.' First, however, she took me to a doctor, a brisk competent man well used to unwinding hypochondriacal Whites. He pronounced my malaria the mildest possible form, advised complete rest for a week and forbade strenuous exercise for a month. A relapse, he warned, might be less mild. My lugubrious friend had been one of many; all the locals, Black and White, dreaded 'the relapse', which can indeed become cerebral malaria.

The Dalkins' simple home – several miles south of Karoi, set high amidst 8,000 hectares of tobacco and overlooking an immense bright expanse of Mashonaland – offered all the comforts I appreciate and none of the luxuries I disdain. Shayne and Gary so graciously absorbed me into the family (themselves and two small daughters) that within hours I had given up thinking of myself as a nuisance and settled down to the serious business of convalescing and modifying plans.

My original plan – to cycle around Zimbabwe, then leave Lear lodging near the South African border, awaiting my return in 1993 – no longer made sense, quite apart from the doctor's ban on 'strenuous exercise'. Having sniffed the air south of the Zambezi,

I felt Zimbabwe to be not a continuation of Black Africa but – both historically and emotionally – the beginning of South Africa. In the old Commonwealth days, Southern Rhodesia more than once came close to being integrated with the Union of South Africa and here, for ninety years, the Black/White relationship more closely resembled what lies south of the Limpopo than anything I had so far encountered. Many white Rhodesians looked on South Africa, rather than Britain, as their spiritual home (to put it politely) and the Blacks had been subjugated as nowhere else in British Africa. Some mosquito, I realised, had been kind to me. Karoi was the appropriate place for this journey to end and the next to begin.

I consulted the Dalkins, who seemed positively eager to have Lear as a lodger. Then for the last time I unfolded my map and planned my return route to Nairobi: from Karoi to Lusaka by bus, from Lusaka to Dar es Salaam on the Chinese-built Tanzam railway, from Dar to Nairobi by bus via Arusha.

Shayne cherished me judiciously and my recovery was rapid. Sitting on the lawn in the sun – here, in winter, one seeks the sun instead of fleeing it – I read Robert Blake's *A History of Rhodesia* and seized upon a passage highly relevant to an argument I had had in Lusaka with an elderly missionary.

> The impact of European conquest on the African way of life was far greater than almost any white man of the time appreciated. It was a complete revolution. To say this is not at all to say that their way of life had been idyllic. On the contrary it had been in many respects nasty and brutish, and it certainly tended to be short. But it was to them an ordered and predictable system – even witchcraft, so fiercely denounced by missionaries and officials, had an accepted and recognized place. It was above all freedom – freedom to live in accordance with customs and usages, superstitions and rituals handed down from immemorial antiquity; and freedom not to live in accordance with the overt and tacit rules of a European cash economy . . . The African man had his tasks both of labour and ritual to perform, just as much as the woman. He was certainly not a drone. Even if we set aside the sexual aspect, his removal for months on end to work for a wage made necessary

261

by the imposition of the hut tax for just that purpose was bound to disrupt the whole traditional, time-honoured order of tribal society . . . The African did not in the least want to work for the white man. He, therefore, had to be compelled by fiscal pressure. It was hoped that, having thus entered, if unwillingly, the advanced wage economy of his conquerors, he would discover new needs, aspire to new luxuries and so be happy to become, as Wilson Fox put it in an important (1910) memorandum, 'one of the privates of the industrial army, in every department of work'.

That was written in the mid-1970s and Lord Blake's understanding of the colonial process gets to the very core of modern Africa's problems. Now one wonders why anyone ever expected (if they did) Africa's new nations to function smoothly. In 1960 Harold Macmillan told the South African parliament, 'This African national consciousness is happening everywhere. The wind of change is blowing through this continent and, whether we like it or not, this growth of national consciousness is a political fact.' But the political fact was anti-colonialism rather than 'national consciousness'. After a generation of independence, young Africans who make 'patriotic' noises seem to be merely striking a pose, to go with their blue jeans and bubble-gum.

When the wind of change blew the Scramblers home the new nations rejoiced in their freedom and all its outward signs: flags, anthems, armies, embassies, presidential palaces, national airlines, UN seats. But of course it wasn't that true freedom to which Lord Blake referred – freedom *not* to live in accordance with a European cash economy. The Scramblers hadn't really gone home. Instead they were being hyper-active, the old familiar faces joined now by (among many others) the Cold Warriors, adding their ideological poisons to an already unwholesome political brew. The harm done during the colonial era has been hideously compounded by the harm done since. To me the ultimate symbols of neo-colonialism were those giant pylons seen marching across Malawi. They march from A to B for the benefit of donor countries and their venal Black allies. Below them crouch countless villages where children do their homework by firelight.

Is it not time we quit Africa – cutting off the corrupting flow of billions of dollars, withdrawing the thousands of parasitical 'experts' and leaving the Africans free to sort out their own future? What is our continued meddling achieving *for the Africans*? Aren't we merely prolonging the process begun a century ago, of undermining their self-respect and self-confidence? The argument about global interdependence at the end of the twentieth century doesn't convince me that Blacks must be forever locked into our manipulative Rich Man's economy. Africa is after all a *continent* and not long ago was self-supporting. The notion that if given enough 'aid' – financial and technical – the Africans can soon acquire a Western lifestyle is simply absurd. This was the pivot of my argument with the Lusaka missionary – who severely reprimanded me. 'You can't think like that! Africans long for cameras, cars, fridges, videos – all of it! And they're entitled to their share of modern goodies and comforts, we can't arrogantly say they must do without them!'

This, however, is not a question of 'entitlement' but of what is realistically attainable. Of course the African has 'discovered new needs and aspires to new luxuries', but these are *not* realistically attainable within his authentic world. The graftings on to Africa of Western systems of education, administration, justice, worship, agriculture, industry and commerce have demonstrably been a failure. None has taken. All are systems so profoundly alien to Africa that they have provoked every sort of collapse – moral, political, economic. Nor is there any reason to hope that in time those graftings will take. Why should they? Why should a complex civilisation slowly built up by one race be assumed suitable for instant adoption by another – by peoples who a century ago or less were without written languages, wheeled vehicles or a cash economy? Western civilisation being more advanced gives us no right to assume it can solve other peoples' problems – an inherently racialist assumption. Yet we still treat Africa as our forebears did in the 1890s, operating behind a different screen with the same (or worse) greed. Now it is our 'duty' to deliver irrigation schemes, factories, grain silos, motorways, agrochemicals, multi-storey hotels and conference centres, multi-party democracies and human rights (our own code of human rights, which some Western countries find easier to preach than to practise.) All this denies African civilisation its own dignity and integrity. But getting rid of the Donors will be harder than getting rid of the Scramblers.

In Lusaka, one of Africa's smaller capitals, I listed the UN agencies involved in Zambia's 'Development Assistance'. It's a sinister list: FAO, IAEA, IDA, IFAD, ILO, UNCHS, UNDP, UNDRO, UNFPA, UNFSDT, UNHCR, UNICEF, UNIDO, UNU, UPU, WHO, WMO, WFP – and of course the World Bank. In addition, eighteen White countries, plus Japan, are also deep into Zambian 'Development'. There are very many more highly paid expatriates in Africa now than there ever were low-paid colonial officers. And for all its problems the continent is still worth exploiting; many would see leaving it to its own devices as an act of lunatic fecklessness – altruism gone mad. Moreover, few African *leaders* will ever want to get rid of Donors. Yet we now know that on the international scene the supposedly impossible can happen within half a decade. Granted, the disintegration of an anti-human political structure is less unlikely than the abandonment of quick-buck opportunities by Black politicians. But the Ugandan academic quoted in an earlier chapter, Professor Ali Mazrui, does see light at the end of the tunnel:

It certainly looks as if the whole post-colonial euphoria about 'modernization' has been a mere illusion of modernity, a mirage of progress, a façade of advancement. The reality behind the façade is grim and devastating. Africa is bleeding; Africa is starving. The reasons lie in a hundred years of colonial history and a thousand years of African culture . . . I think a partial reversal of Westernization is already under way. The schools as major instruments of Westernization are under strain and ceasing to be efficient transmitters of Western culture; the villages are being forced back into areas of self-reliance, because the wider national set-up is unproductive. People are losing faith in currencies not only because they are valueless but because they are susceptible to abrupt change altogether. The money and cash aspects of economic life, which came with colonialism, are losing the sanctity they had . . . Personally I think that a partial reversal of Westernization is not bad. Africans of my ilk ought to be cut down to size. They have enjoyed disproportionate influence for too long. In any case most of us constitute a cultural élite, not an economic vanguard. Therefore we are less relevant to the transformation of our societies than we might be. I'm not unhappy that the ancestors are fighting back, that they are saying, 'Your pact of the post-colonial era is inappropriate and therefore we shall make sure your roads won't work, your trains won't move, your telephones won't ring, your schools won't educate, and your soldiers will take over power every so often. We pronounce a curse upon all your post-colonial arrangements until a new compact of African authenticity is devised.' I'm not unhappy about that curse.

Neither am I.

Bibliography

Anderson, W. B., *The Church in East Africa: 1840–1974* (Uzima, Nairobi: 1977)

Baker, Kristina, *AIDS, Sex & Family Planning* (Africa Christian Press: 1989)

Barnett, Tony, & Blaikie, Piers, *AIDS in Africa* (Belhaven Press: 1992)

Bourenane, N., & Mkandawire, T. (eds.), *The State and Agriculture in Africa* (Codesria: 1987)

Buckoke, A., *Fishing in Africa* (Picador: 1991)

Campbell, H., & Stein, H. (eds.), *The IMF and Tanzania* (SAPES, Harare: 1991)

Chabal, Patrick (ed.), *Political Domination in Africa* (CUP: 1986)

Chirimuuta, R. & R., *AIDS, Africa and Racism* (Free Association Books: 1989)

Clark, John, *A Simple Guide to Structural Adjustment* (Oxfam: 1991)

Davidson, Basil, *Modern Africa: A Social and Political History* (Longman: 1989)

Dinesen, Isak, *Letters from Africa: 1914–1931* (Weidenfeld & Nicolson: 1981)

—— *Out of Africa* (Putnam: 1937)

Donovan, V. J., *Christianity Rediscovered: An Epistle from the Masai* (SCM Press: 1982)

Duignan, Peter, & Jackson, R. H. (eds.), *Politics and Government in African States: 1960–1985* (Croom Helm: 1986)

Dumont, Rene, *False Start in Africa* (Deutsch: 1966)

Erny, Pierre, *The Child and his Environment in Black Africa* (OUP: 1981)

Freund, Bill, *The Making of Contemporary Africa* (Macmillan: 1984)

Gallmann, Kuki, *I Dreamed of Africa* (Viking: 1991)

Hancock, Graham, & Carim, Enver, *AIDS: The Deadly Epidemic* (Gollancz: 1987)

Hancock, Graham, *Lords of Poverty* (Macmillan: 1989)

266

Hansen, H.B., & Twaddle, M., *Uganda Now: Between Decay and Development* (Heinemann: 1988)

Harrison, Paul, *The Greening of Africa* (Paladin: 1987)

Huxley, Elspeth, *The Sorcerer's Apprentice* (Chatto & Windus: 1949)

—— *The Flame Trees of Thika* (Chatto & Windus: 1958)

—— *The Mottled Lizard* (Chatto & Windus: 1962)

Jackson, R.H., & Rosberg, C.G., *Personal Rule in Black Africa* (University of California Press: 1982)

Johnston, Erika, *The Other Side of Kilimanjaro* (Johnson Publications: 1971)

Karugire, S.R., *A Political History of Uganda* (Heinemann: 1980)

Kenyatta, Jomo, *Facing Mount Kenya* (Secker & Warburg: 1938)

Kibwana, K., *Law and the Administration of Justice in Kenya* (International Commission of Jurists: 1992)

King, Preston, *An African Winter* (Penguin Special: 1986)

Lamb, David, *The Africans* (Mandarin: 1990)

MacPhee, A. Marshall, *Kenya* (Ernest Benn: 1968)

Maillu, David G., *Our Kind of Polygamy* (Heinemann: 1988)

Maitland, Alexander, *Speke* (Constable: 1971)

Mamdani, Mahmood, *Imperialism and Fascism in Uganda* (Heinemann: 1983)

Martelli, George, *Livingstone's River* (Chatto & Windus: 1970)

Martin, P.M., & O'Meara, P. (eds.) *Africa* (Indiana University Press: 1986)

Mbiti, John S., *African Religions and Philosophy* (Heinemann: 1969)

Meinertzhagen, Richard, *Kenya Diary (1902-1906)* (Eland Books: 1983)

Melrose, Dianna, *Bitter Pills* (Oxfam: 1987)

Miller, Charles, *The Lunatic Express* (Macmillan: 1971)

Museveni, Yoweri, *The Uganda Resistance War* (NRM Publications: 1986)

Musharhamina, M.G.C., *Traditional African Marriage and Christian Marriage* (St Paul Publications: 1981)

Ndegwa, Philip, *The African Challenge* (Heinemann: 1986)

Okullu, Henry, *Church and Politics in East Africa* (Uzima Press: 1985)

—— *Church and State in Nation Building* (Uzima Press: 1987)

Oppong, Christine, *Middle Class African Marriage* (Allen & Unwin: 1981)

Pakenham, Thomas, *The Scramble for Africa* (Weidenfeld & Nicolson: 1991)

Panos Dossier, *Triple Jeopardy: Women and AIDS* (The Panos Institute: 1990)

Pirouet, M.L., *Black Evangelists: The Spread of Christianity in Uganda: 1891-1914* (Rex Collings: 1978)

Rafael, B. R., *A Short History of Malawi* (Popular Publications: 1980)

Ransford, Oliver, *Livingstone's Lake: The Drama of Nyasa* (John Murray: 1966)

Rimmer, Douglas (ed.) *Africa 30 Years On* (The Royal African Society: 1991)

Rotberg, R. I., *Joseph Thomson and the Exploration of Africa* (Chatto & Windus: 1971)

Rupesinghe, Kumar, (ed.), *Conflict Resolution in Uganda* (James Currey: 1989)

Sabatier, Renee, *Blaming Others* (The Panos Institute: 1988)

Vaughan, Megan, *Curing Their Ills: Colonial Power and African Illness* (Polity Press: 1991)

Waugh, Evelyn, *A Tourist in Africa* (Chapman & Hall: 1960)

Index

Abel (teacher), 135-7
Aberdare mountains, 11
Abraham (Kenyan pastor), 12-14, 40
Acholi people (Uganda), 49-50
Adam (Bukoba bar-owner), 147-8
Africa Highway, 135, 137
African Contemporary Record, 49
African Lakes Company, 212, 214, 226
Africans: patronised by Europeans,
    35-8; impact of Whites on, 261-5
Agnes (Ugandan), 75-6, 80-1
AIDS (*ukimwi*; 'slim disease'):
    prevalence and incidence, 9, 12-13,
    28, 34, 43, 55, 89-90, 101, 145,
    149, 157, 173-4, 177, 185-6, 201,
    206, 245; control programmes, 42,
    68, 184-5, 223; belief in Western
    cure, 52, 90; reactions to, 56-7,
    112-3; Western action on, 59; and
    internal migration, 73, 89, 174;
    interest in Western experience of,
    76; effects, 80; testing and
    screening, 81, 89, 149-50, 194;
    treatment, 85-6; and orphans, 86,
    153-4, 202; and 'behaviour change'
    (monogamy and celibacy), 86-8,
    127, 130, 156, 186, 199, 203, 223;
    and Irish attitudes, 87; social
    distribution, 88-9; and moral
    dilemmas, 89; warning posters,
    111-12; and feminism, 122-3;
    believed introduced by US, 129,
    143; testing costs, 149; Support
    Organisation, 150; and personal
    responsibility, 152-3; and sex as
    commodity, 161; Church and

religious attitudes to, 166, 186, 199;
    proposed solution by polygamy, 181,
    186; and dry sex, 251-2; research
    industry, 252-3.
AIDS & Health News, 251
Albert (of Sotik), 23, 97
Albert (Ugandan driver), 67, 70
Alcock, Sir Rutherford, 191
Ali (of Kyenjojo), 109-10, 168, 266
Alice (Edward's wife), 70
Amin, Idi, 49-50, 67, 71-2, 91, 120,
    143, 146, 152
Amnesty International, 49
Angela (Ugandan), 69
Angoni people, 208, 209
Ankole (Uganda), 123, 126, 130, 133
Arabs: slave trade, 209-10, 212-14
Archer, Jeffrey, 84
Asians: in East Africa, 57-8, 85, 200

backpackers, 73-4, 78, 119, 217
Bagamoya (Tanzania), 165
Baganda people (Uganda), 94, 102
Bahaya people (Tanzania), 147, 160
Bahima people (Uganda), 133-5
Baines (District Commissioner, Kagera,
    1910), 153
Bairu people (Uganda), 133
Banda, Dr Hastings Kamuzu: regime,
    210, 218-21, 223, 227, 236; and
    unrest, 215-17; unpopularity, 230;
    birthday, 235; hostility to Kaunda, 240
Basoga people (Uganda), 94
Basunju (Uganda), 96
Ben (of Chelinda Lodge), 233-4
Bernadette (Mumfi's daughter), 156-7

269